ANTI-AMERICANISM
IN THE THIRD WORLD

Foreign Policy Issues
A Foreign Policy Research Institute Series

Series Editor
NILS H. WESSELL

Managing Editor
ELIZABETH D. DUNLAP

ANTI-AMERICANISM IN THE THIRD WORLD

Implications for U.S. Foreign Policy

Edited by
Alvin Z. Rubinstein
and Donald E. Smith

PRAEGER SPECIAL STUDIES • PRAEGER SCIENTIFIC

New York • Philadelphia • Eastbourne, UK
Toronto • Hong Kong • Tokyo • Sydney

Library of Congress Cataloging in Publication Data
Main entry under title:

Anti-Americanism in the Third World.

  (Foreign policy issues)
  Bibliography: p.
  Includes index.
1. Developing countries—Foreign relations—United
States—Addresses, essays, lectures. 2. United States—
Foreign relations—Developing countries—Addresses,
essays, lectures. 3. United States—Foreign opinion,
Developing countries—Addresses, essays, lectures.
4. Public opinion—Developing countries—Addresses,
essays, lectures. I. Rubinstein, Alvin Z. II. Smith,
Donald Eugene, 1927–   III. Series.

D888.U6A57 1985   327.730172′4   84-20595
ISBN 0-03-001962-1 (alk. paper)

Published in 1985 by Praeger Publishers
CBS Educational and Professional Publishing
a Division of CBS Inc.
521 Fifth Avenue, New York, NY 10175 USA

© 1985 by Praeger Publishers

56789 052 987654321

Printed in the United States of America
on acid-free paper

FOREIGN POLICY RESEARCH INSTITUTE

The Foreign Policy Research Institute is a nonprofit organization devoted to scholarly research and analysis of international developments affecting the national security interests of the United States. The Institute's major activities include a broad-based research program; an internationally recognized publications program; seminars, workshops, and conferences for business, government, and academic leaders; and a fellowship program that provides training in policy analysis to promising scholars.

The Institute's research and publications programs are designed to:
- Identify, explore, and forecast political, military, and economic trends in the international system;
- Analyze the fundamental issues facing U.S. foreign policy;
- Suggest guidelines for U.S. foreign policy that contribute both to American security and to the development of a stable international order.

To accomplish these purposes, the Institute:
- Maintains a staff of specialists in the field of international relations as well as an extensive library of pertinent periodicals, books, and information files. The Institute's library is open to use by scholars, students, and the general public;
- Draws upon the expertise of leading academicians and persons in public life who are concerned with international affairs;
- Convenes and publishes the results of conferences and symposia of U.S. and foreign experts on contemporary international problems.

The products of the Institute's research program include the following publications:
- **ORBIS:** a quarterly journal of world affairs, widely recognized as a leading forum for research in the field of international and strategic studies;
- **Foreign Policy Issues:** a book series (in cooperation with Praeger Publishers) of important studies written by authorities in the field of international and strategic studies;
- **Philadelphia Policy Papers:** analyses of timely issues and developments having serious implications for U.S. foreign and defense policy;
- **Research Reports:** sponsored by various institutions, including agencies of the U.S. government.

The opinions expressed in publications of the Foreign Policy Research Institute are those of the authors and should not be construed as representing those of the Institute.

Contents

Foreword

Anti-Americanism is not an ephemeral phenomenon that sprang up from nowhere and may be expected to pass as inexplicably as it arose. To be sure, as the chapters that follow demonstrate, particular U.S. policies have played an important role in engendering resentment of the United States in the so-called Third World. But the cultural and social roots of anti-Americanism are to be found in Europe in the nineteenth century and its political ramifications will extend around the world into the twenty-first. It is probably an illusion to believe that despite issue-specific sources of anti-Americanism the United States, merely by making accommodative adjustments in its foreign policy, could regain the universal esteem and affection that most Americans in their hearts believe we rightly deserve. As a great power with extensive commitments around a shrinking globe, itself beset with internecine conflict, it is unlikely that the United States will ever be able to so order its policies that no other nation or social group abroad will have cause to resent the influence and example of the United States.

As long as the United States attaches some value—not necessarily an absolute one—to preserving and extending human rights around the world, Americans must expect to earn the animosity of a large number of the world's governments, three quarters of which are authoritarian and, in some measure, repressive. Similarly, any U.S. policy that seeks, however modestly, to contain the global influence of the Soviet Union will engender vocal criticism from Moscow's Marxist-Leninist clients and their political allies. To some extent we can choose our critics, but we cannot choose whether to have them.

Anti-Americanism in the Third World is the eighth volume in the Foreign Policy Research Institute's book series, *Foreign Policy Issues*. The series includes both collectively and individually authored studies on contemporary international relations and provides a publications outlet for work by researchers at the Foreign Policy Research Institute (FPRI) and other authors in the academic and policy communities.

The present volume was conceived by Alvin Z. Rubinstein, Senior Fellow at the FPRI and Professor of Political Science at the University of Pennsylvania, and Donald E. Smith, also Professor of Political Science at the University of Pennsylvania. The reader is indebted to them not only for the remarkable substantive coherence of the chapters that follow but for the promptness with which these essays, produced originally for the Conference on Anti-Americanism in the Third World, held March 21–23, 1984, at the University of Pennsylvania, have been published. It is with particular pleasure that I acknowledge the support of the Howard Heinz Endowment that made it possible for the Foreign Policy Research Institute to cosponsor the conference in conjunction with the Anspach Institute of Diplomacy and Foreign Affairs at the University of Pennsylvania.

Nils H. Wessell
Series Editor
Foreign Policy Issues
A Foreign Policy Research Institute Study

Preface

We are confident that there is much of interest in the pages that follow, but the reader may already have missed a significant point: namely, the book's date of publication. How is it that anti-Americanism in the Third World, a subject of obvious and pressing importance, did not receive systematic attention in a scholarly publication until 1985? This book makes its appearance a full three decades after the phenomenon it analyzes.

We are not sure that we know the complete answer to our question. At the level of general awareness it may be the result of a disinclination to confront unpleasantness combined with the vague suspicion that to identify a problem is to inflate or even create it. It is instructive to recall that until the late 1950s, most Americans doubted that this society had a serious racial problem. Anti-Americanism calls into question our basic self-image, the assumption of a just and benevolent role in the world.

On a more academic level, the neglect of anti-Americanism as a subject for research may be related to the less than satisfactory way in which "public opinion" has been understood in relation to foreign policy making within the United States. In this light, the effort to relate the impact of U.S. activities (governmental and nongovernmental) and indigenous public opinion within a hundred Third World societies of diverse cultures, economies, and political systems poses problems that are formidable indeed. But to say that the challenge is great is not to explain why there has been so little response to it.

In any event, the present volume attempts a first cut. In the editors' chapter "Anti-Americanism: Anatomy of a Phenomenon," we present an overview of the problem and propose the structure of an approach to it, including a typology of anti-Americanism. This is followed by chapters that are country-specific or regional in scope (Mexico, Latin America, the Arab world, Turkey, South Asia, Malaysia, Africa) in which our colleagues flesh out some of the cultural, ideological, and historical factors that have influenced the particular expressions of anti-Americanism in various parts of the Third World. Finally, three colleagues analyze the phenomenon in functional areas (the multinational corporations, the United Nations) and in terms of implications for the United States.

This volume resulted from a conference held at the University of Pennsylvania in March 1984. We are deeply grateful to the conference cosponsors: the University's Anspach Institute for Diplomacy and Foreign Affairs, Professor Chong–Sik Lee, Director; and the Foreign Policy Research Institute, Dr. Nils Wessell, Director. We are very appreciative of the additional support provided by the University's School of Arts and Sciences, Dr. Joel Conarroe, Dean. For efficient handling of the many details connected with the organization of the conference, we extend hearty thanks to the staffs of the Foreign Policy Research Institute and the Department of Political Science. We hope that this book and whatever influence it may have will bring a measure of satisfaction to all those who have contributed to bringing it into being.

Alvin Z. Rubinstein
Donald E. Smith
University of Pennsylvania

ANTI-AMERICANISM
IN THE THIRD WORLD

1

Anti-Americanism: Anatomy of a Phenomenon

Alvin Z. Rubinstein and Donald E. Smith

When word came of the takeover of the U.S. Embassy in Tehran in November 1979, there was elation in the souks of the Persian Gulf: "The United States has been done in the eye," was a commonly repeated phrase. In Islamabad that same month, merely the rumor of U.S. complicity in the attack by religious zealots on the Great Mosque in Mecca sparked an eruption of violence and destruction against U.S. personnel and property. These incidents are illustrative of a growing antipathy in the Third World toward the United States and of a readiness to believe the worst about it.

Anti-Americanism is easy to identify but difficult to define, ranging from suspicion and resentment to disdain and hostility toward the government, policy, culture, and society of the United States. It is widespread and persistent in many parts of Asia, the Middle East, Africa, and Latin America. Important segments of the educated classes of Third World Societies perceive U.S. objectives and actions as consistently misguided or malevolent.

In its moderate form the image of the United States is the not too intelligent Clumsy Giant who runs around the world stamping out brush fires regardless of whose turf they break out on. The more sinister image is the Octopus whose tentacles—the military, the CIA, the banks, the multinational corporations—encircle the globe.

Anti-Americanism is a new phenomenon, differing markedly from the anti-British, anti-French, or anti-Dutch sentiments that surfaced in the heyday of British, French, and Dutch imperial rule. And despite a spreading Soviet presence in the Third World, there is nothing comparable to be found in mass or elite attitudes toward the Soviet Union. Anti-Americanism is *sui generis.*

Throughout the Third World, Soviet and local communist propaganda together can account for but a modest part of the phenomenon. A more important factor in a number of countries is the influence of Marxism on the thinking of political and intellectual elites over the past fifty years, but this explanation also is incomplete. In some cases anti-Americanism is associated with pro-Soviet attitudes but in other cases not; Islamic fundamentalists in Iran need no inspiration from Moscow to vent their wrath on "the Great Satan."

In our analysis we start with the nature of Third World societies themselves. On some points we offer substantive generalizations; on others we simply identify important variables which must be taken into account. Our argument is that one cannot explain anti-Americanism without considering (1) ethnicity, religion and culture, (2) the values of elites, and (3) the political systems of Third World societies.

THIRD WORLD SOCIETIES: PREDISPOSITIONS AND INFLUENCES

Ethnicity, Religion, and Culture

Third World societies are very different from that of the United States. They are different, inter alia, in wealth and power, political system, and ethnicity. It would be plausible to assume that important clues to the phenomenon of anti-Americanism could be found in the very character of, say, a poor, predominantly Muslim black African country with an authoritarian regime.

The differences between the two societies are striking, no doubt, though it is not clear that differences per se generate hostility. What is needed is a theory that shows how awareness of these differences might condition basic perceptions of the other society. The differences might incline some individuals to suspicion or bias in the first instance or reinforce perceptions of threat from the other side. But the connections between dissimilarities and antipathy are frequently inferred with little supporting evidence.

In the United States the dominant majority is white, English-speaking, and Christian; in the Third World we find all three major races, thousands of non-Western languages, animism, Hinduism, Buddhism, Islam, and a majority of the world's Catholics.

Western imperialism was an enterprise of white Christians who spoke English or some other European language. In some cases, the nationalist movements that emerged in response drew heavily on indigenous race, language, and religion as symbols of group identity in the struggle against imperialism. If, as is often suggested, the United States has inherited the European imperialists' legacy as the chief focus of Third World resentment, differences in race, religion, and language should be no less significant in the explanation of anti-Americanism.

This approach would see the Tanzanian reacting as a black African to the white man in Washington, the Indian as a brown Hindu, the Iraqi as an Arab Muslim. In noting the objective differences in ethnic character between U.S. and Third World societies, interesting patterns appear. Jamaica is similar to the United States in language and religion but dissimilar in race; Syria is close in race, very different in language and religion; Chile is close in all three components; Burma is dissimilar in all three.

It is important to remember, however, that objective differences, physical or cultural, are not important unless they have been politicized and define group identities. Africans on the whole are not embarrassed by the adjectives "Francophone" or "Anglophone." Linguistic and tribal identities (e.g., Hausa, Yoruba and Ibo in Nigeria) are vitally important in internal politics, but weaken the sense of national or African racial identity and have little influence in shaping attitudes toward the outside world. It is doubtful that anti-Americanism in most African countries originates with racial consciousness. Alleged U.S. support for South Africa's apartheid regime, however, is clearly important. That is, grievances explain much more than ethnic differences per se. And the relative similarities in race, religion and language of Chilean society to U.S. society have not produced less anti-Americanism than in African countries.

In two important cases, closely related, it does appear that ethnic and religious differences are a significant factor in explaining anti-Americanism. Both the Arab world and the Muslim world are conscious of a conflict with the Christian West which has gone on for centuries but which in its present form has the United States as its standard-bearer. If scholarship in the politically dominant West has served to confirm negative stereotypes of Arabs and Muslims, as has been argued,[1] it is no less true that hostility toward the infidel West has for centuries been part of the Muslim view of history.

Here again, grievances against U.S. actions are more important than prejudices. Our point is simply that this historical consciousness is very much alive among contemporary Muslims, and is unique at least in its intensity. Hinduism and Buddhism also suffered the dislocations and humiliations of several hundred years of Western imperialism but manifest little of the bitterness and hostility still felt within Islam.

Although differences in race, religion, and language are not a primary factor in the explanation of anti-Americanism, it is a factor that must not be overlooked. The evidence of religious, cultural and racial bigotry in U.S. society in the recent past is overwhelming, and serious problems remain. Many members of Third World elites see Americans as a people who assume their own racial and cultural superiority, who are ignorant and disdainful of other civilizations, who are eager to teach but disinclined to learn from others. Many Latin American intellectuals believe that the long history of U.S. interventions and bullying in their region reflected not simply U.S. interests and superior power but also a view of the Latin as an inferior human being.

The Third World, in short, is responding to what it perceives to be U.S. assumptions of superiority in race and culture as well as technology and economy. As Ainslie Embree put it: "Part of the way they look at us is based on how they think we look at them."[2] Specific grievances against the United States government may provide the spark, but there is also an ethnic-cultural tinder that helps to explain the ignition of anti-Americanism.

Paradoxically, some Asian and African elites who proclaim their indigenous cultural roots most vigorously have in fact undergone a profound process of westernization, as we shall see in the next section.

Elites and Their Values

We have already suggested that anti-Americanism is found primarily at the upper levels of a Third World society. In Asia, the Middle East, and Africa it is often knowledge of a Western language that separates this minority from the masses. It is not a single homogeneous elite but a collection of elites differentiated by wealth and occupation, and the extent and intensity of anti-Americanism can be expected to vary among them in a given society.

Anti-Americanism may be most intense among members of the intellectual elite—academics, writers, journalists, students, and so forth. The political elite, like the intellectuals, frequently function on the basis of the connection between anti-Americanism and nationalism, but of course have to pay more attention to the foreign policy consequences. The bureaucratic elite may be inclined to greater moderation, but in most Third World countries its independence is severely curtailed or nonexistent. The military elite, consisting of commissioned officers, has become a prominent actor in Third World politics; its attitude toward the United States has varied widely. Elites holding greater wealth than any of the above might include a landed class, businessmen, and industrialists; in some cases economic interests will dictate generally pro-American views, but in other cases not. The differentiated character of elites must be borne in mind; our primary concern here is with the intellectual, political, and bureaucratic elites.

Many Third World leaders who came to power in the decade or two after World War II were educated in the capital or major center of the colonial power. They had often spent years abroad, in the process becoming fluent in the language of the ruler and acquiring an abiding attachment to his culture. Their agitation for independence was carried on without any diminution in admiration for the culture of the colonizer. During the long-lived age of imperialism, successive generations of young people from the families of native elites spent years in the metropole aspiring to be "proper Englishmen" or "proper Frenchmen." Culturally this seemed possible.

Whether it was London or Paris or The Hague or Brussels or Lisbon, the center of the empire attracted and educated the budding cadres of nationalists, who understood that knowledge of the language and culture of the imperial ruler were essential prerequisites for entrée into the political arena. Regular interaction at social as well as political levels between the ruling elites and members of the aspiring nationalist movements became very much a part of the changing imperial order. This pattern of acculturation helped ease the transition from colony to nationhood and accounts for the persistence of close linkages between many Third World countries and their former rulers.

None of this applies to the Third World's experience with the United States, with the possible exception of the Philippines. Few Third World leaders feel about the United States the way they felt about Britain or France or Portugal; few of them have had the same prolonged, intimate or intellectually intense exposure to U.S. culture or politics. Until recently, elites in the Third World sent their children to be educated in

Europe. This was true even of Latin America, which looked to Europe, not The United States, for culture and education.

This cultural divide cannot be bridged quickly. The result is a relative absence of understanding, of cultural intimacy, of shared perspectives about the world, the lack of which bedevils day-to-day diplomatic, economic, and social relations.

The emergence of the United States as the inheritor of Europe's power ushered in an age of discontinuity. The United States is a global power but, unlike its European predecessors, not an imperial power; it has no possessions, no proprietary stake in spreading its culture, no pretensions to give, as some British defenders of empire had contended, people of the Third World a "high and rewarding civilization."[3]

Most Third World leaders educated in Western Europe, especially in Britain or France, developed a commitment to socialism which was *de rigueur* among the intellectuals who dominated the academic scene. Later, this ideological orientation created some tension between themselves and U.S. officials.

As a capitalist country the United States was regarded as unsympathetic to the socialist aspirations of newly independent countries. Also, in the innumerable meetings of international organizations where ideological preferences dominated discussions of economic, social, and political issues, the Soviet Union had an advantage over the United States. The Soviet emphasis on nationalization of key industries, heavy public sector investment, extensive central planning, and collectivist solutions found a generally receptive audience, even among Third World leaderships opposed to communism and Soviet policies.

Influenced by socialist precepts and preferences, Third World leaderships believed that their countries could not afford the wasteful competition of Western capitalist development, the permissiveness of social systems that allowed private individuals or corporations to accumulate great wealth, or the constant siphoning off of scarce resources to satisfy the conspicuous consumption of a small portion of the population. They also thought the U.S. prescription for curing Third World socioeconomic ills was too conservative, too conditioned by the West's own experience, too wedded to an essentially status quo orientation. The result in the first decade or two of decolonization and diplomatic normalization with the Soviet Union was a readiness to make much of Soviet assistance while belittling U.S. assistance, especially since much of it came in the form of food which the United States had in superabundance and which they believed was easy to give away.

The elites of Asia, the Middle East, and Africa are thus characterized by a culture—modern, western, frequently socialist—that separates them sharply from the traditional culture of the masses. But the "brown Englishman" of the South Asian subcontinent must also come to terms with the traditional culture, particularly if he aspires to political leadership in an age of presumed mass politics. If his acquired English culture gives him a sense of distance from the United States, as we have argued, his identity as Hindu or Muslim or Buddhist is ultimately more critical in defining his nation's special place in the world and in his perception of the United States as Other. The Latin American elites are not subject to such difficult problems of cultural identity, but their ambivalence toward the North has been clear since the early nineteenth century. They have found much to admire and emulate, much to fear and hate, in the Colossus which it is impossible to ignore.

Political Systems

The political elites who came to power in Asia, the Middle East, and Africa following World War II, like those in Latin America a century and a quarter earlier, anticipated democratic political development patterned after Western European and North American models. What has transpired is very different. The vast majority of Third World governments are authoritarian, approximately two-thirds of them military regimes. African states are about evenly divided between military and one-party civilian authoritarian governments. Most Third World governments have little in common with U.S. democracy.

It might be argued that this difference generates complex negative feelings among Third World leaders who started out proclaiming democratic principles. Continuing assertions of the inapplicability of Western democracy combine with serious inner questioning of the legitimacy of their authoritarian alternatives and the suspicion that the West regards their politics as a mark of inferiority. Anti-American rhetoric thus identifies the external villain who is the cause of most problems and relieves the psychological strain.

Whatever the validity of such psychological interpretations, it is important to remember the authoritarian context of much of Third World anti-Americanism. In many cases the press, radio and other forms of public communication are tightly controlled, and few demonstrations take place without the tacit consent of the regime. External enemies are very useful to governments of all kinds, democratic and authoritarian, but in the latter case there is likely to be little criticism of the manipulation of "enemies" by the regime. It is important to note, however, that the largest Third World country, India, has long been both a functioning democracy and an important source of criticism of the United States.

Most Third World governments combine tough, repressive authoritarian practices, which project an image of strength, with corruption, inefficiency, and a general incapacity to get things done, pointing to an inherent weakness of the political system. This intrinsic weakness entails vulnerability to foreign penetration, and leads to the question of the impact of Soviet propaganda and other means of influence in fomenting anti-Americanism.

The Soviet Union "spends at least five times what the United States does on its information and cultural ventures" in an effort to attract supporters in the ongoing competition with the United States in the Third World.[4] Although the range of Soviet activities is extensive, little is known of their effectiveness in fostering anti-Americanism (and, conversely, engendering pro-Soviet attitudes), largely because Western analysts have focused on what the Soviets do rather than what they accomplish.

Part of the difficulty lies in determining the effect the media have in shaping attitudes. For example, during the 444-day Iranian hostage crisis, the broadcasts of the Soviet Union's Radio Peace and Progress upheld the seizure of the Americans, blamed U.S. imperialism for the situation, and encouraged the Iranians to persevere, frequently hinting at the readiness of the Soviet Union to assist the Iranians in their revolution. Did these broadcasts, often highly charged and polemical, encourage the Iranian government to drag out the crisis? Did they intensify the regime's well-developed anti-American campaign? Would the government have had any second thoughts if Soviet broadcasts had ever mentioned, as Foreign Minister Andrei Gromyko did on two occasions in a European context, that the Soviet Union did not uphold infringements on diplomatic immunity? In a word, who pays attention to Soviet broadcasts? And if so, how is their behavior affected?

The Soviet Union finances a global network of communist front organizations. But whereas in Western Europe the organizations can help mobilize public opinion against the U.S. position on prominent issues, in the Third World the situation differs significantly: most regimes, being dictatorships, do not permit private groups to demonstrate freely and all protest movements are subject to government control. Moreover, in such political systems, communist front organizations are generally not trusted and are watched very closely, even though the government may have a pro-Soviet policy orientation. Only in a democratic society such as India can local communists, financed with Soviet money, agitate actively and often against the United States and seek to foster anti-American attitudes.

The Soviet Union wages psychological war against the United States in the Third World. The Russian phrase, *aktivniye meropriyatiya* (active measures), signifies a range of techniques that include disinformation, "media manipulations, forgeries, calculated rumors, falsely attributed radio broadcasts, and the activities of agents of influence."[5] The impact of these Soviet efforts is difficult to assess. One U.S. official argues that it is considerable because governments in the Third World, "often unstable, economically stressed and lacking tested political institutions are more vulnerable to covert manipulation"; that the Soviet Union's "active measures" occasionally help bring to power a regime subject to its influence; and that they distract Third World leaders from "their primary task—development."[6] These contentions, interesting and suggestive, need however to be examined carefully in light of what we know about Soviet policy in the Third World. Furthermore, they need to be concretely related to manifestations of anti-Americanism in specific sectors before their validity can be established.

AREAS OF DISAGREEMENT

In this section we set forth the major areas of disagreement between the Third World and the United States. Anti-Americanism is a post-World War II and post-colonial phenomenon that took root among elites whose policies and perceptions of regional and international issues differed from those of Washington. Although critical of colonialism and generally sympathetic with the desire of colonial peoples for independence, the United States did not play much of a direct role in the decolonization process. There is no denying the ambivalence of the U.S. position in this unfolding situation. It stayed on the sidelines, constrained by the demands of alliance cohesion to mute its criticisms of British, French, Dutch, and Portuguese empires already in an advanced stage of dissolution; but it kept to a minimum the diversions of American military and economic assistance for the maintenance of the status quo in the Third World.

United States (and Soviet) ideological opposition to colonialism meant that the national-liberation forces had to cope only with second echelon powers and that they could campaign freely for support in international forums. Because the United States was content to play the part of observer and referee while the opposing teams settled the score between themselves, decolonization was in large measure peaceful (Algeria and Vietnam were notable exceptions). Yet by the time it was over the United States found itself the target of considerable suspicion and animosity among Third World countries. The reasons vary from country to country and from region to region and, as we shall see, are often difficult to isolate precisely, but four major areas of disagreement surface repeatedly in the criticisms of Third World spokesmen.

We discuss these areas of disagreement primarily from the viewpoint of Third World critics of the United States. There is no systematic effort made to refute their charges, since our purpose is to understand the grievances that give rise to anti-Americanism.

Global U.S. Policy

The United States is perceived as being obsessed with the threat of communism. Although some would trace the cold war primarily to this obsession, perhaps a more typical Third World opinion would hold the two superpowers equally responsible. There would be wide agreement that the anti-Soviet rhetoric of U.S. politicians has frequently been harsh and provocative, as in President Reagan's denunciations of the Soviet Union as "an evil empire."

Neither superpower has demonstrated much willingness to take risks in order to achieve peace, but each is willing to risk nuclear war in the struggle for advantage over the other. Nuclear arms control negotiations drag on year after year, the Third World believes, because neither superpower is willing to make changes that might cost it military advantage.

Many Third World leaders see superpower behavior on both sides as basically amoral. Both sides have perpetrated or abetted violent outrages on innocent people: in Hungary, Czechoslovakia, Afghanistan; in Guatemala and Vietnam. To the Third World, morality in the global conflict, if it exists at all, is ambiguous. Both contenders profess high principles and both give highest priority to the retention and expansion of their power.

Initial disenchantment with the United States dates from the mid-1950s, when it was political in character. The Eisenhower administration, keen to extend the containment of the Soviet Union, sponsored a series of military pacts that polarized the Middle East and South Asia and pitted U.S. policy against the national interests of key regional actors. The "pactomania" that brought Iraq and Pakistan into the military orbit of the Western powers triggered a countervailing animosity from Egypt and India, respectively, each of which saw U.S. policy as a threat and consequently moved to develop closer relations with the Soviet Union. This, perhaps more than any other development, sowed the seeds for the erosion of prevailing goodwill toward the United States, paved the way for Soviet penetration, and gave impetus to Third World attempts to dissociate from the East-West conflict, leading to nonalignment.

Anti-American impulses flowed from political differences over how best to foster security. At the core of these differences was a widely divergent conception of what the danger was and how best to counter it: for the United States, it was the Soviet Union; for Egypt and India—the most prominent of the early critics of the United States—it was regional rivals, if only because neither had ever experienced a threat from the Soviet Union. In time, these political differences were to assume manifold dimensions, though competing conceptions of national security remained a central consideration.

Nonalignment was and is the essence of the Third World's response to the global power struggle. The communist Tito, the democrat Nehru, and the authoritarian Nasser all played leading roles in the founding of the movement, and ideological pluralism has characterized its entire history. Nonalignment became, in the field of foreign policy, the logical extension of the Third World country's political independence. Following centuries of Western imperialism, nonalignment was an expression of Third World nationalism, an assertion of the right to chart an independent course free of great power control.

United States policy was insensitive to the feelings and calculations that produced nonalignment in the 1950s. Seeing the cold war as a global conflict between good and evil, the Third World was admonished that "neutralism is immoral." Having marked out the proper course through such regional alliances as SEATO and CENTO, the United States could not easily come to terms with nonalignment, while the Soviets by 1955 publicly supported the principle.

John F. Kennedy in his 1961 message to the twenty-five members of the nonaligned movement assembled at Belgrade said that the United States shared their commitment to "a world of peace in which nations have the freedom to choose their own political and economic systems and to live their own way of life."[7] But as the membership of the movement grew rapidly in the following two decades, reaching 101 by 1983, it frequently became a forum for criticism of U.S. policies.

Americans tend to see pro-Soviet bias in expressions of anti-Americanism, partly because Third World spokesmen have roundly condemned alleged misdeeds by the United States but reacted to similar Soviet actions with muted criticism at most. Assuming that this generalization about the lack of even-handedness is valid, how do we explain it? Partly it is the continuation of a pre-1945 pattern in which imperialism was Western imperialism (Yankee imperialism in Latin America), while the Soviet Marxist-Leninist tradition was strongly anti-imperialist. Overwhelmingly, the Third World's direct experience with imperialism was at the hands of the West.

Paradoxically, it is also true that Third World spokesmen feel freer to criticize those whom they know better. Harsh criticism of government is part of the Western tradition in which Third World elites have been socialized. In a curious way the vehemence of Third World rhetoric reflects membership in the same extended family, and the West is expected to "understand." No such historic ties link Soviet and Third World peoples; the Soviets must be treated more circumspectly, more cautiously, because they too have vast power but are less well known. This lack of even-handedness has often led U.S. officials to dismiss Third World complaints as biased and therefore unjustified.

U.S. Policy Toward the Third World

The most fundamental perception, and complaint, is that U.S. policy relegates all Third World countries to the status of pawns in the global struggle. All bilateral relationships are subordinated to calculations of utility in the cold war or peaceful competition with the Soviets. The Americans profess commitment to peace, economic development, human rights, and democracy in the Third World, but any of these values may be jettisoned without hesitation or compunction if U.S. military or strategic interests are at risk.

Since most Third World countries are not now within the Soviet orbit, the United States is preeminently a status quo power. That is, the United States finds the present distribution of power and wealth in the world relatively satisfactory and will resist radical changes initiated by others. A Third World society is important to U.S. policymakers primarily because it might go communist. U.S. policy has therefore been: (1) to secure the allegiance of as many countries as possible to U.S.-sponsored military alliances, (2) to secure and maintain U.S. military bases in strategic locations, (3) to promote the economic development of U.S.-aligned or nonaligned countries in which U.S. aid can become a significant factor in limiting Soviet influence, (4) to prevent the overthrow of pro-U.S. governments, whatever their internal character, and (5) to overthrow leftist governments supported by or sympathetic to the Soviet Union.

Taken together, according to Third World critics, these are the elements of U.S. imperial policy. The effort to clothe these objectives in the rhetoric of peace, economic development, human rights, and democracy is an exercise in hypocrisy. When the regional military alliances that were forged in the mid-1950s withered away, the U.S. continued the basic relationship on a bilateral basis in a number of cases. A brutal military regime in Pakistan was supported in the 1971 Bangladesh crisis because it was a traditional anti-Soviet ally facing an internal upheaval. U.S. identification with the Shah of Iran was almost complete until a few months before he was overthrown by the Islamic revolution, with little concern for democracy or human rights. Somoza in Nicaragua, Marcos in the Philippines, Pinochet in Chile, and others were all quite acceptable leaders because they did not disturb U.S. interests.

In the basic grievance we are delineating, the United States seeks the political domination of the Third World, not in the old-fashioned form of colonialism but in a flexible policy of expanding and contracting interventionism which sets clear limits on the freedom, internal and external, of supposedly sovereign states. On the whole, Third World observers see a large degree of continuity in U.S. foreign policy objectives over the past thirty-five years, regardless of who has occupied the White House. If in 1953 the C.I.A. was engaged in overthrowing the nationalist Mossadeq government and restoring the Shah to power in Iran, in 1973 it was busy destabilizing the Marxist Allende regime in Chile in preparation for a rightist military coup. If in 1954 the reformist Arbenz had to be overthrown to protect the United Fruit Company's interests in Guatemala, in 1961 the disastrous Bay of Pigs invasion was launched against Castro's Cuba, and in 1983 the C.I.A. was openly engaged in "covert" operations to overthrow the revolutionary Sandinista regime in Nicaragua. For good measure, in 1983 the U.S. Marines invaded Grenada to remove a Marxist military regime with strong Soviet and Cuban connections.

Third World elites have available to them vastly more information on the C.I.A. than on the K.G.B. Most of this information comes to them from the United States and other western countries in a steady stream of liberal and leftist criticism of the C.I.A. Freedom of the press guarantees the publication and dissemination of this criticism, and debates in the House and Senate on appropriations for C.I.A. covert activities are freely reported. Somewhat paradoxically, the democratic and open politics of the U.S. system operates in this way to stimulate and promote the growth of anti-American sentiment in the Third World. Whatever the allegations of ruthless K.G.B. actions, they are never confirmed by Russian sources.

While most of the U.S. interventions, overt or covert, were of brief duration, the war in Vietnam was different, and perhaps more than any other major event contributed to anti-Americanism in the Third World. The war demonstrated the extraordinary lengths to which the United States was prepared to go to keep a noncommunist government in power in the south, and the enormous losses in human life over the years convinced many that the U.S. obsession with communism had become more destructive than whatever it sought to prevent. That these were mostly Asian lives lost in Vietnam and Cambodia, and mostly civilians, heightened the sense that moral justification for the war was lacking. The fact that successive administrations argued that vital U.S. interests were involved was seen by the Third World as an imperial assertion of a right to intervene anywhere.

The unwavering U.S. commitment to Israel since 1948 has affected relations with so many countries that it must be touched on separately. Although policymakers have frequently asserted that Israel is a "strategic asset" to the United States, cold-war calculations have never been the primary consideration, unlike most U.S. policies in the Third World. Support for Israel has been based on memories of the Holocaust and the considerable political clout of the U.S. Jewish community. A policy strictly calculated to minimize Soviet influence in the Middle East during the past three decades would have favored the Arabs over the Israelis.

In any case, U.S. support for Israel has long been the most obvious cause of anti-Americanism in the region. The Arabs condemn Zionism as a racist and imperialist ideology which, in its implementation by the state of Israel, has robbed the Palestinians of their homeland, national identity, and human rights. Since the 1967 war the bitter debate has centered on the fate of the Arabs in the West Bank and Gaza. The 1979 peace treaty between Israel and Egypt, through a remarkable diplomatic achievement, left the latter issue unresolved.

Egypt's turnabout in international alignment under Sadat, from a model Soviet client to a model U.S. client, signaled a corresponding de-cline in expressions of anti-Americanism. The contingent nature of the phenomenon seemed clear: anti-Americanism was freely expressed when it reflected the authoritarian government's international orientation and when specific grievances against the United States gave it point; anti-Americanism receded as these two circumstances changed.

American Economic Activity in the Third World

Third World grievances over the operations of U.S. capitalism vary greatly in intensity from one region to another, ranging from Latin America and the Caribbean where investments have long been sizable, to South Asia where they have been relatively small. A large and eco-nomically diverse country like India could afford to adjust its trade and investment policies with a declining United Kingdom after independence while keeping the Americans at arm's length. Small countries with a sin-gle major export and thus highly dependent on the world market found their situation to be very difficult.

In Latin America the economic penetration of weak societies began in the nineteenth century and produced an image of Yankee capitalism that has persisted into the era of the modern multinational corporation. At the turn of the century the United Fruit Company owned land in Costa Rica, Guatemala, Nicaragua, Panama, Colombia, Santo Domingo, Cuba and Jamaica, operated a large fleet of steamships, and held title to the Guatemalan Railroad Company. Nicknamed El Pulpo (the Oc-topus), the Company had no difficulty in extracting favorable treatment from successive Guatemalan governments until Arbenz's enactment of an agrarian reform law in 1952, which set the state for the C.I.A.-engineered coup that overthrew him.[8]

Seventy percent of U.S. overseas investment is now in the developed world where there are no coups, and political stability can be counted on. Third World critics see U.S.-based multinationals as continuing to exploit their countries' resources and populations, perpetuating a polit-ical and economic dependency that benefits only a denationalized elite. These critics dismiss claims that the multinationals are beneficial to the host country in terms of capital and technology transfer, managerial training, employment, and genuine development, and see any benefits as marginal and incidental to the MNC's basic objectives. They discount the ability of host governments to bargain effectively, even with the weapon of nationalization in the background. The penetration of the economy by a group of powerful multinationals simply means that the government is no longer in control.[9]

The United States, in this view, has consistently sought to combine its political and economic power to ensure hegemony and the subjugation of the Third World. U.S. foreign policy serves the interests of big corporations; the corporations abroad are agents of the U.S. government in its quest for political domination. Such views are commonplace among Latin American intellectuals and are by no means confined to Marxists.

Two U.S. companies, Kennecott and Anaconda, have operated copper mines in Chile since early in this century. In 1969 Anaconda's return on U.S. investments was 39.5 percent and Kennecott's was 24.1 percent. As in Brazil, Argentina and Mexico, in the 1960s there was a rapid expansion of U.S. multinationals into Chile. U.S. investment doubled during the decade, but profits, part reinvested and part repatriated, rose sevenfold. Twenty-four of the top thirty U.S. multinationals (Standard Oil, Ford, IBM, ITT, General Electric, etc.) were operating in Chile by 1970.[10] These facts constitute part of the economic profile of Chile in the year the Marxist Salvador Allende won a plurality in a free election and became president.

Whatever the economic effects of the American MNCs in Third World countries, their operations are highly visible, and this fact has a strong bearing on the articulation of anti-Americanism. In the 1970s Iran's oil bonanza, combined with the Shah's megalomania, brought swarms of U.S. and other Western businessmen to Teheran. Bell Helicopter and other companies set up huge installations with thousands of employees, and U.S. executives with their dependents were soon ensconced in aristocratic villas complete with servants. By 1976 U.S. companies had over $1 billion invested in Iran, and two years later there were 50,000 Americans living there. As the drama of the following two years unfolded, the large and obtrusive U.S. presence was used to discredit the Shah, and the close U.S. ties with him fanned the flames of anti-Americanism.[11]

Why is there no anti-Soviet counterpart to anti-Americanism in the Third World? Partly because the Soviet Union is marginal to the capitalist international economic order with which the Third World must come to terms, like it or not. U.S. companies, on the other hand, crisscross the globe in the search for economic opportunity. Resentments grow with U.S. profits, and high visibility means vulnerability. The emerging conflict is not between North and South, but between West and South, and the United States represents the West.

Perceptions of U.S. Society

Third World images of U.S. society have always been mixed. In the early 1950s these images were formed largely from popular magazines and Hollywood movies; relatively few people from Third World elites had any firsthand experience of the United States.

There were many negative components in the image. The United States was a land of economic opportunity, but its prosperity had led to crass materialism and secularism. It was a depersonalized, superficial society without the moral restraints of deeply rooted religion. In particular, sexual immorality was common. The dominant Anglo-Saxon Protestants shared but little power with others, and did so reluctantly with the Catholic and Jewish minorities. White racism was rampant, Blacks had no political voice and often no vote. It was a narrow, bigoted society in which Senator Joseph McCarthy could intimidate the highest in the land with charges of communist sympathies.

U.S. society has changed a great deal in the last thirty-five years, and although there has inevitably been a certain time lag, Third World images of the United States have also changed. The election of a Catholic as president in 1960, civil rights advances, the rise of black and Hispanic politicians, Andrew Young's tenure as U.S. ambassador to the United Nations, and other developments have decisively changed the old stereotypes of U.S. society.

The dynamism of U.S. society is viewed as a radical threat by Third World elites intent on the preservation of existing values, institutions, practices, and social relationships. In the Muslim world, the resurgence of fundamentalist groups, inspired by Ayatollah Khomeini's Islamic revolution in Iran and virulent attacks on "satanic" America, drew attention to this dimension of hostility toward the United States. Anti-Americanism is a visceral reaction to the iconoclasm intrinsic to U.S. cultural exports, a recognition that everything American can have socially disruptive and unanticipated consequences. Whether it be rock music, pop art, blue jeans, McDonald's restaurants, television soap operas portraying sex and violence, political activism, the youth drug culture, social permissiveness, or the preoccupation with personal fulfillment, the effect is perceived as threatening to traditional values and authority relationships.

The consumerism of U.S. mass culture is a more dangerous antagonist for groups seeking to ensure the status quo than is communism or the revolutionary message of the Left. But the materialistic aspect of the American dream is only marginally threatening to tradition-bound societies; it is the peculiarly U.S. notion of change for the sake of change that is systemically so profoundly revolutionary in its import. This underlying restlessness is destructive of traditional institutions, and in that sense the United States stands as an exemplar of the world's leading revolutionary system.

Driven by a conscious commitment to use technology to produce wealth and a higher living standard for larger numbers of people than ever before in human history, and willing to accept the searing dislocations and disruptions that are an inevitable part of rapid social, economic, and cultural change, the United States is lunging into the future, impelled by forces that are uncontrolled and non-selective.[12] Governments struggling to control their dissatisfied populations whose aspirations exceed productive capacities fear the diffusion of the United States' consumer-oriented culture and the pressures from below for change that it unleashes.

U.S. affluence also occasions envy, especially among groups who are politically and socially aware. The contrast between their own plight and the superabundance of their U.S. counterparts breeds ill will toward the person and the society possessing the wealth. Even in an age of universal consumerism, the U.S. wealth that is palpably evident in the Third World often stands out as wasteful and ostentatious. It seem ubiquitous and inexhaustible, whether in the hands of transient tourists or resident technicians—most of whom are oblivious to the offense that their appearance and behavior may give.

With the United States, changes continue to make U.S. society more accessible to the Third World. Changes in immigration law and the admission of refugees have opened the country to sizable numbers of immigrants from various parts of the Third World. The pluralization of society has proceeded apace. Cubans and other Latin Americans, Koreans, Indians and Pakistanis, Iranians and others from the Middle East, and refugees from Vietnam and Cambodia have added their numbers to the older U.S. communities of Third World origin and have changed the face of America. International students have settled here in large numbers, and many upper and middle class people in the Third World have relatives or friends living here. Many more are anxious to emigrate to the United States. (Who wants to emigrate to the Soviet Union?)

As in the past, economic opportunity is the most powerful attraction of U.S. society. The possibilities of upward mobility draw the new immigrants with fresh appeal; there are difficulties and complaints, but little or no disillusionment with the system. Continuing poverty and the plight of an underclass disproportionately present in the black community are recognized as unpleasant facts of contemporary America but are outweighed by the positive aspects.

Personal and political freedom in a functioning democracy have a strong appeal. Even the failings of U.S. democracy are instructive, as when Third World readers of *Time* magazine sought to grasp how the peccadilloes associated with Watergate could have brought down a president, in contrast with the unchallenged authoritarian power of many of their own governments.

What impresses many in the Third World is the dynamism of U.S. society. If a kind of rootlessness goes with the dynamism, there is freedom for the individual to incorporate as much of the traditional religion and culture as he wishes. Middle class immigrants find a congenial environment in the freedom of an open society.

A TYPOLOGY OF ANTI-AMERICANISM

The manifestations of anti-Americanism vary greatly from one situation to another; in order of their political impact, from the least to the most serious, they are as follows.

Attitudes. Individuals and sections of elites feel resentment, anger, ill will, and hatred toward the government and/or people of the United States. These attitudes can be deeply felt but remain unexpressed.

Verbal expressions. Speeches, writings, radio and television programs criticize, ridicule or denounce the U.S. government and people.

Demonstrations. Large groups of people, more or less organized, assemble publicly to denounce the United States through marches, speeches, and the shouting of slogans.

Violence. Violent mob attacks on U.S. embassies, consulates, and U.S.I.A. libraries, and the taking of U.S. government personnel as hostages may be carried out in front of television cameras. More typically, terrorist forms of violence, such as the bombing of embassy buildings or assassination of U.S. officials, are carried out clandestinely with the anti-American message conveyed by the deed itself. Any of these manifestations may be associated with the types of anti-Americanism analyzed below.

Our typology attempts to make some sense of the bewildering array of beliefs, situations, and events that taken together have been labeled "anti-Americanism." We identify four basic types of the phenomenon; a critical distinction must be made concerning the major actor or actors involved in each: government, elites, and masses.

Issue-oriented Anti-Americanism

Issue-oriented anti-Americanism is an outburst of hostility, or a pattern of such outbursts, against specific policies or actions of the U.S. government with which a Third World government disagrees. Nongovernmental elites generally play a significant but secondary role in supporting their government's policies and in articulating opposition to the United States. Issue-oriented anti-Americanism springs from the policy disagreements of two governments pursuing their respective national interest; it is not generated by elite attitudes nor instigated by the Third World government for ulterior purposes.

Much of what is regarded as anti-Americanism in the Third World is of this type. The United States has frequently found itself in policy conflicts with India during the past thirty-seven years—conflict over U.S. military aid to Pakistan, over India's nonalignment policy, over India's annexation of Goa, over U.S. support for Pakistan in the Bangladesh crisis, over the U.S. military base in Diego Garcia, and over India's reaction to the Soviet invasion of Afghanistan. On some of these issues the denunciations of U.S. policy in the Indian press and in official statements were strongly worded. However, while these denunciations were regarded in Washington as expressions of anti-Americanism, from New Delhi's point of view the U.S. policies and actions were *anti-Indian*. It could be argued that the Indian interpretation was more plausible, since the U.S. policies in dispute directly impinged on Indian interests in South Asia. There have been differences of opinion but no serious tensions in Indo-American relations over U.S. policies in Western Europe or Latin America.

Thus there is a conceptual problem imbedded in our category of issue-oriented anti-Americanism, which is always but one side of the coin in a bilateral relationship. One can speak of anti-Americanism as a general phenomenon, as contrasted with "anti-Indianism," simply because the United States since the early years of the cold war has defined its national interest in global terms and its policies have impinged on virtually every Third World country, making for a very weighty aggregate of policy grievances and conflicts.

Anti-Americanism is also fueled by Washington's frequently heavy handed approach to specific and important issues and by the alacrity with which it uses pressure rather than conciliation to bring about preferred outcomes, in the process manifesting an insensitivity that worsens existing relationships. In the late 1960s, for example, waves of criticism swept through Peru in reaction to U.S. threats to cut off economic assistance because the government had bought sixteen supersonic Mirage fighters from France and was seizing U.S. fishing boats within the 200-mile zone that was claimed as territorial waters, at a time when the United States considered sovereignty to extend only 12 miles offshore.[13]

U.S. hostility toward Cuba and attempts to isolate it in the hemisphere have often resulted in sympathy for Havana, even among those antipathetic to Castro's policies. Typical of Latin American reaction was the view expressed by the Mexican writer and diplomat, Carlos Fuentes, who has not been to Cuba since 1962 because of political disagreements with Castro: "The day the United States stops attacking Cuba, it will no longer be possible for Cuba to mobilize intellectual opinion in the region. All Latin Americans have felt they must keep silent so as not to help imperialism."[14]

More recently, U.S. efforts to destabilize the Sandinista regime have caused waves of criticism, in large measure from deep-rooted opposition to U.S. interference in the internal affairs of countries in the region. Such specific issues—be they arms purchases, assertions of sovereignty on matters such as territorial waters, or the handling of Cuba or Nicaragua—prompt anti-American outbursts that cut across the political, social, or class spectrum.

As noted earlier, Third World officials believe the United States is obsessed with the Soviet Union and world communism and is interested in Third World nations primarily as pawns or proxies in the ongoing global superpower struggle. As these officials see the situation, aid will be forthcoming if they play such roles; otherwise, neglect. They tend therefore to regard U.S. grants of aid that promote economic and social development as payoffs for political cooperation rather than as expressions of empathy for their problems and aspirations.

This view concerning U.S. motives comes at a time when Third World leaders feel capable of assuming greater responsibility for regional security and cooperative development programs. Though well aware of their vulnerabilities and limited power, they nonetheless insist that the sovereign equality of nation-states requires their greater involvement in decisions affecting their future. Above all, they refuse to accept as givens the traditional monopolization by the great powers of decisions affecting regional security. For example, Latin Americans contend that they could play an important conciliatory role in Central America, moderating the Sandinista Revolution and bringing the principal protagonists in El Salvador to the conference table. A non-communist Nicaraguan nationalist told a U.S. journalist, "The best way to twist the arms of the Sandinistas is by economic and diplomatic pressure from Latin Americans. The more the pressure is managed by Latin Americans and neighbors, the more the Sandinistas will accommodate and save face with neighbors."[15]

Ultimately, the argument goes, countries such as Mexico, Venezuela, Panama, and Colombia (the "Contadora" countries) can more successfully find a solution in El Salvador and Nicaragua than can the United States, especially if all that Washington has in mind is military solutions. Carlos Andres Perez, president of Venezuela from 1974 to 1979, laments the "humiliating lack of respect" displayed by the United States toward Latin Americans, epitomized by the failure of the United States to accord prominence to the Contadora group, which he calls a "symbol of the new Latin American consciousness."[16]

Ideological Anti-Americanism

Ideological anti-Americanism is a sustained, rationally argued antagonism toward the government and society of the United States, and is an important part of the belief system of certain sections of Third World elites. Ideological anti-Americanism is based on (1) a view of history in which the past and present role of the United States in the world is seen as politically and economically imperialist, and (2) a view of the value system of U.S. society, variously described as bourgeois decadence, godless materialism, and so forth. Pitched at a higher level of generalization, ideological anti-Americanism continues to generate hostility even without serious policy conflicts between the United States and the elite's own government; the intellectuals' views are formed on the basis of what is going on everywhere in the world. In its identification of a central villain in world history, ideological anti-Americanism can be compared with Latin American anticlericalism in the past or anticommunism among extreme rightists today.

Three important streams flow into ideological anti-Americanism in the contemporary Third World: nationalism, Marxism, and Islamic fundamentalism. Nationalism is the most universal and easily merges with the other two. Marxism is the most intellectually coherent, but derives much of its political force from its critique of imperialism, a nationalist theme. Islamic fundamentalism is of course limited to the Muslim world, but since this embraces forty-four countries it must be reckoned a major force. What is striking is the similar way in which Fidel Castro and the Ayatollah Khomeini view the role of the United States in the world today. Concepts of imperialism and neoimperialism lie at the heart of ideological anti-Americanism.

Latin America's long tradition of anti-Americanism is historically rooted in hostility to U.S. interference in the region, especially in Central America. As far back in the nineteenth century as the promulgation of the Monroe Doctrine, Latin American elites resented the implicit arrogation of hemispheric hegemony. As a consequence of decades of experience, mistrust and fear of the Yanqui colossus are indelibly fixed in their political consciousness. This is reinforced by the use of force by the United States to depose unfriendly regimes and install friendly ones.

Anti-Americanism is strong among Islamic fundamentalist groups, regardless of their government's official relationship with the United States. In virulently anti-American Iran, as we shall see, the official hostility permeates the society. But even in Egypt, where the government of Hosni Mubarak cultivates close ties with the United States, the Muslim Brotherhood and its ancillary supporters are a source of bitter anti-Americanism. They resist U.S. inroads as destabilizing and antithetical to the perpetuation of traditional values and institutions.

Marxist and Marxist-oriented elites see U.S. capitalism at the center of the system they seek to change. What unifies their diverse radical and revolutionary impulses is alienation from the existing international economic system whose prime defender is the United States and their belief that the United States is the main obstacle to systemic change.

Marxism's appeal to the communist and noncommunist Left alike inheres in its potential for providing, at one and the same time, a critique of capitalism and imperialism, an adaptable model for viewing socioeconomic phenomena, a formula (in its Leninist variant) for acquiring power, and a visionary world outlook. Its adherents use Marx's analytical categories and dialectical approach with varying degrees of sophistication to attack the contemporary international economic system, and especially the preeminent role played in it by the United States. Many theorists of development and social systems, such as the dependencia school established by Raul Prebisch and others, for example, draw heavily on Marxist and neo-Marxist formulations.

In Latin America, a vaguely Marxist outlook pervades the field of literary activity. Among many distinguished authors, "Marxism, either confused or clear, vague or firm, as a mere pretext for desperate protest or as a serious interpretive effort, as the superficial stridency of youth or as the radical belief of maturity, has contributed a fundamental trait to the ideological physiognomy of Latin America."[17]

If ideas are catalysts of change, intellectuals are the agents by which they are spread and popularized. They exercise an influence disproportionate to their power; even in the highly restrictive political environments in the Third World, their voices are heard, especially if regimes can manipulate them for their own ends. According to one longtime U.S. observer of the Latin American scene, it is the intellectuals "who provide respectability to governments in power and legitimacy to revolts and revolutionary movements, they who articulate the ideas and contribute the images through which Latin Americans relate to power, they who satisfy the decidedly Latin need for a romantic and idealistic raison d'être."[18]

Intellectuals of the Left tend to be anti-American partly because they can neither forget nor forgive the success of the U.S. experiment. To the reality of U.S. affluence and power, they can only posit a romantic vision of a bright and indeterminate future. They know that notwithstanding its troubles, inequities, and social tensions, the United States remains a bulwark of stability, evolutionary change, and widely distributed wealth at a time when most Third World countries find themselves in a perilous condition of worsening perplexity.

Instrumental Anti-Americanism

Instrumental anti-Americanism is the instigation and/or manipulation of hostility toward the United States by governments with ulterior motives (1) to elicit mass support by playing on nationalism, (2) to neutralize domestic opposition on the left, (3) to provide a plausible scapegoat for governmental failures, or (4) to justify and strengthen a desired alignment as a client of the Soviet Union.

The typical setting for this type of anti-Americanism is that of an authoritarian regime that controls all the important means of communication. Although the formal institutional means for broad political participation are very limited (sometimes an official party) or nonexistent, the government actively seeks the support of the urban masses, while often ignoring the peasantry.

In such a context anti-Americanism becomes a useful instrument for mobilizing popular support and deflecting frustration away from the leadership toward a foreign, omnipresent, and supposedly omnipotent protagonist. It is convenient, easily generated, and relatively cost-free. As a political instrument for manipulating and mobilizing domestic public opinion, anti-Americanism has been a godsend to Third World regimes. They can exploit it with virtual impunity. As independent actors, they can turn to the Soviet Union or some other source for the wherewithal needed to stay in power. Indeed, a strong dose of anti-Americanism may facilitate the transfer of coveted resources, be they arms, concessionary oil, or long-term loans for development and trade. In the contemporary international system, few Third World countries fear U.S. intervention. For the most part they understand and exploit the systemic tolerance that permits small countries a hitherto unknown flexibility in challenging the great powers.

The use of a scapegoat to deflect criticism from the leadership and mobilize the people against "the enemy"—whoever that may be—is a time-tested technique of rule, whose effectiveness has been enhanced since the advent of mass media. The United States is an inviting target because of mutually reinforcing perceptions of it as an ever-intriguing, intrusive superpower and because it is not apt to respond in kind.

In the absence of institutionalized procedures for permitting criticism of official policy, authoritarian rulers cannot acknowledge having made mistakes without jeopardizing the basis of their rule. Pointing to some outside actor as the source of the trouble can serve to foster cohesion at home. Nasser blamed the United States for Egypt's crushing military defeat in June 1967 and broke diplomatic ties with the United States (as did most Arab governments). In the process, he elicited an emotional outpouring of public support and sympathy in the Arab world, which deflected attention away from his responsibility for the debacle. Fidel Castro has in the United States a natural culprit on which to heap all the blame for the ills and unrest of Central America.[19]

A scapegoat satisfies the need for explanations that are simple, satisfying, and believable. The controlling consideration is reasonableness, not reality. Whatever is complex, disturbing or ambiguous, however germane, weakens the leader's aim of deflecting the blame for an unpopular situation. How much simpler to blame U.S. assistance to Israel for that nation's defeat of three combined Arab armies, rather than face up to the inadequacies and mistakes of the key Arab leaderships. How much more comforting for critics of the United States to attribute the toppling of Salvator Allende to CIA intrigues, rather than to acknowledge the bitter hostility that his policies had aroused on the Chilean political scene.

Blaming an outside force for internal unrest and failure to achieve greater domestic progress is common practice. In early 1982, the Sudan's vice-president, Abdel-Magid Hamid Khalif, accused "foreign conspiracies," an allusion to Libya, of fomenting the riots against price increases.[20] After a series of massacres in the state of Assam in early 1983, Prime Minister Indira Gandhi said that "the agitators may have been getting encouragement from outside," and when asked specifically if the CIA was involved she replied that the situation "is much more complicated, there are many such elements." In this way she left a lingering implication of CIA intriguing—a theme frequently discussed in the Indian press.[21] Railing against "U.S. imperialism" may not enable a leadership to correct shortcomings in the system, but it is a way of rationalizing failures in order to ensure perpetuation of a ruler's power.

Instrumental anti-Americanism also includes government-managed hostility for the purpose of justifying and strengthening a client state's relationship with the Soviet Union. It is a function of pro-Soviet regimes that they be critical of U.S. "imperialism." However, being critical of U.S. policy, even identifying the United States as the enemy, does not always signify that anti-Americanism is endemic in a society. It is important to distinguish between official policy and nonofficial attitudes and behavior.

At a time when the Egyptian government did not have diplomatic relations with the United States and was bitterly critical of U.S. support for Israel, Egyptians liked Americans personally, despite the strains in relations between the two governments and the anti-American biases in the Egyptian press. By contrast, they did not like the Russians even though the Soviet Union had been generous with vital assistance, including the dispatch of combat troops in the spring of 1970, during an extemely difficult period in the country's history. The Egyptian example is, admittedly, not a typical one in the Third World, but neither is it unique.

The existence of significant differences between official pronouncements and popular attitudes suggests that an official policy of anti-Americanism may be instrumental and not at all an expression of permanent hostility, and that there exists a potential receptivity to closer ties with the United States. This should act as a reminder not to mistake a particular regime's attitude for the country's underlying national interest; a regime's attitude may undergo sharp reversals as a consequence of a leadership change that can bring the country onto a course closer to that of the United States. Egypt after the October War and Somalia in the fall of 1977 are two examples of countries whose pro-Soviet orientation was abruptly reversed as a result of a change in their leaders' perception of how to achieve key national goals and of the importance of better relations with the United States. Indeed, a basic characteristic of instrumental anti-Americanism is its reversibility on short notice.

Revolutionary Anti-Americanism

Revolutionary anti-Americanism starts with the ideological anti-Americanism of an opposition group seeking to overthrow a regime closely identified with the United States. Attacking the regime thus involves attacking the United States, which is seen as responsible for keeping the regime in power and hence for its misdeeds. After the overthrow of a pro-U.S. government, ideological anti-Americanism becomes an important tenet of the revolutionary regime itself, which sees part of its mission as transmitting the revolution to other countries. In the process, revolutionary anti-Americanism, unlike the three types discussed above, becomes a mass phenomenon. The new regime will find it useful on occasion to manipulate anti-U.S. sentiment, as in the instrumental type, but the revolutionary process has pushed anti-Americanism to the center of both the regime's ideology and mass consciousness.

Both the Iranian revolution and the Nicaraguan revolution clearly exhibit this type of anti-Americanism. The United States government's support for authoritarian rulers (the Shah, the Somoza dynasty) paved the way for the anti-American orientation of the popular forces that overthrew these rulers and replaced them with revolutionary regimes.

For most Americans the most puzzling aspect of the Iranian revolution was how the United States came to be blamed for virtually everything objectionable in the Shah's Iran. As Beeman notes, "The vituperative, accusatory rhetoric seemed to be aimed at indicting all American leaders since World War II for unacceptable interference in Iranian internal affairs, and destruction of the Iranian culture and economy."[22] The Americans working in Iran, 50,000 of them by 1978, thought that they were simply doing a job under difficult circumstances for high wages, but the Islamic militants saw not only economic exploitation but a veritable invasion of foreign influences that were destroying the spiritual orientation of Iranian society. "Thus a highly complex but very basic issue became concretized in the complex symbolic image of the Great Satan:

the loss of the nation's spiritual core and the assignment of blame for the occurrence to the United States."[23] For the Ayatollah Khomeini, the Islamic Republic was the great achievement of the revolution, but the Great Satan continued to be its deadliest enemy long after the demise of the Shah. The Great Satan had to be fought continuously, in Iraq, in the Gulf states, in Lebanon, and so the holy war continues.

TABLE 1.1: **Typology of Anti-Americanism**

Type	Government	Elites	Masses
Issue-oriented	**X**	X	
Ideological	X	**X**	
Instrumental	**X**	X	X
Revolutionary	**X**	**X**	**X**

X = major actor
X = secondary actor

SUMMARY

By definition, government is the major actor in issue-oriented anti-Americanism; hostility is generated by policy conflicts between two governments, and the role of nongovernmental elites is secondary. In ideological anti-Americanism the reverse is true; the intellectual elite articulates a belief system that influences government. In instrumental anti-Americanism the government manipulates hostility among elites and masses for ulterior purposes. Revolutionary anti-Americanism incorporates the ideological type in a process that mobilizes elites and masses and leads to a regime that enshrines the revolutionary ideology of which anti-Americanism is an important part.

CONCLUSION

Anti-Americanism was an inevitable consequence of Third World disenchantment with the United States. The idealized conception of an America exemplified by Thomas Jefferson, Abraham Lincoln, and Woodrow Wilson was rudely dispelled by the actions of U.S. administrations that became intimately enmeshed in international politics and in the process and on various occasions supported colonialism, apartheid, and dictatorships, sounding the alarm over communism when throughout the Third World the clarion call was for change.

In the early 1960s, C. L. Sulzberger discerned the cause for the spread of anti-Americanism in the contrast between what the United States professed and what it did. Sulzberger observed, "The image of the United States has become both tarnished and obscured by platitudes. The idealism we assume everyone acknowledges as the foundation of our policy has been diminished by time." And this tarnish becomes increasingly evident as the United States lectures Third World countries from "a pedestal of fake morality," as the discrepancy between the benefits U.S. leaders say they wish to bestow on the world and the inequities in U.S. society itself imprint themselves on foreign minds, and as U.S. wealth and power seem not to be directed toward improving the lot of impoverished societies abroad.[24]

The question often heard in Third World countries is: "Why has the United States lost interest in us?" Perceiving a diminished U.S. interest in helping them tackle the myriad problems facing their societies, governments will be less hesitant to sanction unfriendly acts and to attack the United States as a way of enhancing their domestic popularity.

Few Third World regimes still find much of interest or relevance in the Soviet Union's developmental model. Whatever expectations there may have been about it in the 1950s and 1960s have largely dissipated through observation and frustrating experience. Moscow's appeal now is only as a patron–protector against external threats or as a specialist in curbing internal opponents and controlling the masses, in a word, for system–maintenance.

Contemporary anti-Americanism does not state the Third World's final conclusion, but one side of a profound ambivalence felt toward this country. In a preceding section we examined Third World perceptions of U.S. global policy, of U.S. policy toward the Third World, of U.S. economic activity in the Third World, and of U.S. society itself. What we have suggested is that the Third World perceives U.S. foreign policy as frequently irresponsible, belligerent, and imperialist, U.S. international economic activity as frequently exploitive, and the United States as a basically good society. The paradoxical perception of a good society that frequently does bad things in the world captures this fundamental ambivalence.

Third World perceptions of a United States that is indifferent to them and their problems create confusion and dismay. Should these societies come to consider the U.S. experience irrelevant in some profound sense, the result would undoubtedly be further erosion in the long-range prospects for the survival of pluralism and democracy in the world.

NOTES

1. See Edward W. Said, *Orientalism* (New York: Vintage Books, 1978).

2. Comment in a panel on Anti-Americanism, Northeast Political Science Association, Philadelphia, PA, November 18, 1983.

3. A.P. Thornton, *The Imperial Idea and Its Enemies: A Study in British Power* (Garden City: Anchor Books, 1968), 254.

4. Kenneth L. Adelman, "Speaking of America: Public Diplomacy in Our Time," *Foreign Affairs*, Vol. 59, No. 4 (Spring 1981), 917.

5. Lawrence S. Eagleburger, "Unacceptable Intervention: Soviet Active Measures," *NATO Review*, Vol. 31, No. 1 (1983), 9.

6. *Ibid.*

7. Quoted in a letter from Ronald Reagan to Indira Gandhi, *India News*, March 7, 1983.

8. See Richard H. Immerman, *The CIA in Guatemala: The Foreign Policy of Intervention* (Austin: University of Texas Press, 1982).

9. On this, and many other points discussed in this chapter, see Richard E. Feinberg, *The Intemperate Zone: The Third World Challenge to U.S. Foreign Policy* (New York: W.W. Norton & Co., 1983).

10. Dale L. Johnson (ed.), *The Chilean Road to Socialism* (Garden City: Anchor Books, 1973), 13.

11. Barry Rubin, *Paved with Good Intentions: The American Experience and Iran* (New York: Oxford University Press, 1980), 141.

12. The theme of mankind being overwhelmed by forces that have been unwittingly unleashed is explored in the pioneering study by Alvin Toffler, *Future Shock* (New York: Bantam Books, 1970), 366.

13. *The New York Times*, August 18, 1968.

14. Quoted in Alan Riding, "Revolution and the Intellectual in Latin America," *The New York Times Magazine* (March 13, 1983), 35.

15. *The Wall Street Journal*, June 8, 1983.

16. *The New York Times*, August 14, 1983.

17. Luis E. Aguilar, *Marxism in Latin America* (New York: Knopf, 1968), 59.

18. Riding, *op. cit.*, 30.

19. *The New York Times*, December 13, 1982.

20. *The New York Times*, January 9, 1982.

21. *The New York Times*, February 26, 1983.

22. William O. Beeman, "Images of the Great Satan: Representation of the United States in the Iranian Revolution," in Nikki R. Keddie (ed.), *Religion and Politics in Iran* (New Haven: Yale University Press, 1983), 191.

23. *Ibid.*, 192.

24. C.L. Sulzberger, "To Change Their Image of Us," *The New York Times Magazine*, March 5, 1961.

2

Anti-Americanism in Mexico

George W. Grayson

On the spot where the Aztecs once offered throbbing human hearts to appease left-handed Hummingbird, their war god, the Mexican government opened a National Museum of Interventions in September 1981. The facility's seventeen rooms, joined by red-tiled corridors, embrace photographs, documents, and memorabilia revealing the slights, indignities, incursions, forays, invasions, and occupations suffered by Mexico at the hands of foreigners since the country declared its independence in 1810.

The Spanish stayed in Mexico 300 years, and Napoleon III dispatched French troops who occupied the nation for five years in the mid-nineteenth century. Yet, the unmistakable focus of the museum is on North American activities in a manner termed "a blend of anti-Americanism and bruised dignity."[1]

The first room prominently displays the Monroe Doctrine, as well as comments of José Manuel Zozaya, Mexico's first ambassador to Washington. "The arrogance of those republicans does not allow them to see us as equals but as inferiors. With time they will become our sworn enemies," the envoy observed. Maps and commentaries describe "Jefferson's expansionism" and the U.S. determination to conquer the west "at Mexico's expense." Cartoons and engravings recall the 1847 occupation of Mexico by the U.S. army, led by General Winfield Scott. "U.S. meddling" in the Mexican revolution commands a great deal of space. Fading brown photographs depict U.S. Marines seizing the gulf port of Veracruz in 1914. And other exhibits turn Pancho Villa, a feared and despised

31

marauder, into a revolutionary hero because of General John J. "Black Jack" Pershing's punitive expedition" to capture him.

This is "not a place to stress our losses," stated Gaston García Cantú, director of the National Institute of Anthropology and History and the moving force behind the museum. "No country can afford to lose its historic memory. People must understand what happened and why." Many Mexican intellectuals believe that the museum is especially appropriate at this time because of renewed U.S. military intervention in the Caribbean basin.[2]

As revealed by the museum, anti-Americanism in Mexico predates that in any other Third World nation. It became evident when the United States annexed Texas; was exacerbated by the Mexican-American War; manifested itself during the revolutionary upheaval early in this century; increased in response to the nationalization of the oil industry in 1938; reappeared when Washington applied diplomatic, economic, and political pressures on Fidel Castro's regime; and intensified in the 1970s, following both the discovery of rich oil and natural gas deposits in southeastern Mexico and militant U.S. opposition to revolutionary movements in Central America and the Caribbean. As expressed by historian Stanley R. Ross, Mexicans see their relations with the United States as one shaped by "armed conflict, military invasion, and economic and cultural penetration."[3]

This chapter analyzes (1) the cultural roots of anti-Americanism in Mexico; (2) examines how repeated military interventions combined with racism and discrimination have exacerbated anti-American sentiments; (3) describes the middle class character of this phenomenon; and (4) discusses the prospects for anti-Americanism in Mexico.

CULTURAL ROOTS OF ANTI-AMERICANISM

From their respective beginnings as independent nations, profound social, economic, and cultural differences existed between Mexico and the United States. The former emerged from a Hispano-Arabic and Indian heritage that emphasized religious orthodoxy, militarism, personalism, fatalism, centralism, hierarchical control, a manipulative attitude toward law, the importance of leisure over work, and hostility toward change. The United States inherited English traditions, nourished by the Reformation and the Enlightenment which had barely affected Spain, that stressed religious tolerance, civilian control of the military, aggressive competition, the importance of work, exaltation of technology and capitalism, respect for law, and an orientation toward the future.[4]

Distinct outlooks preordained distinct development paths. Furthermore, the United States separated itself from England with governmental machinery and political rules of the game embraced by the majority of influential citizens. The question of institution-building resolved, its people's energies could be focused on economic development and territorial expansion. In contrast, Mexico's eleven-year struggle for independence (1810–21) left the country politically rent, economically debilitated, and burdened by the political domination of churchmen, landowners, and militarists. The armies and revolutionaries who had mauled each other during this conflict devastated the agricultural and mining sectors, which were crucial to the colonial economy. Mexico resembled the newly independent nations of the mid-twentieth century inasmuch as it was beset by instability, low productivity, capital flight, budget deficits, and foreign indebtedness. Economic distress and foreign invasions contributed to Mexico's victimization by predatory ex-generals from the wars of independence. During its first half-century of independence, over 50 governments rose and fell as 30 different men served as president. Sixteen men headed 22 governments during one 15-year period alone.[5] The most contemptible of these men was Antonio López de Santa Anna, "a cryptic, mercurial, domineering military chieftain," who captured the presidency nine times between 1833 and 1855.[6] During this time the name of this Mexican Caligula became synonymous with treachery, intrigue, and betrayal.

Some U.S. leaders viewed with great hope the independence of Mexico and other Latin American nations. Here were prospective allies, optimists believed, joined to the United States by the ideals of the Enlightenment, in confronting Old World monarchies. Such idealism proved more rhetorical than real; the U.S. government discouraged a plan in 1825 by Mexico and Venezuela to free Cuba, because Washington self-interestedly preferred that the island be held by Spain, not Great Britain, into whose hands it might have fallen. Moreover, the enunciation of the Monroe Doctrine demonstrated that the United States would be the dominant party in any partnership with Latin American nations. In addition, Washington's failure to act when Spain (1829) and France (1838) invaded Mexico indicated that the doctrine's lofty principles would be applied selectively, if at all. By the early 1830s, any optimism in the United States had faded as noble constitutions were denigrated by the actions of unscrupulous generals-turned-politicians. "Dictators like Antonio López de Santa Anna seemed to be at best slight improvements over the Bourbon kings or Iturbide I. Ignorance, fanaticism, and military despotism still prevailed over political freedom, civil rights, and general toleration, condemning Mexico to immobility and backwardness."[7] Obtaining independence from Spain had changed little in Mexico's social, economic, and political order. Its dilemma was that of a politically divided, economically hobbled, and territorially defensive nation suffused by values that impeded unification and development living cheek by jowl with a unified, productive, and expansionist neighbor.

The two countries collided over Texas, originally a northeast province linked to the Mexican state of Coahuila into which colonists, most of whom were enterprising and aggressive slave-owning cotton planters from the United States, had been invited to settle. Despite having sworn allegiance to Mexico, both English-speaking and Mexican settlers resented interference in their affairs from Mexico City as they spurred the economic development of what had once seemed a remote and unproductive wasteland. In 1819 the United States had renounced its questionable claims to Texas in exchange for Florida. Mexico rejected subsequent efforts by U.S. presidents to purchase the province. Nonetheless, Washington waited only a few months before acceding to the colonists' request to recognize Texas as a sovereign country. This action was taken in 1837, the year after the Lone Star Republic had wrested its independence from Mexico with the benefit of supplies and manpower from the United States. A series of complex diplomatic maneuvers led to the annexation of Texas eight years later. This move ignited a two-year war between the neighbors that was concluded by a peace treaty signed at Guadalupe Hidalgo on the outskirts of Mexico City on February 2, 1848. By its terms, Mexico surrendered a crescent of territory from Colorado and New Mexico to California, embracing over one million square miles. In return, the United States paid a $15 million cash indemnity, while assuming claims of its citizens against Mexico that would not exceed $3,250,000.

Vehemently criticized by Illinois congressman Abraham Lincoln, South Carolina's John C. Calhoun, and Virginia's Robert E. Lee, the conflict cost the United States about $100 million and approximately 13,000 lives. These figures paled in comparison to the war's impact on Mexico, which lost upwards of 50,000 lives, significant amounts of foodstuffs and livestock, and one-half of its national territory.[8]

The war exacerbated national disunity and political fragmentation. In addition to the areas ceded under the treaty, Santa Anna, through the Gadsden Purchase of 1853, consented to sell the Mesilla Valley in what is today southern New Mexico and Arizona. Mexico and the United States were roughly equal at the time of independence in size, population, and the percentage of the budget expended for the military; the war and attendant accords sharply delineated and permanently set the disparities between the two countries as Mexico shrunk in size to about 760,000 square miles while the United States expanded to over 3,000,000 square miles as it settled the boundary to its own satisfaction. Furthermore, the one advantage that Mexico enjoyed over the United States before the war, namely a standing army several times larger and presumably more powerful, had completely disappeared.[9]

The physical devastation of the war was secondary to its psychological effects. Mexico was humiliated in what is deemed by careful scholars in the United States and Mexico as a U.S. war of aggression.[10] The conflict has long receded in the memory of Americans, who seem always hurrying toward the future. For Mexicans, an indelible scar of "virulent, almost pathological Yankeephobia,"[11] remains from the wound of defeat and humiliation produced by what is officially known as "the war of the North American invasion."[12] In 1877, the Mexican poet Guillermo Prieto visited the United States where he gave poetic expression to a sentiment shared by many of his countrymen:

> They can do everything;
> they can change the shreds
> of my unhappy country
> into splendid nations,
> —booty of deceit,
> victims of outrage!
> They can do anything!
> But they cannot tear
> from my native land
> her nobility, nor rob
> her shining beauty,
> her divine, heroic heart![13]

Resentment in the Deep South toward the military phase of Reconstruction provides the closest American analogy to a bitterness so deeply etched on a people's psyche. Still, Southerners could take solace in the distinguished generalship of Robert E. Lee, Thomas J. "Stonewall" Jackson, Nathan Bedford Forrest, and others, in the impressive victories registered by grey-uniformed troops at First Manassas, Second Manassas, and Chancellorsville, and in the withdrawal of "Yankee" troops and the restoration of local governance following the bitterly disputed 1876 Hayes–Tilden presidential election. Not only did it survive the war, but the South prospered politically, for the control of "safe seats" by Southerners in a seniority-sensitive congress gave the region enormous influence in both the Senate and the House of Representatives until the last third of the twentieth century. For the Mexicans, however, their army failed to win a single major battle; U.S. forces easily and rapidly moved from Veracruz to Mexico City; the United States navy maneuvered at will, virtually lacking opposition; and some commanders refused to obey direct orders of Santa Anna. Indeed, the war's heroes from the Mexican perspective were neither generals nor admirals, but several young military cadets—the much-heralded *Niños héroes*—who jumped to their death from Chapultepec Hill rather than surrender to General Scott's army. To rub salt in the wounds of Mexicans, occupation was followed by the permanent loss of land to a foreign country that had helped provoke hostilities. Worse still, the lost territory encompassed Sutter's Fort in California where, one year after the war's conclusion, prospectors discovered the gold that would help finance the United States' industrial revolution.

U.S. INTERVENTIONS AND RACISM

The Mexican-American war presaged multiple U.S. diplomatic and military interventions into Mexican affairs. Following his assumption of the presidency in 1876, Porfiro Díaz brought order out of chaos and civil strife, using force, when necessary, "to amputate the cancerous political instability that had been eating away at the country since 1810."[14] Peaceable conditions found U.S. capital pouring into Mexico during the rule of Díaz as his country became known as the "mother of foreigners and the step-mother of Mexicans." The overthrow of the dictator in 1911 proved to be among the first in a series of events that represented the six-year military phase of the Mexican revolution. During this period, the United States intruded shamelessly in its neighbor's affairs as U.S. naval vessels patrolled the Gulf Coast to keep the Mexicans "in a salutary equilibrium, between a dangerous and exaggerated apprehension and a proper degree of wholesome fear."[15] Ambassador Henry Lane Wilson, a quintessential supporter of both American business interests and dollar diplomacy, actively plotted the ouster from the presidency of Francisco I. Madero, who had fomented the movement to topple the *Porfiriato*. Wilson may even have given "tacit approval" to the brutal assassination of the so-called "apostle" of Mexico's revolution.[16]

President Woodrow Wilson, who had once expressed a determination "to teach South American republics to elect good men," used as pretext the temporary arrest of North American sailors in Tampico in dispatching U.S. marines to occupy Veracruz for seven months following the bloody seizure of the port on April 21, 1914, ostensibly to prevent the unloading of German arms. Intervention also took the form of a punitive expedition when General Pershing led 6,000 troops onto Mexican soil against Pancho Villa who had, on March 9, 1916, looted and burned the border town of Columbus, New Mexico, killing 18 Americans.

General Pershing failed to capture his quarry. Yet, skirmishes with Mexican forces pushed the two countries to the brink of warfare as Republican jingoists such as Senator Albert Bacon Fall of New Mexico cried for blood. Despite the crusading moralism that guided many of his actions, President Wilson understood the dangers inherent in a major military conflict with his southern neighbor at the very time that his country was increasingly at odds with Germany.

The United States' history of racial and ethnic prejudice, which sometimes found Mexicans and Chicanos as the target of discrimination, nourished the anti-Americanism that sprang from the interventions. Early in the twentieth century, U.S. fruit growers, farmers, and manufacturers welcomed Mexican workers into their farms and factories. However, the Great Depression dried up employment opportunities and sharpened the antagonism toward foreigners who were scorned as competitors for scarce jobs and social welfare largesse. Physical intimidation and ethnic slurs abounded. Signs in restaurants and other public places revealed the ugly popular mood: "No Niggers, Dogs, or Mexicans Allowed."[17] Obviously, impressed by the docility of the Spanish-speaking foreigners, a Kern County, California, deputy sheriff stated that "the Mexicans are trash. They have no standard of living. We herd them like pigs."[18]

In the face of rising unemployment following the Korean War, the U.S. Immigration and Naturalization Service launched the paramilitary "Operation Wetback" to capture and return to Mexico illegal workers. The United States would never have tolerated draconian searches and massive expulsions by the Mexican government to return North Americans unlawfully in Mexico to the United States. As late as 1975, senior officials of the U.S. Environmental Protection Agency approved a plan to use Mexican citizens rather than North Americans as guinea pigs in evaluating the effects on the human thyroid of massive doses of fungicides known to cause cancer in animals. The experiment, to be undertaken in a Mexico City hospital, was cancelled at the last minute because of what newspapers called an "administrative fluke."[19] The asymmetry in influence and power makes unthinkable the use of Americans as subjects of medical tests conceived by Mexican scientists and carried out in the United States.

MIDDLE CLASS PHENOMENON

Anti-Americanism touches all elements of Mexican society. At the behest of their leaders, trade unionists have marched in opposition to the U.S. invasion of Grenada and peasants have swarmed into the Zócolo, Mexico City's central plaza, to protest Uncle Sam's "acts of aggression" against Nicaragua's revolutionary regime. Nonetheless, anti-Americanism is largely articulated and disseminated by sectors of the middle class— principally, journalists, writers, bureaucrats, politicians, university professors, teachers, students and certain professionals such as economists. These individuals sometimes have their views strengthened through contacts with American counterparts, who themselves decry past and present U.S. policies. More inclined to favor cooperation with the United States are industrialists, members of the business community, military men and professionals such as physicians, architects, and engineers.

What explains the middle class character of anti-Americanism? To begin with, the middle class has enjoyed access to high schools and universities, institutions whose curricula illuminate the injustices suffered by Mexico at the hands of the "colossus of the North." University professors often explain the plight of Mexico and other Third World countries in terms of the "dependency" theory, which draws heavily on Marxist and neo-Marxist formulations. The body of the literature on this subject is far from homogeneous; however, certain elements of agreement exist. For instance, Raúl Prebisch, a pioneer of the dependency approach, portrayed the world as divided between a developed center and an underdeveloped periphery, with a confluence of factors—the periphery's deteriorating terms of trade, the competitive disadvantage of developing states in producing manufactured goods, the center's tight grip on technology and finance—continuing if not accentuating the unbalanced relationship. During the mid-1960s, a group of Latin American scholars went beyond Prebisch's perspective and "interpreted the phenomenon of *dependencia* in a holistic fashion and in terms of the capitalist mode of production." These theorists pointed to large business conglomerates or multinational corporations as providing a structural link between internal and external factors of dependency. They argued that transnational firms, such as those that are extremely visible in Mexico, expanded into the economies of weaker countries, conditioning their economic, social, and political behavior. They despoiled them of primary products, controlled capital movements, limited technology transfers, employed undemocratic methods to manipulate local politics and placed on their payrolls energetic members of the middle class, thereby "denationalizing" them, for their loyalties shifted from national priorities to accomplishing the objectives of Citibank, General Motors, Gulf Oil, or some other foreign enterprise.[20]

Dependista ideas have strongly influence Mexican foreign policy. For instance, Luis Echeverría Alvarez, who until his inauguration as president in 1970 had dedicated his life to domestic matters, decided—according to aides—"that Mexico could not achieve true development while it remained politically identified with and economically dependent on the United States.[21] Several factors reinforced this outlook. When Echeverría took office, Mexico shipped 60 percent of its exports to the United States, from which it received 64 percent of its imports. In addition, the United States accounted for $1.7 billion of the $2.2 billion foreign investment in his country. These funds were concentrated in the production of capital goods, the most dynamic, profitable, and strategically important sector of the economy. The annual burden of payments abroad in dividends, royalties, and other obligations to foreign private capital was more than $300 million.[22] Additionally, the economic problems faced by the U.S. economy led the Nixon administration to impose a 10 percent surcharge on imports in 1971. This move, which caught Mexico by surprise, provided further evidence of the vulnerability of peripheral countries to the center of the capitalist world and deepened the anti-Americanism of Mexico's leaders.

Imposition of the surcharge encouraged Echeverría, in concert with Venezuela's President Carlos Andrés Pérez, to spearhead the establishment of the Economic System of Latin America, known by its Spanish abbreviation as SELA to promote national development projects and create Latin American transnational firms, defend the prices of manufactured goods and raw materials, establish cartels in primary products, provide information about the prices of these goods, stimulate food production and encourage multinational ventures for the production of fertilizers, facilitate the acquisition of capital goods for the region, and foster technical cooperation among Latin American and Third World nations.[23]

Echeverría and Pérez convinced their regional neighbors that "the countries of the Third World and those of Latin America, in particular, must unite in defense of their common principles and interests or resign themselves to remaining underdeveloped indefinitely."[24] Divided by "North American expansionism," Latin America would remain the poor cat's paw of the North unless states of the hemisphere banded together, argued Echeverría. Their joint effort bore fruit on October 17, 1975, when 25 nations signed SELA's charter. Included among the signatories was Cuba; excluded was the United States, against which the system was implicitly aimed.

More important than educational opportunities or economic theories in understanding the virulent anti-Americanism of the middle class is the fact that members of this class have dominated Mexico's political life for more than 50 years through the Institutional Revolutionary Party or PRI, as it is commonly called. During this period, Mexican leaders have trumpeted their commitment to advancing social justice and promoting economic opportunities for all of their countrymen. For nearly three decades after the end of World War II, Mexico experienced an economic "miracle" that included widespread industrialization and annual income growth of 8 percent. Yet, the redistribution goals that sparkle on the pages of PRI's program essentially ended with the completion, in 1940, of the presidency of Lázaro Cárdenas, who gave impetus to the distribution of 20 million hectares of land, the unionization of millions of workers, and the nationalization of 17 U.S. and European oil companies.

Hence, Mexican anti-Americanism is predominantly instrumental. The reality of revolution in Mexico has long since given way to rhetoric and symbols, such as Echeverría's expropriation of Northern croplands just before he left office. Hunger, malnutrition, illiteracy, backwardness, and deprivation abound in Mexico where at least one-third of the population lives in abject poverty. Such conditions might be understandable were Mexico an impecunious banana republic, but oil is only the most conspicuous item on a list of mineral resources that includes zinc, copper, silver, coal, and uranium. The legacy of ancient civilizations combines with magnificent scenery and a favorable climate to make the country a potential mecca for tourists. And prolific fishing grounds offer a relatively undeveloped source of protein and foreign exchange.

How can underdevelopment amid such wealth be explained? To attribute it principally to factors within Mexico—centralization, corruption, mismanagement, anti-Indianism, the collapse of higher education, excessive population growth, and so forth—would not only indict past and present leaders, almost all of whom are middle class, it could also undermine the legitimacy of a "revolutionary" regime controlled by a "revolutionary" party.

How much less threatening to point an accusing finger at the United States. After all, Americans occupied Mexico City, carved up Mexico's territory, meddled openly in post-revolution politics, dispatched troops across its border, profited greatly from its oil patrimony, and now—through financial institutions and multinational corporations—are perceived to manipulate its economy. In late 1982, President José López Portillo, who bore prime responsibility for his nation's economic crisis that followed an oil boom, implored his countrymen not to stand with open arms and allow Mexico to be bled dry, gutted, and eaten away. He said that "their nation cannot work and be organized only to have its life blood drained off by the gravitational pull of the colossus of the North."[25]

Attacks often focus on government agencies such as the CIA or U.S.-based multinational corporations as the presumed agents of intervention whose actions are ubiquitous and omnipotent. Seldom is evidence considered a necessary prerequisite to leveling such charges. For instance, in mid-1980 Mexican officials and newspapers had a field day accusing the United States of stealing rain by diverting hurricanes from Mexico's shores. The villain was the U.S. National Oceanographic and Atmospheric Administration, whose hurricane-hunter aircraft had allegedly intercepted a storm named "Ignacio" off Mexico's Pacific coast in October 1979, thereby contributing to the country's worst drought in 20 years. Mexican observers, including the director of the country's National Meteorological Service, apparently believed that Yankee ingenuity was so great that Uncle Sam could bend Mother Nature to his will.[26]

The flames of anti Americanism are fanned by a press renowned for corruption—with many reporters and columnists for allegedly objective publications in the pay of individual politicians, government agencies, or special interests. Until 1968, when Julio Scherer García became executive publisher of *Excelsior*, the nation's most influential ne a prominent politician could buy a front-page story lauding himself for $8,000.[27] Scherer subsequently lost his post after crossing swords with confidants of president Echeverría, a master at media manipulation. Government entities possess special funds to pay reporters assigned to cover their activities. Such covert payments, known as *igualas*, should not be confused with *gacetillas*, stipends given to editors or reporters to carry specific stories in the news columns of their publications.[28] The government's ability to shape what appears in print prompted political scientist Evelyn P. Stevens to comment:

> To read a Mexican newspaper is to venture onto a factual desert in the midst of an ideological hailstorm. Headlines scream, news stories bellow, and columnists and cartoonists belabor 'enemies of the revolution' with sledgehammer sarcasm.[29]

The sledgehammer sarcasm has become increasingly loud in recent years. To be sure, there is profound opposition to U.S. foreign policy that appears as a mixture of "arrogance and opportunism, blindness and short-term machiavellianism, volubility and stubbornness...."[30] Particularly vexing is Washington's unrelenting hostility toward Castro's Cuba, its embrace of the Salvadoran government, and its efforts to capsize Nicaragua's Sandinista regime.

Equally irritating to Mexico's middle class is the the acute—and growing—cultural, military, and economic dependence of its country on its northern neighbor.

U.S. cultural penetration of Mexico became unmistakably evident after World War II, sometimes for the better but often for the worse.

> To the chagrin of those who prized traditional Hispanic values, advertisements and commercials assumed a distinct United States flavor, and hundreds of Anglicisms invaded the language. Somehow *el jit, el jonron, el extra inin* seemed more palatable, and certainly more understandable, than *okay, bay-bay, chance, jipi,* and even *estric,* that exhibitionist fad which swept United States campuses during the warm months of 1974. Quick lunches and the coffee break (*kofi breik*) replaced heavy noon meals and afternoon siestas; Christmas was commercialized to the extent of Mexican children sitting on Santa's knee at Mexico City's Sears, Roebuck; beer supplanted pulque as the favorite alcoholic drink of the lower classes, while Scotch whiskey took the place of cognac among the middle and upper classes.[31]

Rotary and Lions Clubs sprang up in Mexico; fads in North American music swept the country soon after debuting in New York and California; and Mexican television viewers cheered, laughed, or cried at the likes of "Columbo," "People's Court," "Taxi," and "Hart to Hart." In 1974, after driving from one end to the other of the Avenida Insurgentes, one of the capital's longest boulevards, a journalist reported counting 50 hamburger restaurants, all with U.S. names, and only ten taco stands.[32]

Not only does U.S. culture pervade Mexican life, but the United States serves as a magnet for Mexican athletes, singers, and movie stars. Fernando Valenzuela, Plácido Domingo, and Cantinflas are among the nationally renowned personalities who have pursued their careers in the United States.

Although less visible than the cultural sphere, national security represents another area in which Mexico is profoundly dependent on the United States. Because of protection from extracontinental attacks afforded by its neighbor, Mexico's defense expenditures as a percentage of budget outlays are among the lowest in Latin America. Moreover, Mexican decisionmakers realize that their patchwork armed forces, though modernizing, could offer little effective resistance in the extremely unlikely event that the United States invaded Mexico. Despite moves to diversify its arms acquisitions, Mexico turned to the United States in 1981 to purchase the most sophisticated weapons in its arsenal: a dozen F-5 jet aircraft.

Mexico is even more dependent in economic matters. Approximately two-thirds of its trade is with the United States, which supplies a majority of external capital invested in Mexico. Moreover, U.S.-based financial institutions have long been the principal supplier of loans to Mexico whose foreign debt stood at $25 billion when López Portillo succeeded Echeverría in 1976. López Portillo's administration coincided with a dramatic increase in oil production, accomplished thanks to huge newly discovered deposits in the Isthmus of Tehuantepec and in Campeche Bay. While refusing to join OPEC, Mexico became the world's fourth largest depository of oil and the principal exporter to the United States. Billions of petrodollars permitted López Portillo to revive a flagging economy. These revenues also enabled him to launch a highly publicized industrial development plan, designed to promote sustained economic growth, stimulate industries in heretofore neglected regions of the country, promote the activities of small- and medium-sized businesses, strengthen the country's export capacity, and—most important of all—create employment for the millions of Mexicans who lack jobs or work only a few weeks each year. As the then head of Pemex, the state oil monopoly, expressed it:

> for the first time in its history Mexico enjoys sufficient wealth to make possible not only the resolution of economic problems facing the country, but also the creation of a new permanently prosperous country, a rich country where the right to work will be a reality.[33]

The black gold and green dollars helped Mexico achieve a key goal of its development program: gross domestic product rose by approximately 8 percent each year between 1978 and 1981. This expansion generated vast profits for the private sector and helped create one million new jobs annually. Mexico's growth became the envy of the world floundering in recession. Such glamour, however, diverted attention from the beginnings of "petrolization"—a neologism connoting an overheated economy fueled by oil revenues, growing reliance on foreign creditors to pay for surging food, capital, and luxury imports (which rose from $6 billion in 1977 to $23 billion in 1981), a convulsed agricultural sector, and—above all—outsized budget deficits. Rather than raising taxes, Mexican leaders chose to cover the growing deficits by printing crisp new peso notes—a move that fueled inflation.

The shift in early 1981 of the seller's market in petroleum to one favoring buyers combined with Mexico's determination to maintain unreasonably high prices triggered a precipitous decline in export earnings in 1981, drove the inflation rate even higher, and helped plunge the nation into its worst depression in modern times. Mexico, which teetered on the brink of bankruptcy, averted disaster thanks to the U.S. government. Washington guaranteed $1.7 billion in grain purchases, prepaid 1 billion for crude oil imports, helped obtain a $1.85 billion loan from the Bank of International Settlements, and urged that a fresh line of credit be extended by private bankers who agreed to postpone for 90 days payments on Mexico's foreign debt which had swollen to $83 billion.

PROSPECTS FOR ANTI-AMERICANISM

Frequency of contact between the two countries has intensified rather than reduced anti-Americanism in Mexico. While many close personal and family relationships exist across the border, Americans in Mexico often appear overbearing, arrogant, and insensitive—characteristics magnified by both the visitors' affluence and innocence of Spanish. To know Americans is not necessarily to love them—although Mexicans do admire the economic and technological achievements of the United States—and the likelihood of increased bilateral contacts between the two nations will be accompanied by more not less anti-American sentiments.

Based on past experience, renewed economic growth in Mexico will also nourish anti-Americanism. A lowering of the decibel level may take place during hard times because of dependence on U.S. financial assistance, the imperative of attracting foreign investment, and the critical need to stimulate tourism. In contrast, prosperity has sparked stridency as evidenced during the 1978 to 1981 period. Emboldened by his country's impressive level of economic expansion and status as a surging oil exporter, López Portillo publicly rebuked President Carter for America's "surprise moves and sudden deceit," pledged solidarity with the Sandinistas against the "satanic ambition of imperial interests," and visited Cuba in mid-1980 in a demonstration of solidarity with the Castro regime during a time of deepening economic problems illuminated by the flight of Cuban refugees to Florida. Economic growth saw a major expansion of the public sector, thereby enhancing the influence of anti-American nationalists, at the expense of the generally pro-American business community.

Novelist Octavio Paz contends that affluence in his country would accentuate differences with its northern neighbor.

> . . . we have only to imagine a Mexico suddenly turned into a prosperous, mighty country, a superpower like the United States. Far from disappearing, the difference would become more acute and more clearcut. The reason is obvious: we are two distinct versions of western civilization.[34]

Joint ventures in foreign affairs as opposed to freelance or individual actions by Mexico may tend to soften the country's anti-American pronouncements. A case in point is its pronouncement of the Contadora Group whose other members—Venezuela, Colombia, and Panama—appear, initially at least, to have moderated Mexico's bitter condemnation of U.S. policy in the Caribbean Basin. Nevertheless this moderation gave way to acerbic criticism following the landing of U.S. troops in Grenada and the CIA-directed mining of Nicaraguan ports.

The growth of the Mexican–American community, its numbers enlarged by illegal immigrants, could provide Mexico with an influential ally within the United States just as Israel benefits from the lobbying activities of Jews and Greece from that of Greek-Americans.

Virtually without dissent Mexicans have opposed immigration reform in the United States. Such reform is viewed as harmful to their nation's economic well-being and an encroachment upon the nation's sovereignty. Mexico has used a number of tactics to thwart changes in the law, not the least of which has been appeals to the humanitarian sensibilities of the U.S. people, whose immigration policy has been among the most liberal in history. Its public officials have also implicitly linked the sale of oil to a flexible border policy.

Agreement in Mexico over what U.S. laws should be is contrasted with the discord in the United States over appropriate legislation. Public support for reform, even among Hispanics, is overwhelming—a fact that should be determinative in a democracy. Yet, an array of interest groups, whose objectives are lauded by Mexico, have delayed and diluted legislation—so that the likelihood appears remote that legislation to slow the influx of unlawful workers, even if passed, will stem illegal entries. Chicano leaders, encouraged by Mexican politicians, have even excoriated this modest congressional initiative on the grounds that it will accentuate civil rights abuses and produce a latter-day Third Reich.

Keeping open the safety valve may prove inimical to Mexico's long-term interests because it not only facilitates the exodus of highly motivated, often skilled young workers, who compete with Chicanos and Blacks for jobs in the U.S. market. It also removes the pressure from Mexican notables to accomplish the political, economic, and social reforms needed to generate opportunities in their country. At some point, it could provoke a militant backlash against foreign workers, especially in the sunbelt, thereby fanning the flames of anti-Americanism below the border.

Mexican-American organizations favor flexibility and compromise in U.S. policy toward Mexico. This fact is not lost on Mexican presidents who, at times, have cultivated Chicano leaders.

Increased political influence by the Mexican-American community—a condition assured by single-member congressional districts and the electoral college—may well inspire anti-American rhetoric and behavior by Mexican elites, particularly if they believe that their Chicano brethren can mitigate or blunt any retaliation from Washington.

NOTES

1. *Washington Post*, December 28, 1981, p. A-21.
2. *Washington Post*, December 28, 1981, p. A-21.
3. Stanley R. Ross, "Mexican-U.S. Relations: An Historical Perspective," in *U.S. Policies Toward Mexico: Perceptions and Perspectives*, eds. Richard D. Erb and Stanley R. Ross (Washington: American Institute for Public Policy Research, 1979), p. 9.
4. Octavio Paz, "Mexico and the United States: Positions and Counterpositions," in Tommie Sue Montgomery (ed.), *Mexico Today* (Philadelphia: Institute for Human Study, 1982), pp. 1-21.
5. Roger D. Hansen, *The Politics of Mexican Development* (Baltimore: Johns Hopkins University Press, 1971), pp. 11-12.
6. Peter H. Smith, *Mexico: The Quest for a U.S. Policy* (New York: Foreign Policy Association, n.d.), pp. 6-7.
7. Karl M. Schmitt, *Mexico and the United States, 1821-1973: Conflict and Coexistence* (New York: Wiley, 1974), pp. 42-43.
8. Justin H. Smith, *The War with Mexico*, 2 vols. (Gloucester, Mass.: Peter Smith, 1963), pp. 253-67, and 318-19; see Schmitt, *Mexico and the United States*, p. 67.
9. Karl M. Schmitt, *Mexico and the United States*, pp. 67-68.
10. Michael C. Meyer, "Roots and Realities of Mexican Attitudes toward the United States: A Background Paper," in Richard D. Erb and Stanley R. Ross (eds.), *United States Relations with Mexico: Context and Content* (Washington: American Enterprise Institute, 1981), p. 30.
11. Michael C. Meyer and William L. Sherman, *The Course of Mexican History* (New York: Oxford University Press, 1979), p. 352.
12. Smith, *Mexico: The Quest for a U.S. Policy*, p. 8.
13. José de Onís, *The United States as seen by Spanish American Writers* (New York, Hispanic Institute in the United States, 1952), p. 120 and quoted in John T. Reid, *Spanish American Images of the United States 1790-1960* (Gainesville: University Presses of Florida, 1977), p. 69.
14. Frank Brandenburg, *The Making of Modern Mexico* (Englewood Cliffs, N.J.: Prentice-Hall, 1964), p. 37.
15. Secretary of State Philander C. Knox quoted in Howard F. Cline, *The United States and Mexico* (New York: Atheneum, 1965), p. 155.
16. Smith, *Mexico: The Quest for a U.S. Policy*, p. 8.
17. *Washington Post*, August 31, 1975, p. 31.
18. *The New York Times*, December 6, 1970, p. 23.
19. *Washington Post*, May 11, 1977, pp. A-1, A-7.
20. Heraldo Muñoz (ed.), *From Dependency to Development: Strategies to Overcome Underdevelopment and Inequality* (Boulder, Co.:Westview, 1981).
21. *Washington Post*, August 31, 1975, p. 31.
22. *The New York Times*, December 6, 1970, p. 23.
23. *Facts on File*, April 5, 1975, p. 210; and *Proceso*, November 20, 1976, pp. 11-12.
24. *Times of the Americas*, April 2, 1975, p. 1.
25. *Daily Report (Latin America)*, November 2, 1982, V-1.

26. *Washington Post*, July 7, 1980, pp. A-1, A-12.

27. Marvin Alisky, *Latin American Media: Guidance and Censorship* (Ames: Iowa University Press, 1981), pp. 40–41.

28. Alisky, *Latin American Media*, p. 35.

29. Quoted in *Protest and Response in Mexico* (Cambridge, Mass.: MIT Press, 1974), p. 30.

30. Ibid.

31. Meyer and Sherman, *The Course of Mexican History*, p. 687.

32. Meyer and Sherman, *The Course of Mexican History*, pp. 687–88.

33. Quoted in the *Christian Science Monitor*, August 8, 1979, p. 22.

34. "Reflections: Mexico and the United States," *New Yorker*, September 17, 1979, p. 136.

3

Latin America, Anti-Americanism, and Intellectual Hubris

Irving Louis Horowitz

Few areas in the life of American letters are so riven with intense polarization as the field of Latin American studies. The concept of two cultures, differences between humanistic learning and scientific technology, appears somewhat tepid in comparison. In Latin American studies the question: "which side are you on?" preempts the more prosaic concerns of evidence and scholarship: "do you know what you are talking about?" Consequently, anti-Americanism must be seen as part of a broad policy dissensus within the field of Latin American studies, rather than an indigenous response to United States policies.[1]

Anti-Americanism, valiant efforts at definition notwithstanding, is an ambiguous concept. In relation to Latin America it is also an anomolous concept. "American," after all, refers to all people who inhabit the Western Hemisphere, which includes Latin America as well as North America. Even North America can be divided into regions: Canada, Mexico and the Caribbean, and the United States. Perhaps no one in recent times has better summed up long-run hemispheric continuities than His Majesty Juan Carlos, King of Spain, in his 1981 address before the Organization of American States. He noted that "Spain perceived from the beginning of the Discovery that America was a unit. Nei-

---

*The author would like to express his appreciation to Professor Douglas C. Bennett of Temple University for his thoughtful critical reading of an earlier draft. Hopefully, his concerns are adquately reflected in this final version.

ther the vastness of its territory, nor the long time elapsing between the arrival of the different discoverers, nor the variety of its climates prompted the initial idea of unity; nevertheless it was so."[2] It is within such a context that anti-Americanism deserves to be probed. This vision of hemispheric dissensus is related to current attitudes toward the United States, or some aspect of its social system or political order or economic functioning.

Without belaboring the obvious, perhaps this situation is best explained by contrasting it with what Mazher Hameed has recently termed "Arab anger at the United States." We are informed that the Arab nations exhibit "a new kind of anti-Americanism, a deeper resentment not merely of American government policies but also of American values and the internal economic system."[3] To be sure, Thomas L. Friedman, one of the more sober reporters of middle eastern affairs, attributes the new levels of terrorism sponsored by states in an area to an increasingly anti-American political atmosphere, attitudes found not only among religious militants, but also among average students, shopkeepers and businessmen.[4]

But it would only compound the fiction if anti-Americanism were perceived to be a phenomenon afflicting Third World countries. European radical elements, fueled by a variety of harsh probing criticisms made by U.S. commentators, have seized the opportunity to legitimate their own resentments and criticisms. Arthur F. Burns, the United States ambassador to West Germany, gave keen expression to this sophisticated form of anti-Americanism.

> Anti-Americanism, in one or another guise, is a symptom of a far more serious ailment that has afflicted a number of Europe's educated classes: the rejection of Western society itself and its values. And as the leader of the West, America has become their number one enemy. This attitude is not born out of ignorance. On the contrary, America is seen correctly as the bulwark of everything they despise—parliamentary democracy, dynamic capitalism, modern technology and robust anti-communism. The root of the matter is that alienation of certain European intellectuals from the values and institutions of their own democratic society.[5]

My own sense of the situation is that the Latin American case differentiates itself sharply from such sentiments. It is not that animosity toward the United States is absent; clearly it is omnipresent. Rather, such attitudes are ephemeral and confined to a narrow stratum of the intelligentsia. It is part of a cultural and political mythology, as Carlos Rangel appropriately calls it, and in that very fact, isolated from the general democratic traditions of Latin American theory and practice.[6]

The connections between Marxism and anti-Americanism are both pandemic and axiomatic. Clearly, the two *isms* are not confined to any single geographical area, but Latin America has produced a greater share of Marxist theorists and self-declared revolutionists than any other portion of the Third World. Further, if by definition the United States is the center of late twentieth century capitalism and imperialism, by extending the definition, it is the country that is the main danger, the main enemy of the Third World. This sort of axiomatic reasoning has been projected so often and with such frequency, that the line between negative doctrines of anti-Americanism and affirmations of radical revolution are often blurred. Marxism in Latin America is not unlike Freudianism in North America—a frame of reference that organizes the common discourse of an intellectual class.

Problems arise at "tactical" rather than "principled" levels. It becomes far simpler to organize cadres around the evils of U.S. capitalism than to forge a positive doctrine of socialism or communism that can elicit broad popular support. Anti-Americanism has marvelous consensualist properties; it is able to unite contending radical forces who may be divided on questions of Soviet style of rule in Western Europe or the Cuban system at home and politics in the Western hemisphere.

Anti-Americanism is furthermore a mobilizing as well as organizing concept. It permits broad, mass participation in select circumstances that would otherwise elicit a loud yawn. Even events that are relatively remote from immediate United States participation, such as the dispute between England and Argentina over the future of the Falkland/Malvinas Islands, took on anti-American overtones once it became clear that Argentina's military adventurism was not going to be underwritten by U.S. policy. Thus it is, as in all ideologies with a healthy staying power, that anti-Americanism—whatever its intellectual content—serves quite real needs of political movements in Latin America. In such a context, Marxism becomes the cherry on the whipped cream— the architectonic heaped upon the rhetoric.

Whatever may be the situation in other parts of the world, for most people of Latin America, a sense of common and shared values with North America is taken for granted. The source of anti-Americanism is more often than not the failure of the United States to keep faith with its own highest ideals and values. José Marti, who is frequently trotted out as the exemplar of anti-Americanism, set the tone for Latin American intellectuals. He shares with North Americans a faith in democracy and a dismay that its ideals are often breached. There is not even a hint of the sort of fanatic fundamentalism and revanchist spirit typical of some regions, such as the Middle East, or the sophisticated vanguardism characteristic of European critics of U.S. life and systems.

> A good American statesman is not one who knows how the French and the Germans are governed, but one who knows what elements make up his country, and how to lead them to reach, through indigenous methods and institutions, that desirable state where each man knows and applies himself and all enjoy the bounty of the country that they make fertile with their work and defend with their lives. Government must be that country. The form of government must suit the peculiar composition of the country. Government is more than harmony among the natural elements of a country.[7]

Anti-American feelings are often the work of Marxian intellectuals, both north and south, who share a cluster of premises: anticapitalism, anticolonialism, and anticommercialism. Capitalism, colonialism, and commercialism are presumed to be the essential features of the United States and must therefore be opposed if liberation is to occur.[8] But perusing the literature one finds a peculiarity: U.S. scholars reflect what might be referred to as neosocialist frames of reference, writing from the point of view of discontent with abundance, whereas Latin American scholars often reflect postfeudal discontent with modernism as such. While there is a commonality of rhetoric, they by no means share a commonality in the sources of their discontent with the United States as a civilization.

A sophisticated "cultural" version of this kind of anti-Americanism is presented by Darcy Ribiero in *The Americas as a Civilization.* Ribiero sees getting out from under the colossus of the North as "an effort in self-improvement." Without quite explaining why, he goes on to claim "that no American people, except Mexico with her 1910 revolution, Bolivia with her 1952 uprising, and recently Cuba, has been able to face it successfully." Ribiero sees patrician-patronal interests, originally founded on the plantation system, continuing to exert control through modernizing neocolonial formations. "The confrontation and overcoming of this retrograde framework cannot be done through any intensification of its reflexive modernization, because that would perpetuate the backwardness. It can be attained only through a prior restructuration of society through a social revolution capable of eradicating the existing power structure."[9]

Ribiero and many who share his viewpoint fail to address what happens after the revolutionary phase. What is the evidence that Mexico, Bolivia, and Cuba have fared better in correcting longstanding social ailments than have Brazil, Venezuela, and Costa Rica? Certainly, the economic data suggest that the latter three have come farther and faster than the former three. Furthermore, have these "restructurations" yielded such extraordinary outcomes among the three nations who presumably have uniquely broken the yoke of North American domination? Single party rule characterizes Mexican democracy; a series of near-endless military coups in Bolivian backwardness; and Cuba has near-total dependence on Soviet aid and trade. These outcomes provide little comfort to those who believe social revolution will uniquely resolve social problems. The ultimate irony is that even the postrevolutionary leadership continues to place current ills at the doorstep of U.S. imperialism and colonialism.

While the radical wing of anti-Americanism draws most attention of critics, there is also a restorationist aspect carved deep in the Latin pensador. Octavio Paz, in *The Labyrinth of Solitude*, compares Latin America to the United States and sees the former as the "true fountain of life." Catholicism, unlike Protestantism "nourishes the activities, the passions, the virtues, and even the sins of both lords and servants, functionaries and priests, merchants and soldiers." Latin America is thus a "true organism" rather than a pyramidal agglomeration imposed by the Protestant culture of New England.[10] While this view reverses North American contempt for Latin America, they are simply the same stereotypes in reverse. The virtues of medievalism, of tradition, permit aristocratic nationalism to close ranks with revolutionary Marxism to forge an unholy alliance of anti-Americanism, of anti-bourgeois spirit, and anti-bourgeois praxis.

One must understand also the long history of anti-American bias in official U.S. political circles. The hemispheric system has displayed strong biases in both directions. There is dislike for the Spanish colonial heritage and its spirit of conquering rather than settling. There is furthermore the Protestant animosity toward the homogeneity of Roman Catholic culture throughout Latin America. There is thinly veiled contempt for the abstract style of thought characteristic of many Latin American writers and novelists. And finally, there is disbelief in the ability of Latin America to get beyond its imagined geographical handicaps or its quite real military dictatorships. These are each aspects of an

American backlash, one which seeps through the entire North American culture, making attitudes toward immigrants from Latin America different from attitudes toward European immigrants.[11] At the level of stereotypes we have a two-way bridge rather than a single undiluted assault on the North American value system by Latin American intellectuals.

In terms of international politics, there is growing North American frustration, as its national power and prestige decreasingly provide a basis for the leadership of advanced nations to justify international involvement in their people. There is also growing Latin American conviction that nationalism as a fact if not as an ideology integrates people and politics and power in Latin America. Roger Hilsman has shrewdly pointed out that advanced civilizations use multinational organizations, military technology, and global warfare as mechanisms to get beyond nationalism, whereas the less developed nations, and here Latin America is very much in the forefront, lack such global propensities and must fall back on nationalism.[12] The rhetoric of anti-Americanism is the source and fulcrum of nativism and nationalism becomes a global rationalization of the hemispheric political processes.

In 1904 Theodore Roosevelt announced as a corollary to the Monroe Doctrine that European governments would not be welcomed if they tried to interfere in the political processes of the hemisphere, and that the region was uniquely part of the U.S. sphere of influence. Outside of a few Latin American intellectuals, little opposition was voiced then. Indeed, even the most vocal opponents of this policy accepted the premise that collective action in the face of dictatorial governments is acceptable.[13] Throughout an era extending from William Howard Taft, who announced the need to use Latin America to relieve the U.S. of its own surplus, to Calvin Coolidge's secretary of state, Charles Evans Hughes, who declared flatly in favor of establishing a Pax Americana, little effective protest to U.S. hegemonic claims were mounted.

Only with the era of Franklin Delano Roosevelt's Good Neighbor Policy in 1933, the establishment, during the Harry S Truman administration of the Organization of American States in 1948, the Alliance for Progress announced by John F. Kennedy in 1961, and the establishment of human rights as the cornerstone to U.S. foreign policy by Jimmy Carter in 1977 did growing intensification of anti-Americanism become apparent. As U.S. policies improved, relations between the North Americans and Latin Americans deteriorated. Expectations grew exponentially, while structures improved arithmetically. Why? First, the disparity between policies and actions: U.S. support for military intervention in Guatemala and the Dominican Republic, its frank opposition to the Cuban and Nicaraguan revolutions for their communist implications, and supervening global demands over regional demands, as in the U.S. support of the Malvinas/Falkland Islands invasion by Argentina. The rise of nationalism as a linchpin throughout the hemisphere took its toll on goodwill. Military regimes often supported U.S. claims, but they also helped to unleash ideological forces that could not readily be bridled. Opposition to "U.S. hegemony over Latin America" united radical and nationalist and militarist.[14]

At a somewhat different level, intellectuals became increasingly involved in hemispheric affairs. Organizations of Latin American studies began to flourish in the United States after the Second World War, reaching a crescendo of ideological opposition to U.S. foreign policy during the Vietnam period in the 1960s. If social scientists chose new organizational forms to express broad area studies interests, the natural scientists and physicians became actively involved in human rights struggles through mainline professional organizations. Parallel efforts emerged in Latin America aimed at producing greater independence from U.S. economic and political influence. Normal liaisons between intellectuals and academics took on manifest political purpose. These linkages became, in some measure, lobbying efforts against established U.S. positions on hemispheric issues. This congruence and confluence of events and organizations served to give anti-Americanism a patina of intellectual respectability absent in an earlier policymaking context. More important, it provided a platform for stimulating political opposition in a manner relatively immune from punishment or responsibility for consequences.

The standard rhetoric became highly simplified: the U.S. must put an end to interventionist politics in the Caribbean; it must underwrite weak economies by a better North–South fiscal balance; and generally it must support or at least not reject or oppose revolutionary forces in the hemisphere. An aura of inevitability and infallibility came into play with the shared acceptance and promotion of Marxism–Leninism and dependency theory. History, the people, the masses, the need for progress, divine Providence itself all in due course came to justify anti-Americanism. Increasingly, any failed Latin revolution—Allende in Chile—any stalemated situation—the civil wars in El Salvador—were placed at the doorstep of the United States and its administrations. In short, even when the wave of the future failed to materialize, it became not a failure of history, but a consequence of U.S. policy.

One can dredge up myriad examples of Latin American ideologists and sociologists condemning the United States. But such condemnations have uniformly come upon the troubled conscience of the better analysts and sociologists. The outstanding Venezuelan writer, Carlos Rangel, put the matter of Latin American backwardness in a more disquieting context. "Paradoxically," he writes, "the fact that we Latin Americans are an extension of Western culture compounds our frustration, since we cannot explain satisfactorily why we have been unable to capitalize on the advantages we have over the real Third World. Argentina takes no satisfaction in being ahead of Australia, New Zealand, or even Canada, as indeed it is, but resents its failure to reach the level of the United States."[15] Rangel sees the infatuation of elites with Marxism as a function of abstract greed rather than concrete need. Anti-Americanism in Latin America is in such close proximity in values and orientations to Americanism, that not only do the "normal" developmental problems in "stage-skipping" manifest themselves, but the "extraordinary" problems that beset two civilizations with sufficient similarities arouse sibling animosities or outright resentment.

Immediately after the Cuban Revolution in 1959, a veritable torrent of anti-American commentary was unleashed. Years of bridled, muffled resentment toward U.S. insensitivities and incursions were released. Castro himself well understood this critical supranationalist aspect of his revolution. He constantly appealed to the Latin American, not just Cuban, sources and ambitions of his revolution. He coopted Bolivarism as the answer to Monroeism. As Federico Gil put the matter at the time: "The challenge of the Cuban revolution to the influence, might, and prestige of the preponderant power of the Western Hemisphere changed the foreign policies of the Latin American countries."[16] But with the steady Sovietization of the Cuban Revolution, even its most enthusiastic early intellectual supporters have either switched causes (to support the El Salvador guerrillas or the Nicaraguan Sandinistas for example) or have been reduced to stunning silence (often as a result of specific Cuban policies—from its overseas military adventures to its repressive treatment of minorities such as homosexuals).[17] Since many of these intellectuals were North American, the erosion of Cuban autonomy translated into a clear diminution of anti-Americanism as a successful revolutionary ideology.

It is dangerous and erroneous to view anti-Americanism as an indigenous phenomenon within Latin America. The broad masses of the region have shown little inclination to follow its Marxist intellectuals down such a primrose path. Present-day anti-Americanism is ironically an attribute much more likely to be found and celebrated in elite intellectual circles of North America than in the hovels of Latin America. In this connection, and most recently, it is curious to note that a portion of the North American establishment has opposed the Bilateral Commission with much more vigor than have the Latin Americans. The following remarks by James Chace are not uncharacteristic of this North American response.

> Today America's "credibility" is indeed in question because of the obtuseness of its foreign policy. By continuing a long history of relying on repressive local military forces to effect change in Central America, the Reagan administration does not appear to be planning for a future that would allow countries with fragile democracies to grow stronger and hardy democracies to flourish. If it were to do so, if it were to concentrate on negotiating security guarantees for the region, then it might find its credibility was indeed improved because countries both friendly and unfriendly would recognize that America was acting with good sense. The exercise of American power should derive from an unblinkered assessment of American interests. To the extent that America is found wanting in this respect, then its alliances will suffer, and its enemies rejoice.[18]

On the other hand, it is Eduardo Ulibarri, the editor-in-chief of *La Nación*, the largest daily newspaper in Costa Rica, who leads the charge against the Contadora proposals of his fellow Latin Americans and is highly supportive of the Kissinger Commission report:

> The Kissinger Commission on Central America, no matter what its political constraints are, has two basic advantages over the Contadora Group: a wider mandate, which resulted in a more complete set of suggestions for facing the many problems in Central America; and the U.S. government's stronger position than Contadora to take the appropriate actions required without fear of a Cuban reaction. The Kissinger Commission does not equate peace with truce. Peace is not looked at as an absolute value, but as something that must result from justice, democracy, progressive development and a lack of foreign manipulation in the area. This is why there is no contradiction between pressuring the Sandinist government to change while providing military support to El Salvador. To the extent that the Sandinistas keep building a Marxist totalitarian society in Nicaragua, there will be a potential danger for the future of the area. On the economic side the

commission has emphasized aid and resources, while on the political side it has stressed democratic legitimacy. There are important difficulties in both areas that demand more thinking. With all the problems of the Kissinger report, the existence of a fairly good recipe for Central America—which the report is—is better than having none, or having to depend on more limited ones such as that offered by the Contadora Group.[19]

What we have then is not so much a transvaluation of values but a transmigration of values. Anti-Americanism has become an American preserve, sometimes to the embarrassment and other times to the chagrin of Latin American intellectuals. To paraphrase Pogo: One does not have to look far afield for anti-American phenomena: basically it is us. The consequences of a politics of self-flagellation remains to be determined. But the actual state of intellectual affairs within the inter-American system is quite beyond dispute: what is evolving is the search for a middle way between the superpowers at the level of tactics, and the need to choose between the United States and the Soviet Union at the level of principles.

When Latin American intellectuals express anti-American sentiments in raw, undiluted form it is often less an ideological charge than a cultural aping of the Northern Colossus. For example, the anti-hero in Carlos Fuentes' novel, *The Death of Artemio Cruz*, gives vent to a sense of treason, of betrayal of fundamental culture and national values within Latin America, rather than any systematic denunciation of the United States.

> The financing operations, the stock holdings, the administration of the the company formed to lend money to the railroad, the legal representation of North American firms, the directorships of banking houses, the foreign stocks—dyes, steel, and detergents; and one little item that does not appear on the wall: fifteen million dollars deposited in banks in Zurich, London, and New York. Yes: you will light a cigarette, in spite of the warnings you have had from your doctor, and to Padilla will relate again the steps by which you gained your wealth: loans of short terms and high interest to peasants in Puebla, just after the Revolution; the acquisition of land around the city of Puebla, whose growth you foresaw; acres for subdivision in Mexico City, thanks to friendly intervention of each succeeding president; the daily newspaper; the purchase of mining stock; the formation of Mexican–U.S. enterprises in which you participated as front-man so that the law would be complied with; trusted friend of North American investors, intermediary between New York and Chicago and the government of Mexico.[20]

There are strong feelings about race, culture and nationality invoked here, including a folkloric anti-developmental bias no less than anti-capitalist bias *per se*. That the United States is identified as the central agency, the root source of these corruptions is not surprising. What is more surprising is that U.S. values as such are viewed as less a source of moral degradation than of material domination.

I am struck by how little in classical, radical Latin American scholarship (and here I have in mind historians like José Luis Romero, or Marxist philosophers like Rodolfo Mondolfo, or sociologists like Gino Germani) ever yielded to the temptations of an anti-American posture. Even present-day Latin American *dependistas* uniformly reveal a keener sense of internal hemispheric problems and a much less shrill notion of overseas domination. In this regard, the work of people like Julio Cotler, Fernando Cardoso, Guillermo O'Donnell, and Celso Furtado comes readily to mind. However strong the feelings may be about inequities within the U.S. system, the sharp empirical sense of bearing witness to actual Latin American inequities is more often than not preferred to the kind of usual sloganizing typical of their North American counterparts.[21]

The work of many of the above-mentioned figures has recently settled on the bureaucratic-authoritarian model of Latin American rule. And while there remains an extraordinary myopia, indeed downright unwillingness to mention, much less examine how communist states like Cuba partake of such a model, it is nonetheless the case that political structures of the region are being examined firsthand, and on their own terms. No longer does the sort of dependency model approach characteristic of an earlier decade in which the United States was held uniquely responsible for every shortcoming in the hemisphere hold unquestioned sway. In this, the essential level-headedness of many Latin American intellectuals has resurfaced, albeit with some hesitations, to reestablish the need for internal, structural analysis in place of external, global mystification.

At its best, this kind of development is touched with a power analysis in reverse, which at least has the merit of being clear-eyed if not particularly hopeful. Typical in this regard are the concluding passages in Helio Jaguaribe's monumental work on *Political Development*.

> In the present and foreseeable future, the best possible interrelation between the American and the Latin American societies is an enlightened rule and management by the United States of her imperium, giving possibilities for enlightened forms of radical or progressive reformist in Latin America, along the lines formerly discussed. The economic,

technological, and military advantages already accumulated by the United States, vis-à-vis Latin America, are of such a nature that even within the framework of an empire, the autonomous development of Latin America—after a period of difficulties of about three decades— would be a factor for future substantial improvement, including all sorts of benefits, in the relations between the two areas. Moreover, given the present general primacy of the United States and the fact that the most successful level that Latin America could achieve, in the next three decades would be one of simple international autonomy, the relative strength of the former would remain untouched.[22]

What one detects among Latin American intellectuals is a deep and at times tragic sense of inequality, but by no means the sort of rabid anti-Americanism that one has come to expect or at least anticipate from the popular literature. Thus, the ultimate turn of the screw on this anti-American phenomenon is that we are dealing essentially with a heresy within American elite culture; more a collapse of nerve from within than any presumed attack by Spanish and Portuguese speaking guerrillas from without. Patrick Glynn, in a recent essay on nuclear arms, uniquely summed up the situation. It stands as well as anything that I could add as a fitting postscript to this anti-American ideology.

> For whole sectors of our culture, it should be recognized, moral thinking now finds its starting point in the *rejection* of received moral and political values. This loss of faith has had a profound effect on the perspective that many people bring to the problem of national defense. In particular, it has undermined in many minds the idea that the United States, at least a political entity, is something basically good and worth preserving. Thus while protest is inevitably directed against the weapons, for many people it is the United States government that is the real object of distrust. At its roots, the contention of these people is not that the administration has a bad defense policy, but that in the end the United States, or at least the United States government, is hardly worth defending.[23]

If one substitutes the problem of hemispheric defense for that of national defense, the Glynn comment stands as an eloquent reminder that beneath so many discourses on ideologies are rooted deeply felt ethical premises about U.S. culture and the U.S. system. This is not intended as a policy paper, but if we fashion policies on faulty premises, the outcomes can hardly be salutary. In this instance, it would be better to get beyond the rhetoric of anti-Americanism if we are to see the realities of the *inter*-American environment. Few leaders have stated this need more eloquently, nor with better qualifications than the late Romulo Betancourt. "There are two different ways of behaving in commercial relations with the powerful industrial states when you are responsible for the affairs of a small country...one can posture demagogically in public meetings; or one can persistently and without fanfare undertake action designed to achieve justice."[24] One need only add that the same requirement is true for large nations addressing the needs of small nations. The antidemocratic currents that fuel anti-American sentiments will not readily dissolve under the weight of slogans and policies.

I have not focused extensively on why the phenomenon of anti-Americanism has such staying power because that would be the task of a much larger effort. Rather I take the concept as a piece of datum in trying to piece together an ideological formation in Latin America that will persist over time whatever the actual policies of the United States may be toward any particular nation in the region, or even toward the region as a whole. One cannot emphasize too strongly that there is hardly any correlation between actual United States performance and imputed policies. In point of fact, over the past several decades, there has been a long-run trend (admittedly not uniformly carried forth) for the United States to reduce its military appropriations, increase its social supports, and permit a relatively wide variety of regimes to flourish unimpeded. Generally, from El Salvador to Argentina, it has been made clear that as a nation the United States supports centrist, democratic regimes rather than either leftist or rightist positions and parties.

But during that same period anti-Americanism has thrived. The situation is analogous to the famed Davies "J-curve" in describing revolutionary phenomena: as Latin America undergoes a series of revolutions of rising expectations, its relative standing vis-à-vis the United States becomes the touchstone of success. Thus, the fact that Argentina is a relatively affluent nation, one equal to, if not greater in farming and mineral wealth, when compared to nations such as Australia (with which it has many statistical commonalities) becomes unimportant. It is its inability to perform as a world power equal to that of the United States that becomes critical. Thus it is the politics of relative deprivation that helps to underwrite the politics of revolutionary discontent. These are dangerous alliances. They threaten not only regional stability but the survival of regimes that accept or promote anti-Americanism on tactical grounds.

Anti-Americanism has clearly become a global phenomenon. As

such, Latin American variations on that theme should be seen in a context of asserting its own Third-Worldness. That is to say, Latin America,
which has a historical and geographical coherence all of its own, has now
been placed in the position of a key linch-pin in the activities of
the Third World as such. Hence, in a variety of nonaligned conferences
and agencies, Latin Americans have been compelled to dampen any sense
of area uniqueness in favor of global commonalities. Since this is patently
difficult, if not impossible to do upon a close reading of events and
structures—say comparing South America with Southeast Asia in gross
national product—attitudinal rather than structural elements become central. And among these attitudinal factors none is more ready-to-hand
and serviceable than anti-Americanism. The global role of the United
States becomes the missing link cementing Third Worldism.[25] It serves
to override normal considerations of acute differences between regions
and peoples of the world, leading to organizational formations and transformations of old organizations like the United Nations into forums for
the promulgation of such demands.[26]

Furthermore, just as anti-Americanism at the national level blots out
differences amongst radical groups, so too at the international level, anti-
Americanism enables nations to cohere at the policy level, despite their
strong differences toward the Second World of the Soviet Union. It is
nothing short of astonishing that voting patterns at the United Nations
involve alignments among nations having little else in common other
than a shared animus toward the United States. Alignment politics at
the global level thus conspire to move Latin America reluctantly and
unevenly into a Third World orbit. The price of admission into that orbit, the veritable touchstone of underdevelopment loyalties, often are attitudes toward the United States.

It would be fallacious to assume that anti-Americanism would either
dissolve or disappear if U.S. self-interests could be satisfactorily defined.
This is not to deny the need for such a constant reevaluation of U.S.
purpose. But even if by some magic stroke, such a statement of U.S. purpose could gain wide capital domestically, it would have little bearing
on the rise or fall of anti-Americanism. The vocabulary of motives is
virtually infinite. The imputation of negative performance is inherent in
the estimates of any given policy pronouncement or actual behavior.
Hence, the achievement of a national consensus would not relieve the
anguish of being loathed overseas. For what is at stake is not the type
of U.S. power being exerted in a specific region, but the very existence
of that power as such. That is to say, it is the United States as a global

power rather than specific policy dicta that exacerbate and inflame anti-Americanism.

Nor should one expect specific defeats of U.S. foreign policy to dampen anti-Americanism, or even modulate it. Quite the contrary, defeats for U.S. interests or goals only serve to heighten the uses of anti-Americanism. Thus, whether United States interests suffer defeat in Nicaragua or victory in Grenada, anti-Americanism is a constant. It provides an organizing and mobilizing force that serves a variety of purposes, not the least of which is the refusal of these nations to explain poor economic performance or political repression self-critically. Thus, in Mexico, anti-Americanism serves to disguise a deep fear of radical politics that might topple or transform the PRI. The politicians of Mexico have been consistent in excoriating the United States and in so doing placating Cuba; while at home increasing the size of its own bourgeoisie and dealing harshly with peasant revolts or concerns in backward areas. One might argue that it would be far more salutary for Mexico's leaders to aid its peasantry and lower its rhetoric; but it is clearly far simpler to heat its rhetoric and repress its peasantry. Hardly a better or more ready-at-hand device to achieve such goals exists than anti-Americanism.

Ultimately, it is less the contents of anti-Americanism as a negative ideology than the function of the concept itself that has acquired a compelling force. In Latin American internal affairs, anti-Americanism has permitted the temporary alignment of revolutionist and restorationist. In Latin American foreign affairs, anti-Americanism has permitted a relatively permanent alignment with other segments of the Third World, which are equally unsure and unsteady about their long-range ambitions. In relationships between Latin American states having different socioeconomic systems, anti-Americanism has allowed for the maintenance of a status quo by defusing possible forms of adventurous behavior. And with respect to the United States, anti-Americanism serves as a bargaining chip in negotiating with the establishment, while also providing a bridge to radical intellectuals in North America searching for revolutionary common grounds.

Under such circumstances, it is futile to point out the essential intellectual paucity of the idea of anti-Americanism or its specific contradictions as a model of political behavior. Ideologies rarely have sustaining power as a result of their sophistication or exactitude. Long ago, in a paper on Averroeism, I noted that the magnetism of this peculiar medieval concept was such that as late as the mid-nineteenth century it was invoked to argue the case against secular society. I doubt seriously that anti-Americanism will have a seven hundred year career. It is both too ephemeral and too negative not to run its course more quickly. But the analogy should at least caution analysts to study ideological concepts as if their rise and fall were organizationally rooted in the rise and fall of nations and empires.

NOTES

1. While each chapter must, perforce be judged as a unique and discrete item by the reader, I think it fair to point out that in the corpus of my own work, I see this chapter as part of a longstanding effort to understand United States–Latin American relationships in a policymaking context. I would draw the attention of the readers particularly to the following essays of mine: "The Political Ideology of Political Economy," *Cultural Factors in Inter-American Relations*, edited by Samuel Shapiro. London and Notre Dame: University of Notre Dame Press, 1968, pp. 285–312. "United States Policies and Latin American Realities: Neighborliness, Partnership and Paternalism," *Latin America: The Search for a New International Role*, edited by Ronald G. Hellman and H. Jon Rosenbaum. New York and London: John Wiley & Sons (Halsted Press Division), 1975, pp. 39–56. "Democracy and Development: Policy Perspectives in a Post-Colonial Context," in *The New Caribbean: Decolonization, Democracy and Development*, edited by Paget Henry and Carl Stone. Philadelphia: Institute for the Study of Human Institutions, 1983, pp. 221–33. Hopefully, those who wish to pursue the foundations of my position will consider examining these earlier statements, which I do believe are entirely consistent, and indeed, an extension of, these arguments.

2. Cf. Raul Allard, "The Pluricultural Unity of America," *Americas*, Vol. 36, No. 2 (March/April) 1984, p. 50 (King Juan Carlos' statement quoted therein).

3. Mazher Hameed, "Arab Anger at the United States," *The New York Times* (Op Ed), February 20, 1984, p. 19.

4. Thomas L. Friedman, "State-Sponsored Terrorism Growing," *International Herald Tribune*, January 4, 1984, pp. 1–2.

5. Arthur F. Burns, "This Anti-Americanism is Firstly Anti-Western," *International Herald Tribune*, January 2, 1984, p. 8. Initially delivered as a speech in Munich, Germany, December 17, 1983.

6. Carlos Rangel and Vladimir Tismaneanu, "Revolutionary Thought in Latin America: Mythology, Ideology, Practice." A research proposal submitted to the Foreign Policy Research Institute. Mimeograph. 14 pp.

7. José Marti, *Thoughts on Liberty, Government, Art and Morality*, edited by Carlos Ripoll. New York: Las Americas Publishing Co., 1980, p. 53. See also Carlos Ripoll, *José Marti, the United States, and the Marxist Interpretation of Cuban History*. New Brunswick: Transaction Books, 1984.

8. Andre Gunder Frank, "On the Mechanisms of Imperialism," in *Imperialism and Underdevelopment*, edited by Robert I. Rhodes. New York and London: Monthly Review Press, 1970, pp. 89–114.

9. Darcy Ribeiro, *The Americas as a Civilization*. New York: E.P. Dutton & Co., 1971, pp. 461–62.

10. Octavio Paz, *The Labyrinth of Solitude: Life and Thought in Mexico*. New York: Grove Press, 1962.

11. George P. McLean, "Intervention is Often Necessary," in *Intervention in Latin America*, edited by C. Neale Ronning. New York: Alfred A. Knopf, 1970, pp. 50–56.

12. Roger Hilsman, *The Crouching Future: International Politics and U.S. Foreign Policy*. Garden City, N.Y.: Doubleday & Co., 1975, pp. 609–26.

13. Marcos Falcon Briceno, "Nonintervention Should Be Interpreted in Relation to the Other Pillars of the System," in *Intervention in Latin America*, edited by C. Neal Ronning. New York: Alfred A. Knopf, 1970, pp. 183–89.

14. Octavio Ianni, "Imperialism and Diplomacy in Inter-American Relations," in *Latin America and the United States: The Changing Political Realities*, edited by Julio Cotler and Richard Fagen. Stanford: Stanford University Press, 1974, pp. 23–51.

15. Carlos Rangel, *The Latin Americans: Their Love-Hate Relationship With the United States*. New York: Harcourt, Brace, Jovanovich, 1976, pp. 112–15.

16. Federico Gil, cited in Peter Nehamkis, *Latin America: Myth and Reality*. New York: Alfred A. Knopf, 1964, p. 11.

17. Irving Louis Horowitz, *Cuban Communism* (fifth edition). New Brunswick and London: Transaction Books, 1984.

18. James Chace, "Deeper into the Mire," *The New York Review of Books*, Vol. 31, No. 3 (March 1), 1984, p. 48.

19. Eduardo Ulibarri, "*Cooking up Solutions for Central American Problems*," *The Wall Street Journal* (February 17), 1984, p. 31.

20. Carlos Fuentes, *The Death of Artemio Cruz*. New York: Farrar, Straus & Co., 1964, pp. 10–11.

21. Guillermo O'Donnell, "Tensions in the Bureaucratic-Authoritarian State," in *The New Authoritarianism in Latin America*, edited by David Collier. Princeton: Princeton University Press, 1979, pp. 285–318.

22. Helio Jaguaribe, *Political Development: A General Theory and a Latin American Case Study*. New York: Harper & Row, 1973, pp. 554–56.

23. Patrick Glynn, "Why an American Arms Build-up is Morally Necessary," *Commentary*, Vol. 77, No. 2 (February) 1984, pp. 17–18.

24. Romulo Betancourt, *Venezuela: Oil and Politics*. Boston: Houghton Mifflin Co., 1979, pp. 391–92.

25. Carlos Rangel, *El tercermundismo* (Protogo de Jean-François Revel). Caracas, Venezuela: Monte Avila Editores, C.A., 1982, pp. 19–43.

26. Irving Louis Horowitz, "The United States and the Third World," *Three Worlds of Development: The Theory and Practice of International Stratification*. New York and London: Oxford University Press, 1972 (second edition), pp. 240–69.

4

Anti-Americanism in the Arab World:
Memories of the Past in the Attitudes of the Present

Adeed Dawisha

Attitudes of nations are shaped by the experiences of the present and the memories of the past. It is in the present that policies are formulated, implemented and make their impact on a people's psyche. But this psyche is no virgin land: it is the repository of national images, symbols, even myths which in their totality constitute the collective memory of a people. The relationship between past and present is a dynamic one. The past influences a people's perceptions of the present; but the present provides an ever changing environment that constantly expands the limits of the human intellectual and perceptual horizon. This in turn modifies a people's memory of its past.

So it is with the analysis of Arab attitudes toward the United States. In examining the currents of anti-Americanism in the Arab world, it is analytically perilous to see such attitudes either as mainly the result of post-World War II U.S. policies in the area, or as purely a function of historically and culturally molded anti-Western orientations. The analyst of the Arab world must be aware of Arab history, for the "only hope of discerning the forces actually operative in the [contemporary] world is to range them firmly against the past."[1] But the analyst of contemporary life must use history intelligently: not everything in the past is relevant, not everything is constant. The analyst should discern from history those patterns and contours of human behavior that continue in some ways to influence the contemporary world around him.

One of the most powerful and enduring factors of contemporary

Arab life has been the Arabs' attachment to the memory of their "glorious" past. The period that spanned the rise of the Arab/Islamic civilization in the seventh century and its final eclipse in the fifteenth century is seen by most Arabs as the epitome of Arab and Islamic endeavor, constituting their own substantial offering to the progress of human civilization and proof of what Arabs are capable of.

The Arabs of today savor the memory of a point in history, a mere hundred years after the Prophet's death, when their Arab forefathers had expanded the realm of Islam into an expanse that stretched from Transoxiana and Northern India in the east to Spain in the west. Crucial also to the way contemporary Arabs view the West was the great victory of Salah al-Din al-Ayyubi over the Crusader army in 1187 which relocated Jerusalem into the Islamic fold after eighty-eight years of Christian occupation. Salah al-Din himself was a Kurd, but what Arab today would consider him anything but a true-blooded Arab?

The nostalgia is heightened when Arabs contrast their mediocre intellectual present with their brilliant past; and no period was more brilliant than the golden age of Islam which spanned the eighth century right through to the twelfth. It was then that Baghdad of the Abbasids, Cairo of the Fatimids, Qairawan of the North African Aghlabids and Cordoba of the Spanish Umayyads became the cultural centers of a Moslem world that established and maintained a "paramount influence upon Western scientific and literary thought." For it was essentially Moslem scholars of the vibrant Arab empires who "developed the philosophic and scientific heritage of ancient Greece, Egypt, Persia and India, brought it into line with the religious precepts of a monotheistic world, and so provided the essential link between the teachings of Aristotle, Galen, Euclid and Plato and the thinking of the modern Europeans."[2]

Like Salah al-Din, many of these scholars were non-Arabs, but they flourished under an Arab/Islamic order that provided the environment for the flowering of a whole civilization. And in their memory of the past, contemporary Arabs see those great philosophical and scientific advancements as a product of an entire social order rather than of the individuals within it. What Arab today would consider Ibn Sina (Avicenna, died 1037), a Persian by ethnic origin, whose medical encyclopedia, written in Arabic but translated into Latin continued to be used in Europe until the seventeenth century, anything but a true blue-blooded Arab? What Arab today would judge the works of the Andalusian philosopher Ibn Rushd (Averroes, died 1189) which, along with Ibn Sina's, introduced Aristotelian logic to the Latin Christian theologians,[3] as anything but examples of Arab intellectual masterpieces? These and other ethnically non-Arab intellectual giants—men like the theologian al-Ghazzali, the philosopher al-Farabi, the mathematician al-Khawarizmi, and the physician and astronomer al-Biruni—who, along with their ethnic Arab contemporaries such as al-Kindi, al-Ma'avi, and Ibn Khaldun, produced their greatest works under an all-encompassing Arab civilization, are firmly ensconced in the contemporary Arab psyche as manifestations of the vast intellectual superiority attained by their forefathers over an undistinguished West.

Whether this perception is, in the words of the historian Bernard Lewis, a blatant case of invented history,[4] is not that important to our argument. The point is that Arabs today do see the superiority of medieval Islam over Europe as the achievements of a basically *Arab* social and cultural order. Indeed, this intellectual superiority was transmitted to contemporary Arabs by the Islamic medieval men of learning themselves. As late as the fourteenth century, the great North African Arab historian Ibn Khaldun[5] would remark: "We have heard of late that in the lands of the Franks, that is, the country of Rome and its dependencies on the northern shore of the Mediterranean, the philosophic sciences flourish...and their students are plentiful. But God knows best what goes on in those parts."[6] While the medieval Arabs could justifiably use these contemptuous terms three or even two centuries earlier, the intellectual balance of power had tilted so rapidly in favor of the West that, by the fourteenth century, any talk of Arab/Islamic superiority was hopelessly out of date.

Indeed, the beginning of the Arabs' long decline had started much earlier. The long drawn-out sectarian and regional schisms that by the fourteenth and fifteenth centuries had almost destroyed the political order were accompanied by an intellectual schism that was destined to have far-reaching effects on the Arab/Islamic civilization. In the battle between the theologians, with their emphasis on revelation and mysticism, and the philosophers, who insisted on the primacy of reason and rationalistic free thinking, a battle that spanned the best part of three hundred years, the former were able to muster popular support to win the day. The result of this intellectual evolution was "to throttle almost all innovations in Moslem science and philosophy."[7] And so it came to pass that the dawn of the European era, an era that was to be characterized by rational thought and scientific endeavour coincided with the final suffocation of Arab intellectual creativity.

From about the fourteenth and fifteenth centuries until the nineteenth century, the Arabs went through five hundred years of intellectual coma. The Europeans, on the other hand, made spectacular advances in the fields of science and philosophy. When the Arabs in the nineteenth century finally began to stir from their long and deep slumber, they awoke into a world that was dominated politically and culturally by Europe. At first, European superiority fascinated the Arabs; some were seduced by the science, the technology, the rationality; by the age of reason, by the era of secular liberalism. But not before long, European political and cultural imperialism reared its ugly head. There was little the Arabs could do to stem Europe's military and political dominance, but they could at least try to avoid falling into the pit of cultural emasculation.

The defensiveness was nurtured by the Europeans' clearly articulated sense of superiority over the Arabs. Thus, for example, Sir Samuel Baker wrote of Colonel Ahmad Arabi who had led the revolt against British and French political and financial domination of Egypt, and who for his pains had suffered a crushing military defeat at the hands of the British in 1882: "He (Arabi) stirred up the latent fanaticism of his coreligionists by inciting them against the Christians. . . . Here was 'young Egypt' in the flesh, burning with enthusiasm, determined to show the world that Arabi was an incarnation of a great principle. . . . At the prick of the bayonet the bubble burst; the ass in the lion skin galloped across the desert in cowardly flight."[8] The passage is indicative of European attitudes: not only was Arabi, a man who had become something of a national hero in Egypt, a fanatical bigot, but he was a stupid and cowardly one at that.

On the intellectual level, too, the Europeans revelled in the superiority of their cultural order, based on "reason" and "science," contrasting it with the contemporary Arab situation, allegedly caught up in the dead end of retrogressive Islam. Thus, a leading French orientalist, Ernest Renan, would assert in a public lecture in 1880 that anyone could see the actual inferiority of the Moslem countries, the decadence of states governed by Islam, and the intellectual vacuity of the races adhering to Islam. He went on to condemn Islam as a religion incompatible with science and with new ideas.[9] And Renan was hardly alone among nineteenth century European orientalists[10] in contemptuously dismissing the Arabs and their religion as not only irrelevant to the present but, because of the backwardness and rigidity of the religion, even more irrelevant for the future of humanity and its progress.

The Arabs, filled with the awareness of a militarily and intellectually dominant Europe, could counteract with the only weapon they had: a reaffirmation of their "glorious past," of their once immense military and intellectual superiority, and a return to their "true" religion. For their choice was a stark one: they could disown the past and embrace Europe's secularist rationalism which, according to the Europeans, had been responsible for catapulting Europe into the position of paramountcy, or they could delve back into their origins and use their past as the moral and intellectual barrier to Europe's onslaught. There was no question that they would choose the latter, but in their hearts and minds they realized too that much of Europe's contempt was justified. Somehow they had to defend and reaffirm their roots, for there lay their identity. But simultaneously they had to incorporate Western intellectual and scientific advances into their stagnating societies. Part of the struggle was to counteract Renan's argument: to prove that Islam, the rock upon which Arab culture rested, was not necessarily antithetical to reason; that it was not necessarily anti-science or anti-innovation.

Jamal al-Din al-Afghani (1839-97) was perhaps the first champion of Islam and Arab culture against the Christian European tide. He defended Islam as a religion that allowed in its past the rational sciences to flourish. Indeed, Islam was "in harmony with the principles discovered by scientific reason, was indeed the religion demanded by reason."[11] But Islam, or rather Moslems, after centuries of cultural, as well as military, achievements had become lethargic in the recent past, and what was needed therefore was an Islamic "reformation" and a Moslem "Luther." Apart from that, Islam and reason could and did live side by side; indeed, the two could creatively complement each other. There would be no discarding of Islam, therefore, but in Afghani's political thought there was an awareness of the weakness of the world of Islam, and an appeal to traditional, conservative Moslems to open up to Western sciences and rationalism before the world of Islam is engulfed by the European tide.

Afghani's ideas were taken up by a number of disciples who later were to become intellectual and political leaders of their time. This "reform" movement flourished particularly in Egypt in which, unlike other parts of the Arab world, suffering as they were under repressive Ottoman rule, the interchange of ideas was tolerated by a far less suffocating British control. Indeed, compared with earlier periods, the second half of the nineteenth century in Egypt could be said to have gone through "a true literary and intellectual renaissance."[12] Schools of thought about the regeneration of the Arab world differed and indeed secularists, primarily composed of Christian intellectuals, began to challenge the Moslem reformers. Yet, on the whole, as long as the Western threat to Arab values continued to dominate the Moslem psyche, a reaffirmation of Islam constituted an assertion of identity, a way to emphasize cultural distinctiveness. In other words, it was through Islam that nationalism was being unequivocally asserted.

The cultural struggle ran parallel with, indeed was heightened by, the political struggle. Afghani and some of his most talented disciples, particularly Mohammad Abdu, were contemporaries of the failed revolt of Colonel Arabi; they lived in the succeeding period of British colonialist domination; and ultimately they inspired the generation who fought for independence in Egypt in the first half of the twentieth century. With the collapse of the Ottoman empire after the First World War, and the division of the Arab world into British and French spheres of influence, the various Arab regions of the defunct Ottoman empire began to fight, in most cases independently of each other, to gain political independence from European domination.

To contemporary Arabs, this period of the recent past constituted the reawakening of the Arabs from their deep and long sleep. The century spanning the mid-nineteenth to the mid-twentieth centuries was the period in which the Arabs stretched back into their history to rediscover the tools by which they fought European domination. Anti-Westernism in this period was, unlike the early Islamic period, not borne out of contempt for an inferior social order. Quite the opposite, it was a defensive emotional response, borne out of the intense fear of a dominating civilization on the march threatening to sweep the Arabs, their culture, and religion into historical oblivion.

With time, the absorption of Western ideas into Moslem society, aimed initially at regenerating the stagnant Arab world began to change in subtle forms the intellectual basis of the political struggle. European ideas of secular nationalism espoused primarily by intellectuals of the Levant began to compete with the more traditional Islamic emphasis. The divide was subtle but crucial. The Moslem thinkers looked into their past and saw a religion that carried the Arabs to towering heights. The secularists conceded the role of Islam, but saw its Arab essence as the primary motivating spark. Whatever the orientation, by the mid-twentieth century, the western and eastern Arabs were united in their mistrust of, and hostility toward, the dominant imperial, and in some cases colonial, European order.

It was the Second World War that undermined the dominance of Europe. Britain and France emerged victorious but highly scarred, hardly able to protect interests abroad when so much was needed to be done on the home front. The inherent weakness was not immediately apparent. The struggle against Communist domination in Malaya by the British and in Vietnam by the French continued the facade of greatness and power. Yet it was a facade that obscured the reality of an already collapsing imperial order. It was perhaps Suez in 1956 that spelled the end of the European era in Arab eyes. The two ailing great powers still had colonial possessions in the area, but by then the imperial bubble had already burst, and the responsibility of maintaining the interests of the West, or more appropriately in Arab eyes, the domination of the West, had already passed to the United States, a virtual newcomer into Middle Eastern and Arab politics and society. The U.S. era had begun.

The dawn of the U.S. era occurred at a time when Arab hostility against the West was rampant. Anti-Western sentiments at the popular level had reached a crescendo after the Arabs' defeat at the hands of the new state of Israel in 1948–49. The Palestinian population was fired by the idea of a return to the original homeland. In a sense, therefore, Palestinian radicalism became the focus of, and was itself reinforced by, the rising tide of militant Arab nationalism, as well as by the emergence of President Gamal Abd al-Nasser as the charismatic leader of Arab nationalism and the keeper of its conscience. In such an atmosphere, the times ahead for U.S. policy were bound to be trying.

The United States had actively supported the concept of a Jewish state in Palestine. Indeed, in Arab perceptions, Israel would not have been born had it not been for the policies of President Truman, a perception that incidently seems to have been shared by Israelis themselves. Merle Miller, in his oral biography of Truman, records an occasion in 1949 when "the Chief Rabbi of Israel came to see the President and he told him, 'God put you in your mother's womb so that you could be the instrument to bring about the rebirth of Israel after two thousand years.' At that, great tears started rolling down Harry Truman's cheeks."[13] To the Arabs, the imposition of a Jewish, western-oriented state in their midst was an act that was abhorrent both to Islam and Arab nationalism. And U.S. efforts in bringing this about were bound to make a negative impact on the Arab psyche.

The United States' second handicap in its initial entry into the Arab world was conditioned by the structure of the international system as it had developed after the Second World War. The intense U.S. hostility toward the "forces of international Communism" as manifested primarily by the Soviet Union and China, contributed to feverish U.S.

efforts to stop the perceived expansionism of this new menace. And no man was more determined than John Foster Dulles, the U.S. Secretary of State during the Eisenhower administration, to enforce this policy of containment. In May 1953, Dulles visited Cairo to convince the new and young leader of Egypt of the Soviet Communist threat and the necessity to protect the area from this danger by joining a Western military alliance. Abd al-Nasser, seemingly unmoved by the alleged threat of a power "whose forces were five thousand miles away,"[14] relates his response:

> I told him that he could by his own ways and means exert pressure over any Arab government to join the Western camp and give them military bases on its own territory...[but] he would find that the government which submitted to their presence would be divorced from its popular support, and would be unable to lead the people.... The military bases obtained under pressure would be of no use when they were needed. This was because there would be tens of bases working against this base.[15]

These were prophetic words indeed, as further events were to illustrate. And Dulles himself seemed to have calculated in 1953 that Egypt and the Arab world were not yet ready "to create a Middle East pact parallel to NATO."[16] But the bad-faith model of the Soviet Union continued to dominate the attitudinal orientations of U.S. policy-making elites, so that the rising tide of nationalism in the Arab world was increasingly being interpreted in Washington as a masked Communist upsurge. Acting on this perception, the Eisenhower Doctrine was enunciated in January 1957, pledging U.S. assistance including the dispatch of armed forces to nations requesting U.S. help "against overt armed aggression from any nation controlled by international Communism."[17] This was followed by U.S. political interventions in Jordan to help the king against a nationalist Prime Minister, and in Syria where an aid agreement with the Soviet Union, concluded incidentally by the wealthy land-owning Defense Minister, was interpreted by Dulles and Eisenhower as a sign of an impending Communist takeover.[18] To the Arabs, these and other similar U.S. activities "seemed both a distraction from their local quarrel with Israel and a new form of veiled colonialism."[19] All this emphasized to the Arabs that the United States was simply carrying on the imperialist traditions of Britain and France, and John Foster Dulles was singled out for "special" treatment, as the lyrics from the following Arabic song, popular at that time, illustrate:

Dulles, O Dulles, O Hatcher of plots
Stop intimidating us, O Beloved of the Sixth Fleet
Dance on Your Fleet,
You accuse us of Communism, while your eyes covet oil
Do not accuse us, you will not move us
Syria is free and honest, You'll never deceive us.[20]

I return here to a point I made at the beginning of the chapter. People tend to interpret the events of the present through the prism of the past. To the Arabs in the 1950s and 1960s, nationalism was the means by which a glorious past would be transformed into a heroic future. Through nationalism, with its obsession with ethnic heritage, Arabs drew courage from their long and distinguished history: through nationalism, with its emphasis on state-building, modernization and scientific development, the Arabs, for the first time in almost five hundred years, could begin to become excited about their future. Yet this vehicle for material and intellectual advancement was being attacked, even humiliated and derided, by the West, not only politically but also in cultural terms.[21]

In their interpretation of history, these attacks were analogous to the European onslaught against Islam in the nineteenth century. Indeed, the situation at hand was even more serious, for in Arab eyes the West this time had been able to create a puppet in its own image, an extension of its own ideological and social order, and plant it in the midst of the Arab "nation," so that Western domination could be perpetuated. The terms of reference in this contemporary period may have changed from those that existed in the nineteenth century. But to the contemporary Arabs, the fight waged by Jamal al-Din al-Afghani then was their fight now. In other words, if, as I argued earlier, developments in the present tend to modify perceptions of the past, then in this case, they only went to confirm the mistrust of the West held by the Arabs. Only the players changed. Up until the Second World War, the West meant Europe, particularly Britain and France, and it was primarily these two great imperial powers that took the brunt of Arab anger and hostility. Increasingly in the 1950s and 1960s, it was the United States that to the Arabs signified Western malevolence.

The picture was, of course, not as simple as this. There was always deep, but hidden, admiration for U.S. scientific and intellectual achievements. U.S. films particularly, depicting an advanced civilization and a vibrant social order buttressed by a seeming quality of life that was beyond even the most rampant imagination of any Arab, were obviously leaving their imprint on the Arabs' view of their world. Yet at the same time, this "show" of U.S. cultural dominance, this seeming flaunting of the superiority of the United States' way of life, was seen by Arabs increasingly as an obscene case of "cultural imperialism." To be sure, the Arabs admired, even secretly envied, U.S. culture, but they also resented it and feared what it might do to their own social order. Again the memory of the nineteenth century was constantly invoked, but now the danger was much greater. In their use of advanced modern communications, such as the cinema, the radio and later the television, the Americans, unlike the British in the earlier period, were reaching beyond the admittedly important but nevertheless small upper level of Arab society to a much wider, and perhaps more vulnerable audience.

In a sense, this combination of the Arab admiration for, and their fear of, the seductive U.S. culture contributed to the cementing of the rising nationalist tide. Arab admiration for the United States meant that they demanded a "modern" social order, emphasizing scientific and cultural advancements. The traditional elites were, therefore, increasingly seen in the context in which they presented themselves: status-quo oriented, slow to accept change, believing in evolutionary rather than revolutionary transformation of society. If the Arabs wanted to catch up with the West quickly, they became convinced that they had to circumvent the existing political leaderships. Moreover, to be able to satisfy quickly and effectively the demands of an *entire* society, when eyes had been opened to better things by exposure to a superior civilization, the emphasis had to be on an egalitarian political order in which the rewards would permeate society as a whole. This awareness was of course far more acute in the relatively more advanced societies of Egypt and the Fertile Crescent. And indeed it was in those countries that nationalism, socialism and rule by the modernizing military became the ideological trademarks of a generation who felt destined to deliver the Arabs and their lethargic world into a new heroic age of assertion and power. And spearheading the translation of these dreams into reality was Egypt and its young military leader, Abd al-Nasser, who had closely observed and learned well from the United States' cultural drive into the Arab world.

From the mid-1950s onward, Egypt used its own relative cultural superiority in the Arab world to compete with, and in many cases eclipse, the U.S. effort. And in the Arabic language, Egypt had a powerful weapon. Rock'n'roll and U.S. ballads might have gained many new adherents among Arab teenagers, but the songs of Um Kalthoum, Mohammed Abd al-Wahab and Abd al-Halim Hafiz continued to form the backbone of most Arabs' entertainment. Similarly, Egyptian films more than held their own in the Arab world against U.S. imports, and Egyptian books, magazines, and newspapers continued to dominate the intellectual life of the Arab world.[22] And in all these different media, the political message became increasingly and consciously visible.

When it came to delivering a political message directly and forcefully, the transistor radio, which in the 1950s was to revolutionize communications in the Arab world, played an indispensable role. In an endless stream of fiery speeches and commentaries, Egyptian radio bombarded the Arab world throughout the 1950s and 1960s with nationalist rhetoric evoking anti-Western, particularly anti-American, sentiments. They reminded the Arabs time and time again of their glorious past, of their military achievements, and of their rich culture. When the British and French were forced to withdraw from Suez, this was likened to the Arab/Moslem defeat of the Crusaders. Nor did Egyptian radio show any bashfulness about the obvious benefits in comparing Nasser with Salah al-Din.

Beyond the memory of the past, Egypt would promise a brilliant future based on the present "achievements" and "victories" of nationalism and socialism. Much of this was of course rhetoric, but the people accepted, approved and encouraged it, for the stand against imperialism was as much language as it was concrete policies; and to the applauding multitude, who had suffered the humiliation of colonial domination, hurling insults at the once invincible and powerful was as good as defeating them militarily or overhauling them intellectually. Why should they not dance in the streets deliriously when they hear the young leader of Arab nationalism publicly tell mighty America: "We shall cut the tongue of anyone who dares to insult us.... We do not tolerate pressure and we do not accept humiliation. We are a people whose dignity cannot be sacrificed."[23] These were the heady days of nationalism, the force with which the Arabs would recreate their distant past and the vehicle by which they would erase the humiliations of the recent past. Nationalism would thus constitute, or so people believed, the morality upon which the ultimate triumph of the Arab social order over U.S. political and cultural "imperialist designs" would be achieved.

But then Arab nationalism met its Waterloo in June 1967. On the crucial Arab nationalist issue of Palestinian rights, it failed ignominiously, and with the failure sank the hopes and aspirations of the "nationalist generation." For after a whole decade of nationalist rhetoric and radical politics, the Arabs went to war against the "Zionist entity," confident of their inevitable victory under the banner of Arab nationalism, only to suffer the most humiliating defeat of their contemporary history. And in the shocked aftermath, the Arabs, bewildered by their own impotence, began slowly to reassess their present situation and their relationship to their past.

There were initially efforts to blame the Arab defeat on anybody and anything but the Arabs themselves and their system of values, and for a very short while the United States bore the brunt of Arab hostility. But it did not take long for a serious process of self-criticism to emerge. Thus, beyond the feverish efforts of disgraced leaders to cover their tracks "lay a more profound and interesting set of developments: the honest soul-searching of intellectuals for the roots of the Arab ailment; the quest of a younger generation for a new political thrust and for concrete solutions to harsh realities. . . ."[24] And in this, the debate would inevitably center on the utility of the past to the present and future: should the Arabs rebel against their history, tradition, and heritage; should they once and for all liberate their present from the confines of their past; or should they completely discard modernism, as manifested by the concepts of "nationalism" and "secularism," and return to Islam, like virgins who have sinned returning to the forgiving confines of the confessional; should they, in other words, hasten a return to self, essence and authenticity?[25]

It was very quickly evident that secularism, nationalism and revolutionary leftism were on the wane. Disgraced and discredited, these concepts and slogans were no longer able to fire the imagination of the people. So it was only natural that the search for authenticity, in the form of Islam, would gather momentum. But although the alternative was renewed Islamic assertion, it was a deradicalized form of political Islam that dominated the Middle Eastern political scene. The disillusionment with revolutionary politics following the June 1967 *al-Hazima* (massive defeat) was the springboard for a process of regional deradicalization that gathered momentum with the defeat of the Palestinian guerrillas in Jordan in September 1970, reaching a zenith during the October 1973 war. In the 1970s, the Arabs put their faith in devout, conservative Moslem leaders like King Faisal and King Khalid of Saudi Arabia, and President Sadat of Egypt. The accent was on pragmatic politics emanating from a form of cautious institutionalized Islam.

The Arabs seemed to have learned the necessary lesson. In their international relations, they would henceforth deal with other international actors in a more pragmatic, more rational and less stereotyped manner. "We have tended," Mohammed Hasneen Haykal, Abd al-Nasser's major publicist, told them, "to establish relations on the basis of black and white without any regard to other colours. We must understand that only God can face his servants with two alternatives—Paradise or Hell. . . ."[26] And the Arabs in the 1970s seemed to have heeded the advice. Within this context, the United States could still be condemned for its pro-Israeli orientation, for its continued adherence to the concept of containment; for its seeming propensity to monopolize external influence in the region, and for its often insulting and patronizing self-righteousness. But there was also an increasing awareness that the United States was a superpower with immense influence that could not be ignored. And the analogy with the nineteenth century was appropriate. The Moslem and Arab intellectuals did fear and mistrust European imperialism, and they certainly delved into their roots to combat its spread and possible domination of their culture. But they also dealt with it, and in some cases manipulated it politically, and advocated learning from it intellectually.

The men who led institutionalized Islam in the 1970s began the new era by arguing that the Arabs had to deal with the United States, because it was only the United States which could deliver Israel, thus neutralizing this mortal danger to Islam and Arabism. It was indeed ironic that the pragmatist paradigm would even entertain such a simplistic prognosis. But disillusioned with radical politics, people believed the new slogans and allowed their Moslem conservative leaders, who by then had occupied the center stage of Arab politics, to usher a revitalized U.S. drive into the area, spearheaded by Secretary of State Henry Kissinger.

The 1970s was indeed the decade of America on the march. Arab political consciousness was dominated by Sadat's catch phrase that the United States held 99 percent of the cards. And the new power-brokers of Arab politics, the oil barons of Saudi Arabia and the Gulf, enthusiastically approved, for in the new post-1973 oil boom environment where the attraction of *tharwa* (wealth) was beginning to replace the seemingly discredited concept of *thawra* (revolution),[27] the United States' free enterprise value system had found a vigorous and powerful ally. Indeed, it was not only the conservatives of Egypt and the Peninsula who seemed to tie their destiny to the whims of the United States. Radical Syria also was prepared to flirt with the U.S. experiment. Kissinger, with such powerful backing, was thus able to bring about the disengagement agreements between Egypt and Israel and Syria and Israel. His "shuttle diplomacy" and his advocacy of "step-by-step peace process" entered the main vocabulary of everyday political discourse in the Arab world, and the man became far better known to ordinary Arabs than many of their own leaders, and his alleged prowess far more respected. Kissinger, for a while, was the new prophet, and U.S. power and values were the new religion, in the land of prophets and religions.

The post-1973 period, what I have depicted as the revitalized U.S. era of Henry Kissinger, went beyond the political domain. In the words of Edward Said, writing in 1977-78, "the Arab world today is an intellectual, political and cultural satellite of the United States...Whereas Britain and France once dominated intellectual horizons in the East by virtue of their prominence and wealth, it is now the United States that occupies that place.... And while it is certainly true that some students from the Arab world continue to go to Europe to study, the sheer numerical preponderance comes to the United States.... Besides, the patronage system in scholarship, business, and research makes the United States a virtual hegemonic commander of affairs."[28] Said, however, may have overstated his case. Cultural fascination there certainly was, but political hegemony to a large extent depended on the U.S. promise to deliver Israel. And that promise continued to be alive in the Arab psyche until the 1979 Camp David accords. In Arab eyes, rather than delivering Israel, U.S. power and diplomacy delivered Egypt into the bosom of Israel. For the Arabs, the historical analogy was there for everyone to see: when it comes to Israel, the West always betrays the Arabs. The United States did it in 1979 and Britain and France did it in 1917.

Historical analogies meant an Arab return, yet again, to their past and heritage. To the Arabs, institutionalized, conservative Islam, led by men politically and strategically tied to the United States, was put to the test and was found wanting. And the United States, seemingly inexorably tied to Israel, had no intention to deliver Israel; indeed, it betrayed the Arabs by taking Egypt out of the Arab-Israeli conflict, thus making the Arab world an even greater hostage to Israeli military and strategic power. The United States, therefore, in the late 1970s was being seen no longer as the honest, even-handed broker, but a distinctly biased and perfidious manipulator. Even the United States' staunchest allies in the Arab world were becoming singularly frustrated with it. Prince Abdulla, later to become Saudi Arabia's crown prince, lambasted a group of U.S. businessmen and newspapermen:

We hear constantly that the Soviet Union and Communism constitute the greatest danger to the Middle East. But as a friend, I tell you that you Americans constitute the greatest danger. The reason is your total alliance with Israel. The Arab masses feel abandoned by the United States and find it convenient to look to the Soviet Union instead. The policies the United States offer make it difficult for your friends to maintain that friendship. It is approaching the point where we will be helpless, where we can no longer stand up and defend that friendship. If the United States persists in a pro-Israel policy, the only beneficiary will be the Soviet Union.[29]

The prince, of course, was concerned about more than just Soviet influence; he was concerned about his own safety, and about the credibility of the then dominant order, one of whose main pillars was his own House of Saud. He could no doubt see that the failure of institutionalized Islam was allowing the radical version of political Islam to come into its own. The Moslem Brothers, believing as they do in the utility of violence, were gaining new adherents and taking bolder initiatives. The Brotherhood's activities spanned not only Egypt, but also Syria and Jordan. Other Moslem fundamentalist groups became more active in Saudi Arabia and the Gulf sheikhdoms, and radical Islam generally began to challenge vigorously the established orders in countries such as Sudan, Morocco and Tunisia. And in most cases, the thrust of these radicals' anger was aimed not only at the perceived corrupt rulers, but also at the powers backing them. In almost all cases (with the notable exception of attacks on Russian advisors in Syria), the United States took the main brunt of this hostility.

It was in the midst of this mood of increasing Islamic rebellion that the Iranian revolution exploded on the Middle Eastern political stage. Moslems everywhere saw the revolution as a proof of what they would be able to do if they were to cling doggedly to their faith; if they were to reach back wholeheartedly and without reservations to their own heritage and history, to the glorious days of Islamic assertion. The overthrow of the "westernized" Shah, the United States' much vaunted ally, and the subsequent humiliations inflicted on the United States by an uncompromising frail cleric was perceived by the admiring masses as a great Moslem victory over a dominant U.S. order, equaled only by the great Arab victories over Byzantium and Europe in the early days of Islam.

It is too early yet to predict the extent of the power and permanence of revolutionary Islam, just as it is still too early to assess the hold of the latest bout of anti-Americanism over people's hearts and minds. Islamic revolutionary fervor may be on the wane: the revolution in Iran has stalled; its atrocities have travelled through and beyond the mist of Tehran's propaganda, and people, even those filled with the earlier enthusiasm, are beginning to hedge their bets, waiting to see whether the revolution can be redeemed; whether it will come good in the end. In other countries, Islamic fundamentalism has been taken on and ruthlessly cast aside by state power in Saudi Arabia, in Iraq, in Egypt, and most strikingly in Syria. On the other hand, however, the Arab perception of Israel and the United States is one of a symbiotic relationship, which does not bode well for the United States' image in the area, for its standing and influence, and ultimately for its own friends in the area.

When Arabs look back into the annals of their history, they see a people whose military power struck fear into people's hearts, and whose cultural achievement was the marvel of the times. Those very people then went through a seemingly endless journey into oblivion, only to come back into a world that was no longer theirs. When they set out to reclaim it, or at least to have a share in the new order, they had to contend with failure and humiliation. The new order, whether European as it was in the nineteenth and early twentieth centuries, or American as it has been since the Second World War, has proved resiliently dominant. The Arab world, having tried unsuccessfully to break this dominance, sits today at the crossroads between revolution and pragmatism, between struggle and peaceful coexistence, between a risky confrontation with the dominant order and appeasement of it.

NOTES

1. Geoffrey Barraclough, *An Introduction to Contemporary History* (Harmondsworth, Mddx: Penguin Books, 1967), p. 16.

2. Anthony Nutting, *The Arabs* (New York: Mentor Books, 1964), p. 126.

3. William McNeill, *The Rise of the West: A History of the Human Community* (Chicago: The University of Chicago Press, 1963), pp. 501–503; see also Philip K. Hitti, *Makers of Arab History* (New York: St Martin's Press, 1968), pp. 219–37.

4. Bernard Lewis, *History: Remembered, Recovered, Invented* (Princeton, New Jersey: Princeton University Press, 1975).

5. Ibn Khaldun ranks as perhaps the most original historical thinker of medieval times. For the best and most concise English commentary on Ibn Khaldun's famous work *al-Muqaddima*, see Charles Issawi, *An Arab Philosophy of History* (London: John Murray, 1950).

6. Quoted in Bernard Lewis, *The Arabs in History* (New York: Harper and Row Publishers, 1966), p. 165.

7. McNeil, *op. cit.*, p. 503.

8. Norman Daniel, *Islam, Europe and Empire* (Edinburgh: Edinburgh University Press, 1966), p. 552.

9. Albert Hourani, *Arabic Thought in the Liberal Age 1798-1939* (London: Oxford University Press, 1970), p. 120.

10. See Edward Said, *Orientalism* (New York: Vintage Books, 1978).

11. Albert Hourani, *op. cit.*, p. 123.

12. Nadav Safran, *Egypt in Search of Political Community* (Cambridge, Massachusetts: Harvard University Press, 1961), p. 57.

13. Quoted in Richard H. Curtiss, *A Changing Image: American Perceptions of The Arab-Israeli Dispute* (Washington, D.C.: American Educational Trust, 1982), p. 35.

14. *Sunday Times* (London), June 24, 1962.

15. United Arab Republic, Information Department, *President Gamal Abd al-Nasser's Speeches and Press Interviews, 1959*, p. 600.

16. William R. Polk, *The United States and the Arab World* (Cambridge, Massachusetts: Harvard University Press, 1969), p. 271.

17. P.E. Zinner, ed., *Documents of American Foreign Relations, 1957* (New York: Harper and Brothers, 1958), p. 201.

18. Dwight D. Eisenhower, *The White House Years: Vol. II, Waging Peace* (New York: Doubleday, 1965), p. 197.

19. Patrick Seale, *The Struggle for Syria: A Study of Post-War Arab Politics, 1945–1958* (London: Oxford University Press, 1965), p. 231.

20. Quoted in Karen Dawisha, *Soviet Foreign Policy Towards Egypt* (London: Macmillan, 1979), p. 18.

21. This is aptly demonstrated by Edward Said in his *Orientalism*, pp. 284-328.

22. For the extent of Egyptian "cultural efforts" in the Arab world, see A.I. Dawisha, *Egypt in the Arab World: The Elements of Foreign Policy* (London: Macmillan, 1976), pp. 173-77.

23. *Al-Ahram* (Cairo), February 24, 1967.

24. Fouad Ajami, *The Arab Predicament: Arab Political Thought and Practice Since 1967* (London: Cambridge University Press, 1981), p. 25.

25. *Ibid.*, pp. 23-75. In this section of his book, Ajami synthesizes brilliantly the main contours of the intellectual debate that occurred in the post-June 1967 Arab world.

26. *Al-Ahram* (Cairo), June 30, 1967.

27. Mohamed Heikal, *The Sphinx and the Commissar* (New York: Harper and Row, 1978), p. 262.

28. Said, *op. cit.*, pp. 322-23.

29. *Time Magazine*, November 9, 1981, p. 11.

5

Perception, Preference, and Policy: An Afro-Arab Perspective of Anti-Americanism

Mohammad Beshir Hamid

The evil in the world almost always comes of ignorance, and good intentions may do as much harm as malevolence, if they lack understanding. On the whole, men are more good than bad; that, however, isn't the real point. But they are more or less ignorant and it is that we call vice or virtue; the most incorrigible vice being that of an ignorance which fancies it knows everything and therefore claims for itself the right to kill...

Albert Camus, *La Peste* (1947)

Anti-Americanism, as such, is not a new phenomenon. Nor is it one originating in, or confined to, Third World countries. Consider the following expressions: "Degraded thinking, lying, deception, and unlimited greed are the natural and inescapable consequences of the commercial spirit, a spirit that like a tidal wave inundates the highest and lowest ele-

For going over the preliminary draft of this paper and for their valuable advice and comments, I am grateful to Professor L. Carl Brown, Director of the Program in Near Eastern Studies, Princeton University, Princeton, N.J.; to Professor Richard P. Stevens of the Center for Contemporary Arab Studies, Georgetown University, Washington, D.C.; to Professor Alvin Z. Rubinstein of the Department of Political Science, University of Pennsylvania, Philadelphia, Pa.; and to Professors Richard and Carolyn Lobban of the Department of Anthropology and African Studies, Rhode Island College, Providence, R.I. Needless to say, I am solely responsible for the perspective and the shortcomings.

ments of American society." "In this [American] society composed of a mixture of all peoples, freedom is purely materialistic and lacking in all idealism." "Just read the newspapers of opposing parties during a presidential campaign, and rest assured, you would believe the candidate for this highest honor in the United States deserved life-imprisonment sooner than residence in the White House." "Cheating is an old American custom."

These statements, independent of any value judgement on them, have a familiar ring and could have been uttered by such certifiable anti-Americans in the Third World as Kwame Nkrumah, Mu'mar al-Qaddafi or Fidel Castro. In fact, these sentiments were expressed by German writers in the mid-19th century.[1] That most famous of all German intellectuals defined the ultimate aim of *Capital* as "laying bare the economic law of motion of modern society," which entailed a thorough and systematic criticism of capitalism. The "guiding thread" of Marx's teachings was expanded and diffused, through the German Social Democratic Party, to expound the tensions and conflicts generated by capitalist development and to provide radical critiques of capitalism as an economic and social system. Theorists such as Lenin, Kautsky, Luxemburg and Hilferding sought to link the development of imperialism to the continued strength of capitalism. They, thus, laid down, in a variety of ways, the ideological framework of anti-capitalism and anti-imperialism as expressions of anti-Americanism. European anti-Americanism was by no means historically and intellectually monopolized by German writers and Marxist intellectuals. Samuel Johnson stated that, "I am willing to love all mankind except an American";[2] while Clemenceau noted that "America is the only nation in history which miraculously has gone directly from barbarism to degeneration without the usual interval of civilization."[3]

This European anti-Americanism could have influenced the evolution of a similar sentiment in the Third World in two, rather paradoxical, ways: first, through the process of acculturation during the period of Western colonialism; and, second, through the association of the United States with the colonial powers during the decolonization process. On another level, European anti-Americanism, in its past and contemporary forms, as well as its intellectual (Marxist) and political (Gaullist) manifestations, was bound to be reflected in the thinking of those in the Third World who were fascinated by the ideological content of the former, or admired the independent-mindedness of the latter.

Anti-Americanism is thus a relatively older phenomenon than is generally assumed; the origins of its Latin American variety in fact dates back to the Monroe Doctrine and the encroachment of "Yankee imperialism."[4] Although anti-Americanism is not necessarily an immediate product of the postcolonial period or a function of cold war rivalries, both the emergence of the Soviet Union as a superpower and the extensive projection of U.S. global strategies to contain it, tended to fuel the intensity of the sentiment and its proliferation on a world scale. The U.S. intrusion into the postcolonial settings in the Third World merely triggered what—for lack of better terms as well as of tangible evidence—may be called *latent* or *instinctive* anti-Americanism.

Another related point is that even in its contemporary form, nowhere was anti-Americanism so clearly and vehemently manifested than in the United States itself during the youth rebellion of the 1960s. The intensity of this manifestation ranged from the rejectionist counterculture of the U.S. "anti-American" generation, to the apparent absence of any significant social group that seemed to be affirmatively pro-American. One U.S. observer of the social scene noted at the time:

> The flower children are indeed the enemies of mass, industrial society; the revolutions that so often fascinate and beguile them have never brought to power a social-system that would accept them, even when those revolutions succeeded in bringing a considerable measure of political power and social amelioration to the previously disadvantaged classes. . . . The major social contribution of beleaguered hippies and student militants may be to provide us with a salutary reminder that a reexamination of the traditional association between freedom and equality which, in the democratic myth reinforce each other, is long overdue.[5]

It must be remembered that it was about this time that many African and Arab countries, recently emerged into statehood, were entangled in, and trying to cope with, the acute problems of nationhood. During these formative years, the turmoil and burning issues (both literally and figuratively) in U.S. society left little to emulate from an "American way of life" so demonstratively rejected by many of its own young people. At the same time, U.S. policy (particularly in Vietnam) seemed blindly determined to fashion the world according to America's own image.

In short, the United States appeared to be a society internally divided by lack of understanding between social groups, while at the same time pursuing foreign policies also characterized by an equally incomprehensible lack of knowledge about the realities of the outside world. It was, indeed, a time when it was very difficult in the Third World (just as it was for many young Americans) not to be anti-American.[6]

THE DYNAMICS OF IDENTIFICATION

Perception and the Ideological Political Factor

For the educated Africans and Arabs, political education begins at an early age and is largely shaped by the hard political and socioeconomic facts of life. During the formative years of politicization (mostly in school) they are exposed to different and competitive ideologies that they must relate to their own indigenous experience. As a result of this interaction, ideological identification usually evolves in three main ways: the rejection of Western values and culture and the assertion of precolonial roots and values (e.g., Islamism, Arabism, négritude); the adaptation of European ideologies to local needs and indigenous circumstances (e.g., Arab socialism, African socialism); or the option for what is considered a universally valid and applicable ideology (e.g., Marxism, communism of either the Soviet or the Chinese types). The ideological diversity of Europe and the clear lines of demarcation in the political systems, provide viable ideological options, while the indigenous culture and tradition provide either a basis for implanting the new ideology or an alternative to it. Central to this readaptation process is a constant reaffirmation of indigenous roots, of what Cabral called the "return to the source," which essentially involves "not only a contest against foreign culture but also complete participation in the struggle against foreign political and economic domination."[7]

In this search for workable ideological and political formulae, the U.S. model receives scant support since it is conceived by most of the educated elite as being devoid of ideological content. Even the liberal democracy favored by some of the nationalist elite, and in many cases inherited from the colonialist era, has more in common with British parliamentary liberalism than the U.S. presidential type which, within the African and Arab context, seems to make for the kind of "imperial presidency" most closely associated with pro-American authoritarian regimes (e.g., Egypt under Sadat, Sudan under Numayrí, Zaire under Mobutu, and Kenya under Moi).[8]

Although many of the educated elite, notably among university students, are familiar with the U.S. political system, such familiarity has meant little in terms of ideological identification. Indeed, it has tended to generate a view of the U.S. system in which the lines of ideological demarcation are so blurred, if not nonexistent, as to provide no real political alternatives and therefore, no real claim to democratic practices. Even when social differentiation was sufficiently illuminated, as during the unrest of the 1960s, it showed middle class radicals pitted against an establishment whose main support came from a working-class "silent majority." It was not a matter of class conflict but rather a manifestation of displaced and repressed interclass hostility.

Americans may have little patience for ideological interpretations and even less for such notions as social differentiation and class conflict. But within the Third World context these are important, particularly among the educated elite, as a function of perception and identification. From a U.S. perspective, for instance, it may be easier to blame anti-Americanism in the Third World on the malevolent influences of communist propaganda. The evidence, however, indicates that Western propaganda is more prevalent than communist, and, paradoxically, more likely to generate anti-Americanism than anything else. More people listen to the BBC and the Voice of America than to Radio Moscow. In the Sudan and Egypt, the immense popularity of U.S. movies is only equaled by the negative images they project of U.S. society.

Thus increased exposure to and knowledge of U.S. culture and politics tend to arouse antipathy not sympathy, while the relative lack of knowledge of the Soviet Union leaves untarnished the appealing ideology with which the educated elite is familiar. The issues again are related to ideology and perceptions. When the West talks of "democracy," it raises the question in the educated African mind of why the West, particularly the United States, is always supporting authoritarian and, in the case of South Africa, racist regimes. The concept of freedom conjures up unpleasant reminders in the view of many Arabs of Western complicity, past and present, to deprive them of it. To people in the Third World, the image of the "unfree" world that comes most readily to mind is not that of the Gulag but of their own continued economic subjection by the West, not to mention that of ethnic and unprivileged minorities in the West itself.

This negative picture is actually reinforced by direct contact with the U.S. experience. The perceptive African and Arab observer of the U.S. scene is often profoundly struck by the discrepancy between democratic ideals and political practice; between the warmth of individual Americans and the insensitivity of society and the body politic as a whole; and between technological advancement and an educational system that seems geared to the arithmetical functioning of an opportunity-structured society but not to any profound understanding of the algebra of its history and, still less, to that of any other society. The United States is acknowledged as the land of opportunity yet it is also seen as the land of "scarcity in abundance"; and the society that could send men to the moon seems incapable, at the level of social justice, of providing equal rights in practice for its black citizens.

This impression of U.S. society is, obviously, not shared by all. Some manage to develop a taste for U.S. life and values which makes it that much more difficult for them to relate to their own culture and/or to readjust to the harsh realities at home, while others are genuinely impressed by some positive aspects, such as freedom of expression, which they find lacking in their own society. Yet even the sympathetic few cannot articulate their sympathy in terms of identification either as preference or ideology, unless they are also members of the privileged elite. Ironically, those who enjoy the American way of life do not want to see it duplicated at home. The "free enterprise" system in the Sudan and Egypt produced all the evils of capitalism without any redeeming gains except for the ruling and rich classes. To identify ideologically with capitalism is thus incompatible with identification with the masses of the people. For the educated elite it also means incurring the intellectual stigma of being proimperialist and, for those in leadership positions, of being U.S. puppets.

By contrast, the very internationalism of Marxist ideology enables communists to uphold their ideological credentials without necessarily being discredited as foreign agents, although pro-Western regimes often use such accusations to persecute them and other noncommunist opponents. These measures are usually counterproductive because they tend to endow communist movements with acceptance and popularity, particularly among circles of the educated elites in authoritarian regimes. In Africa and the Arab world, the idea of communism is potentially attractive because it has proved itself in the Soviet Union and in China as the foundation of a society knit into a strong fabric. On an intellectual level Marxist ideology has a particular appeal:

> The spread of Marxist-inspired regimes in the Third World is no aberration of history. For Marxism, as a theory and a practice, contains elements that have proved of considerable relevance to the Third

World in the epochal struggles of the 20th century. Its emphasis on material causation, on class conflict as the motor force of history, and its totalizing theory of society have provided the intellectual underpinnings for a powerful moral philosophy advocating social justice, equality, and freedom from exploitation, both national and social. In the harsh conditions of the impoverished continents of Asia, Africa and Latin America, it is not difficult to understand the attractions of such ideas.[9]

If the African and Arab peoples are intrigued with these ideas, they naturally want to know what the local communists have to say. When communists are persecuted by established authority, they seem to thrive under proscription and their popularity proportionally increases.[10]

The U.S. depiction of communism as an evil force in postcolonial settings proved to be self-defeating. In Africa, the Americans were seen as somehow adopting the British ideals of the nineteenth century a hundred years too late. When Europe put down the "white man's burden" the Americans picked it up in the name of anti-communism.[11] This anti-communist crusade, which indiscriminately classified those who were not pro-American as essentially communist, seemed to leave Africans with little alternative except, perhaps, communism. It was, in effect, a crusade against the forces of history and the prospects of change. A prominent Kenyan journalist put it this way in the mid-1960s: "The easiest way to push the African towards communism is to tell him he needs to be protected from it. . . . Russians are interesting to us simply because [Americans] hate them so much."[12]

This self-defeating U.S. approach was paradoxical in yet another sense. In ideological terms, the "wind of change" in Africa and the Arab world, if its momentum were allowed to develop naturally, was moving in a direction not necessarily parallel to, or in conformity with, "international communism." Religious, ethnic and cultural consciousness was more inherently anti-communist than anti-American. The legacy of colonialism and the intrusion of neoimperialism had, indeed, induced many nationalist leaders, who would not proclaim themselves sympathetic to Marxism, to denounce imperialism in Marxist–Leninist terms because of the relevance of the phraseology to local conditions. "But Marxism is also at odds with the many forms of indigenous oppression and mystification which have arisen in the context of the anti-imperialist upheavals of the past decades, which seek to enlist the support of all opposed to imperialist domination."[13]

In the Arab world, the two main driving ideological forces in the postindependence period were Ba'thism and Nasirism. Both aimed to provide focal points for Arab nationalism as ideological alternatives to communism and capitalism.

In Ba'thist ideology the emphasis is more on Arabism, *al-'Arúba* (not without a hint of racism) and less on Islam, because giving priority to religion would exclude non-Muslim Arabs and include non-Arab Muslims.[14] The preference for an ethnic identification over a religious one (although the latter was by no means rejected or ignored) did not mean that Ba'thism was any more anti-American than it was anti-communist, except in so far as, like many other nationalist movements, it sought freedom from Western domination. Indeed, the emergence of Ba'thism in the early 1940s predated active U.S. involvement in the Arab world and also reflected the disillusionment of the movement's founders ('Aflaq and Bitár) with communism, to which they were earlier attracted. It is significant that when Ba'thist leaders went to President Násir in early 1958 to plead for an Egyptian–Syrian union (the ill-fated UAR) one of their primary concerns was to preempt a possible communist takeover in Syria.[15] Khálid Bakdásh, the leader of the Syrian Communist Party hurriedly left Syria when the proposed union was consummated. It was only in reaction to the projection of U.S. power and the increasing involvement of U.S. policy in Middle East politics that Ba'thism in both its Syrian (*al-Qiyada al-Qawmiyya*) and Iraqi (*al-Qiyada al-Qutriyya*) forms became a strong source of anti-Americanism and a chief ally of the Soviet Union.

The same was true of Nasirism. As an ideology and a political movement, Nasirism was more pragmatic and less inconsistent and factionalized than Ba'thism. Its socialist orientation was acquired piecemeal through a trial-and-error approach and culminated in the socialist charter of 1962.[16] But its driving force lay more in the charismatic personality of Násir than in its ideological content. The popularity of Nasirism among the Arab masses was such that the Egyptian Communist Party, which had opposed the revolution from the beginning, finally dissolved itself in the mid-1960s and came under the wing of Násir's ASU. Nasirism provided the main ideological bulwark against communism, yet at one and the same time it entailed a massive Soviet presence in the Arab world for the first time. The paradox can be explained and the explanation demonstrates, as we shall later see, how the U.S. anti-communist fixation was instrumental in bringing about the very eventuality that it sought so zealously to avert.

In Africa, the intellectual and ruling elites who turned to socialism ranged from those who wanted to adapt socialism to the African condition and proclaimed Africa's right to its own indigenous "road to socialism," to those who rejected Western European socialism in favor of "scientific socialism." The latter were more in evidence in those African countries which gained independence not through a nationalist movement led by Westernized elites but through violent armed struggle. It was no coincidence that the United States—with its peculiarly blinkered understanding of political realities—had supported the established colonial authority and thus placed itself on the losing side. In all of these countries, anti-Americanism was evident, though in varying degrees of intensity.

It is conceivable that this might not have been the case had the historical process of change and ideological interaction taken its natural course. The result, obviously, could have been more socialist and Marxist ideological identification among African states. But it is unlikely that there would have been a Cuban and Soviet presence in Angola and the Horn of Africa. Nor does the prospect of the emergence of socialist, or even Marxist, regimes in Africa necessarily mean an extension of Soviet power—unless the United States makes such a "linkage" not only possible but inevitable. The experience of Yugoslavia vis-à-vis the Soviet Union and Vietnam vis-à-vis China actually point in a different direction.

Another emergent form of the dynamics of identification outside the established elites is the growing *popular* anti-Americanism of the underprivileged masses under pro-American regimes or those regimes which had switched from a pro-Soviet stance to a pro-American one, mainly, but not exclusively, in the hope of getting more aid from the United States (e.g., Egypt and the Sudan). There is no comparable sentiment flowing in the opposite direction in pro-Soviet regimes although the economic situation in these is often even worse.

Preferences and Models of Development

In Africa and the Arab world the attainment of formal independence brought in its wake new informal forms of external control and influence more corrosive than the old imperialism insomuch as they encouraged the trend toward oppressive and authoritarian rule. The economic structures of these emerging regimes were perceived as either "socialist" ("communist" or "leftist" in U.S. eyes), "free-market" ("capitalist" or "conservative" in Soviet eyes), or "mixed-economy" (viewed by both as capitalist disguised beneath a socialist rhetoric). According to Richard Falk, the ideological leanings of these regimes are better understood in terms of the developmental crunch that has generated a wide array of authoritarian solutions. "Socialism and capitalism, although each is manifest in a variety of forms, provide the ideological underpinnings for the principal choice between developmental options."[17]

The case for a capitalist model of development in Africa, as presented from a U.S. perspective, is based on three interrelated premises. First, the "African mentality" must rid itself of the "self-deception" implicit in the claim that the West is largely responsible for the underdevelopment of Africa (Kenneth Adelman), and adopt "the old-fashioned American virtues of thrift, honesty, tolerance, civil discipline and hard work" (George Kennan). Second, the West offers the only means to escape the vicious cycle of economic crises (Kennan), and economic development can be achieved by encouraging internal change and interplay with the ouside world (George Ball). Third, not only should Africa adopt traditional Western values, but it should accept the legitimate efforts of the United States to promote its own economic interests on the continent (Adelman).[18]

These prescriptions, based on the United States' own experience, are seen by many African intellectuals as having their own limitations within the West itself as well as being politically unacceptable and economically suspect within Third World contexts. It is, obviously, legitimate for the United States to give a proper regard to U.S. interests but these are not necessarily compatible with African interests nor really conducive to the economic advancement of Africa. If African leaders tend to blame their own troubles on real or perceived Western influences, it is precisely the continuing Western interventionism that provides such complaints with moral force and political justifications.

To many Africans and Arabs, the past is not irrelevant to the present and the future. As Coker rightly noted:

America's own values are as foreign to Africa as they are to the rest of the Third World.... The African's suspicions are after all rooted in a colonial past which formed a historical prologue to the present predominance of Western interests.... Indeed, the material change to African societies produced by contact with the North explains why their experience of Northern models has served to reinforce the scepticism of an entire generation of African leaders and made hypocrites and self-servers of the rest.[19]

The record of those countries that have opted either for a "capitalist" system or for shifting from a "socialist" to a "mixed-economy" model, usually under U.S. denationalization pressures, is evidence of the bankruptcy of the capital-intensive approach to development. The image of such a model drawn from U.S. values was conjured by one leading Sudanese capitalist in the following terms: "This area is changing and we are taking the American route. You'll see, we'll have Wimpy burger stands, Kentucky fried chicken shops, blue jeans and popcorn."[20] He, somehow, failed to mention "apple pie."

The economic situation in Kenya is belied by a glaringly widening gap between rich and poor that has produced a security situation bordering on an undeclared state of class war. Even in a country exceptionally endowed with resources, such as Nigeria, the western economic and political institutions have proved to be a recipe for coups, corruption, and conflict. If, in terms of economic growth, South Africa is an exception to the general rule, it is an exception that in human, political, and economic terms, actually proves the rule of the "unacceptable face" of capitalism.

In Egypt, private enterprise has replaced socialism since the mid-1970s. Egyptian intellectuals have condemned this transformation as a betrayal of the earlier socialist ideals and a surrender of Egypt's independence. Ghàli Shoukri argued that "the laws opening the way to economic dependence on the West, approved 'in the name of free economy' follows a course parallel to the stages of political dependence on the United States and Israel, justified 'in the name of peace.' "[21] Haykal noted that:

> The conditions affecting Egypt were to be found to a greater or lesser extent in most Third World countries. These, being on the whole exporters of raw materials and importers of manufactured goods, were usually at the wrong end of any trading bargain.... Indeed, Egypt was not being transformed from a planned economy to a market economy but to a supermarket economy. The disrupting effect which this transformation had on Egyptian society can hardly be exaggerated.

To Haykal, "An Egypt whose economy was controlled from outside, in effect from Washington, would be isolated from the Arab world, and oil money would be used simply to keep Egypt afloat rather than allowing her to exercise her natural role as leader of the Arab world."[22]

An Egyptian political sociologist in the American University of Cairo described the U.S. presence in Egypt as "a shadow government," complete with departments corresponding to the official governmental and administrative organs. This massive U.S. penetration of Egypt's political, economic, and even cultural institutions, is seen as part of a well-coordinated plan to make Egypt "psychologically," as well as politically and economically, "subservient" to the United States. The old inferiority complex toward the "foreigner," *'ugdat al-khwaja* (submerged under the national self-assertion of Nàsir's rule), was being subtly revived and cultivated.[23]

Western writers, such as David Hirst and Irene Beeson have also indicted Sádát's regime for his "Americanization" of Egypt through the policy of *infitáh* ("open door" economic policy).[24] It is clear from the chain of events from the "food riots" of January 1977 to Sádát's assassination in October 1981, that the military, political and economic association with the United States has unleashed an anti-American sentiment within Egyptian society which far surpassed that of the "official" anti-Americanism of the Nasirist period, if it had not indeed confirmed and evoked it.

A related factor in the resurgence of this popular anti-Americanism is the resentment of economic packages imposed by the IMF and the World Bank. The economies of Egypt, Zaire and the Sudan seemed to have been placed under the management of these international institutions and other Western financial circles. The enforced adoption of the austerity measures prescribed by these institutions almost amounted in practice to a performance of political *hara-kiri*. In the Sudan, just as in Egypt, the imposition of IMF measures led to spontaneous antigovernment and anti-American popular uprisings which on several occasions came close to toppling the pro-American Numayrí regime.

Obviously, neither the IMF nor the World Bank are, technically or formally, organs of the U.S. government. But in the popular mind they are perceived as such—a perception which, given the degree of U.S. leverage in these institutions, is not that much of a misconception.

In both the Sudanese and Egyptian cases, the governments blamed communist agitation and Soviet machinations for the "disturbances." Such explanations readily fell on receptive ears in Washington and all they helped to produce was more doses of the same medicine. In the meantime, local communists must have been bemused by—without failing to take due political note of—the fact that they were being credited, not discredited, with having more political muscle than their own estimate of their political strength would allow for. The communists may not have invented the IMF and the World Bank, but they certainly stand to thrive and to make political capital out of the existence and activities of these institutions.

The very orientation of the international economic institutions tend to defeat their declared objectives. The right-wing ideology and private-investment priorities of the World Bank and IMF seek to promote reliance on the free play of market forces and to ensure the avoidance of debt defaults, nationalizations and restrictions on imports and on outflow of profit. The recipient governments are expected to adjust to their resulting problems through devaluations, removal of subsidies, cuts in government expenditure and wages, balancing the budget, and restricting credit. While these policies may make economic sense in the developed capitalist system, their impact on developing economies can be devastating, not the least because of their insensitivity to political and social considerations. It is mostly the poor classes who are hit economically while the projected growth remains elusive.

The 1973 oil crisis triggered a trend toward a new international economic approach based on the premise that the world economic order had outgrown the classical concept of independence and the assumptions of limited national interests. In essence the new interdependency seeks to redefine "North–South" relations in such a way as to accommodate the interests of both by contributing to the development of the poor "South" without affecting the growth and prosperity of the developed "North." As expressed in the Brandt report, this approach argues that "the self-interest of nations can now only be effectively pursued through taking account of mutual interests."[25]

However, the concept of interdependency, noble as it may seem, is still fallacious.[26] It assumes a measure of equality and partnership that in fact does not exist, and given the nature of the world order, it is extremely naive to assume that it ever will. The concept is also not unbiased since the economic model presented seems to favor a capitalist orientation and to safeguard existing Western interests. Implicit in the approach is an economic "domino theory" that is related to Western global strategy.

Thus, countries like Somalia and the Sudan which are seen as having no major economic importance to the West are to be kept economically afloat because they are of vital strategic importance within the context of the conflicts in the Horn of Africa and Northwest Africa. As Edward Heath (a member of the Brandt Commission) put it, ". . . like so many other least developed countries in Africa and Asia, their stability is threatened by radical forces whose success is nurtured by economic deprivation and inequality. If these radical forces are given the opportunity to make progress, others like them around the world will also be encouraged. Moderate leaders will conclude that they cannot rely on the West to support them."[27]

This is in line with U.S. aid policy and its proclaimed aim of preventing Third World countries from passing into the communist bloc. More suspect and alarming to many people in the Third World is the connection of U.S. aid policy and the activities of multinational corporations.[28] Hayter argues that it is doubtful, to say the least, whether the recent growth in manufactured exports as a result of foreign investment can be said to be of benefit to the peoples of underdeveloped countries:

> They are, much as before, doing the dirty work of the West, and they are being unmercifully exploited. The increase in export-processing activities in underdeveloped countries is a special phenomenon; it is not a balanced process of industrial growth.... In addition, in most underdeveloped countries, the supposedly blind forces of the market are, in reality, much helped by the repressive apparatus of the state, which in turn is aided by the West.[29]

In this sense, the motif of Third World countries is less that of *interdependence* as *independence* from dependence on foreign trade, technology, finance or values.[30] Capitalism in both its internal and related external forms, is unattractive and unacceptable in economic, political and human-rights terms. Within a Third World context, it is "a recipe for doom."

By contrast, therefore, socialism is seen as the more attractive model for development. African socialism is based on the debatable proposition that the "primitive communalism" of the African "tribal" society facilitates the setting up of modern socialist structures. The interpretation of this indigenous socialism varies from Nyerere's *Ujamaa* program, to Sekou Touré's earlier emphasis on agrarian cooperatives and trade unionism, to Senghor's intellectual concept of *négritude*. Arab socialism of the Nasirist type gave priority to an extended public sector and to central control of planning.

While the preference for socialism is a reality, its record in practice, as Falk pointed out, is too poor at present to support the preference. "Socialism *as applied* to date in the Third World deprives it of the moral advantage associated with socialism *as theory* or as an ideological perspective."[31] Yet despite the unsatisfactory record of socialism in practice, the pertinent question of preference in this context is one in relation to capitalism.

The Egyptian masses might not have fared well under the socialism of Násir but they have fared even worse under the *infitáh* policy of Sádát without, one may add, enjoying some of the positive attributes (the sense of independence and dignity) imparted by the former. The ordinary Tanzanian may not be economically better off than his Kenyan, Zaïrean and Sudanese counterparts but the economy under which he labors is still indigenous or at least not a captive of a manipulative international economy.

The main challenge to socialism comes not from capitalism but from Marxism. African Marxists have dismissed the notion of building socialist models on the communal traditions of tribal society on the gounds that communalism had, in fact, been eroded under the impact of historical processes culminating in colonialism and modernization and had given rise to antagonistic social differentiations. Even where the vestige of "tribal communalism" is still manifest, it has already assumed the form of embryonic class conflict; its natural evolution would, therefore, be toward a capitalist mode of production, not a socialist one.

According to Samir Amin, the real world of expansion of capital has produced a form of "transition" which was not forecast: "a series of 'national liberation' revolutions...where elements of bourgeois revolution are inextricably linked with elements of socialist revolution." Amin argues that the outcome of this "transition" could take different forms. "This outcome may be socialist (in the sense of the abolition of classes) or statist (in the sense of the "revisionist" model magnified by contemporary Soviet reality), or even be only a transition towards a higher stage of capitalist development."[32]

To Amin, the ideological evolution of Arab socialism reflects its contradictions and poverty. He argues that a radical critique of Nasirism is essential and must be undertaken in association with that of "revisionism," by which he means not only a critique of Soviet state policy but also, and above all, a critique of the theoretical basis, the class analysis, and the strategy of what he calls *"pseudo-marxisme."*[33]

Most African and Arab Marxist intellectuals, as distinct from communist movements and parties, tended to prefer the Chinese model of development. Thus, Fanon's concept of national violence (which is not the same as terrorism) and his emphasis on rural authenticity as the repository of national values,[34] have much in common with Chinese Marxism, although Fanon himself had not adopted scientific socialism as such. The preference is shared by some African-socialist regimes as is evident in the *Ujamaa* approach of Tanzania.

In the political setting of Africa and the Arab world, dominated by competing ideologies, revolt and revolution, the reaction of the United States has been to equate revolution with subversion, and to confuse "the concrete processes and consequences of unrest, subversion or dissidence, which vary country by country, with the generalised threat to U.S. national security. This failure to distinguish between the particular and the global is a major cause of interventionism."[35]

THE FOREIGN POLICY DIMENSION

Continuity in Discontinuity and the "Self-Fulfilling Prophecy"

One of the striking features of U.S. policy is a remarkable consistency which, despite the drastic changes and the radical transformations sweeping throughout Africa and the Arab world, remained as rigid as it was self-defeating. The succession of different administrations (from Truman to Reagan) has not interrupted the consistency of approach. Although there have been shifts in emphasis there has been no change in direction. This phenomenon, incidentally, has called into question some of the basic assumptions of democracy in the two-party system.

From the strategy of "containment" of the late 1940s to the policy of "strategic consensus" of the early 1980s, the main policy objectives have remained the same, namely: to prevent Soviet "expansionism" and to preserve the *status quo* either through suppression or support of "friendly" suppressive regimes or, at best, through inducements of social "reform." Both objectives had little relevance to the political and socioeconomic realities of Africa and the Arab world, and U.S. persistence in pursuing them rebounded badly on the United States. Not only did the U.S. nightmare (Soviet expansionism) turn into a reality in the Third World but it did so because of, and not despite, U.S. policy, and in the process, it was the United States which was projected as the *real* enemy and the main obstacle to social and economic transformation.

In the first place, most countries in Africa and the Arab world did not regard Soviet "expansionism" as a direct threat. U.S. efforts to press them into believing in the Soviet threat produced the opposite effect, even in those countries that desired to remain or become pro-American. Second, the political forces at work in the postcolonial period tended toward radical socioeconomic transformation—a transformation that was incompatible with either the existing order or with gradual reformism (e.g., of the kind administered by the Shah in Iran). Thus, U.S. policy was perceived, on the one hand, as entailing unnecessary and potentially dangerous entanglements in cold-war politics and, on the other, as trying to arrest the inevitable and irresistible processes of historical change.

In the Arab world, the decolonization process was a period of turmoil in which competing nationalisms and new ideologies were asserting themselves as the old order disintegrated. In inheriting the interests of colonialism, the United States also became the recipient of the animosities generated by the forces of nationalism. The United States had become a world power but Americans had little experience in this role and still less of the local and regional realities with which they had to deal.

The irony is that most Arab nationalist leaders, to whom the Soviet Union was a remote and largely unknown entity, were well disposed toward the United States despite the negative and disappointing U.S. role in the decolonization struggle. It was, in fact, to the United States that Násir at first turned for military and economic assistance. The Americans, however, wanted Egypt, in return, to join the proposed Western regional defense system against the Soviet Union. To Násir, the real danger to Egyptian (and Arab) interests came not from the possibility of a Soviet attack but from the actual presence of British troops stationed in the Suez canal and the threat posed by Israel. More to the point, Násir realized that a communist threat was more likely to come from within and that the position of local communists would be greatly strengthened by Egyptian participation in Western defense pacts. He told the Americans so.[36]

The Americans, apparently, were not impressed with these arguments. Egypt's encounter with the United States thus turned into a confrontation with all the disruptive marks of an escalating cycle of action, reaction and counteraction. Násir felt threatened by the Baghdad Pact, the Israeli raid on the Gaza strip, and the machinations of the CIA.[37] In the face of U.S. reluctance to provide him with arms, Násir turned to the Soviet Union and thus effectively broke the Western monopoly of arms supplies and influence in the region. When the Americans, partly in retaliation, withdrew the offer to finance the building of the Aswan dam, Násir reacted by nationalizing the Suez canal. The counteraction of the West was the tripartite invasion of Egypt in 1956.

Násir emerged from the Suez crisis with great political prestige not only in Egypt but in the Arab world where, paradoxically, the Americans then enjoyed for a time a certain measure of good will for their successful pressure on Britain, France and Israel to withdraw from Egypt. But this goodwill was rapidly eroded by the introduction of the Eisenhower Doctrine, the landing of U.S. marines in Lebanon in 1958 (the forerunner of the United States' current predicament), the continuing support of Israel, and generally, the persistent obsession to view developments in the area through cold-war binoculars.

From an Egyptian viewpoint, U.S. attitudes toward the Egyptian revolution varied from efforts to "tame" (*tarwid*) and "contain" it (*ihtiwà*), to attempts to "punish" (*'igáb*) and use "force" (*'unf*) to destroy it.[38] Instead of coming to terms with the new nationalist forces in the Arab world, as opposed to traditional conservative elements, the United States regarded these forces as a threat to Western interests and/or an instrument of Soviet policy in the region. When the United States, in the mid-1960s, became the main direct supplier of arms to Israel and the conservative regimes in the Middle East, and tried to exert pressures on the radical Arab states, the anti-Americanism sentiment and rhetoric of the latter intensified while their reliance on the counterweight of the Soviet Union correspondingly increased.

The radical Arab movement saw itself on an inevitable collision course with the United States "so long as the goals and means of American policy in the Middle East remained incompatible with Arab interests and as long as the United States continued to play its world role in a manner inconsistent with the interests of peace and progress."[39] The crunch came in June 1967. Yet even when, in the wake of defeat, the Arab nationalists were preoccupied with undoing some of its shattering consequences, U.S. policy showed neither the flexibility that could have served its own interests, nor the impartiality that might have redeemed it in the Arab world. The June war of 1967 led to the October war of 1973 with all the inevitability of some supernatural force.

Fouad Ajami viewed these developments in terms of both their political implications and cultural impact. He argued that the Arab world was witnessing the simultaneous advance of the "civilization" that technology promised and the determined resistance to it:

> The bitterness of the 1967 defeat pushed the Arab world still further from the United States—further even than the Arab elite may have wanted. This would be borne out by the turn of events after October, 1973. The success of October enabled the Arab elite to indulge their

tastes in alliances, in technology, in models of development—and the American advantage was there for all to see. Americanization and anti-Americanism are two sides of the same coin. The political anti-Americanism displayed in the Arab states and in Iran as the 1970s came to an end was in great measure an expression of the region's rage at itself; it was a display of agony over cultural surrender. The American push into the region has succeeded all too well.[40]

The U.S. "success," such as it was, succeeded in swelling the wave of Islamic and nationalist reassertion that, as an expression of the "popular culture" of the masses, threatened to sweep away the "Westernized culture" of the ruling elite.

It is sometimes argued that the Kissinger diplomacy of the post-1973 period broke with the traditional rigidity of previous U.S. policy. The United States, by establishing a monopoly of influence in Egypt, succeeded in the exclusion of the Soviet Union—a feat later crowned with the Egyptian–Israeli peace treaty.

Yet the evidence seems to indicate that Kissinger's diplomacy, and subsequent U.S. policy, is merely the continuation of the old strategy with the emphasis shifted to different local actors. As to American gains, they have been more illusory then real. True, Egypt has, for the present, been "tamed" as was the Iraq of the 1950s; but it is doubtful whether the implication of this situation is necessarily conducive to the United States' best interests, not to mention those of its Egyptian client. The Arab world has been "balkanized" as never before and the PLO, though sharply split, has become even more radicalized (Yasir 'Arafat is now considered a "moderate"). The Palestinian problem remains as elusive as ever, while the Reagan "peace plan" has floundered in Lebanon where a quarter of a century ago the Eisenhower Doctrine met the same fate.

The implications of the new-old realities seem lost on U.S. policymakers. The U.S. response is the "rapid deployment force" operating within a new "strategic consensus" (to many Arabs, the old Baghdad Pact in new guise) which even the United States' traditional "friends" in Saudi Arabia and the Gulf states are wary of and which, ironically, reflects U.S. concern for the stability of their regimes. The main destabilizing agent is still identified in Washington as the Soviet Union despite the fact that the history of the Middle East since the 1950s indicates that the major source of tension and anti-Americanism is continuing U.S. interventionism.

Nowhere is this more clear than in the case of Egypt. To many Egyptian intellectuals, the alliance with the United States and the peace treaty with Israel, far from leading to stability, have injected a new instability in the region by enabling Israel to redirect its military expansionism to the Lebanon and other Arab countries.[41] The failure of the United States to modify its total commitment to an expansionist Israel is seen as amounting to the creation of "the era of Imperial Israel." As Haykal noted, "This is a prospect which can only be regarded with the greatest foreboding, particularly for the West which probably stands to lose by it more than even the Arabs."[42]

The almost universal Arab resentment of Sádát's policy centered mainly on his "Americanization" of Egypt. But Egyptians, in particular, also resented his decision to provide military facilities to the Americans (as during the ill-fated attempt to rescue the U.S. hostages in Tehran) and to give asylum to the Shah of Iran. The latter move was seen as no more in Egypt's interest than it was for the Americans who hypocritically applauded the gesture that relieved them of responsibility toward their former client.[43]

It is often assumed in the West that Sádát's friendship with U.S. leaders enabled him to present the Arab case and, for the first time, to give Western opinion a proper understanding of the Arab world and its problems. Haykal, rightly, argued that this was not the case:

> What the West was watching was the performance of a superstar; the public in the West appreciated the posture of one man, not the problems of millions. Nor was there any realization of the price at which superstardom had been bought.... It is not the mark of a good general to capture a new position at the cost of losing his own base.[44]

By starting down the road to Jerusalem that would eventually lead him to Camp David and the peace treaty with Israel, Sádát achieved a new apotheosis in the Western world, but not in his Egyptian constituency and certainly not in his Arab environment. Paradoxically, Sádát's main bargaining power was his increasing readiness to make even more concessions. The irony of his position was that the more he tried to make Egypt the principal bastion of U.S. and Western interests in the Middle East, the more he alienated the other Arab states and, conversely, the less valuable his role was bound to be to the United States.[45] Like his U.S. patrons, Sádát was caught up in a web of dazzling but ultimately self-defeating illusions. The cost of U.S. "friendship" was, in fact, to unleash in Egypt violent and unpredictable counterforces, the vehemence of which was manifested in that swift and inevitable moment of retribution so terribly visited on President Sádát on October 6, 1981.

It is perhaps a measure of the intensity of anti-Americanism in Egyptian society that one of the most widely held conspiracy theories following Sádát's assassination assumed the complicity of the CIA in his demise. The premise of this assumption was that "Sadat had served his purpose, particularly by his recognition of Israel; [he] was now a liability rather than an asset, and so had become expendable, like Diem and other earlier American protégés. It was time for him to be replaced by someone liberal and so more acceptable."[46]

The significance of this view is not its plausibility or the lack of it, but the fact that it gained currency among Egyptians and many other Arabs. This reflected the deep-seated suspicion of the United States, which was not without foundation in contemporary history. It also caught the mood of an anti-Americanism that has now become instinctive. A Saudi diplomat was probably not referring to U.S. complicity but nevertheless arrived at the same conclusion when he remarked after Sádát's assassination: "First the Shah, now Sadat. It is fatal to be America's friend."[47]

Even within the context of regional geopolitics the balance of power situation is not to the United States' advantage. Paradoxically, the Soviets' painful experience in Egypt might have taught them the important lesson of the dangers of high visibility and of putting too many constraints on their Arab allies. It is Syrian, not Soviet, policy which is now relentlessly and successfully being pursued, although from a Soviet perspective, the interests of the two are not incompatible.

For the United States, history keeps repeating itself but the lessons are largely left unheeded while the cost of reflexive interventionism continues to mount. Compared to what the Americans had experienced in Iran, what they are experiencing in Lebanon, and what they may experience in Saudi Arabia and the Gulf region, the anti-American reactions and manifestations of the 1950s and 1960s might, in retrospect, seem a model of moderation and restraint.

In Africa, just as in the Arab world, the *fact* of revolution and the *fear* of revolution have also dominated U.S. policy. John Girling noted that:

Both fact and fear converge in the belief that 'indigenous' insurgencies and urban mass struggles as well as explicitly communist-led revolutions can be manipulated—at first by 'international communism,' then by Moscow or Peking—in a chain reaction of revolt against 'transitional' structures of authority in one Third World country after another. This is seen as a 'universal' threat, encompassing America's own security; thus it requires an equivalent response.[48]

The U.S. policy objective in Africa is two-fold: first, to install proAmerican regimes (the Congo-Zaire) and to protect insecure clients (even when the insecurity is a result of internal opposition, as in the Sudan) or allies in a hostile and insecure environment (South Africa); second, to destabilize or overthrow communist or suspected communist regimes. U.S. military intervention by proxy in the Congo crisis succeeded in installing a pro-American regime in the mid-1960s but this "success," coming against a background of increasing involvement in Vietnam, actually damaged U.S. prestige among some newly independent African states, and aroused suspicions and overt anti-Americanism in others.

The main operative factor in the "linkage" mentality of U.S. policy manifested itself in the U.S. approach to African liberation movements. In Algeria, Angola, Mozambique and Zimbabwe, the liberation movements combined both the forces of nationalism and social revolution. The French, the Portuguese and the South Africans labeled the liberation movements as "communist-inspired" or led by "communist agitators." These labels fitted nicely into the U.S. concept of a global strategy that absurdly generalized local or regional developments into a universal threat to U.S. security. As a result, the United States placed itself solidly on the colonial side of the struggle. This left the liberation movements with little option but to turn to the Soviet bloc for support, and, in the process, what started as genuine nationalist movements that increasingly identified with communism or at least with a pro-Soviet and anti-American stance.

The process had a dynamic of its own. As the liberation struggle intensified, the liberation movements became more radicalized and, consequently, their anti-American sentiment and posture became more pronounced. When the sudden collapse of the colonial power in Angola left the United States with no established authority to support, the Americans intervened on the side of Holden Roberto's FNLA and, by so doing, probably facilitated the eventual victory of Agostinho Neto's Marxist MPLA and, not coincidentally, the Cuban presence in Angola.

But the destabilization process continued with the South African intervention, in collusion with Jonas Savimbi's UNITA, in southern Angola. U.S. policy remained in line with that of South Africa, both in

Angola and neighboring Namibia, where SWAPO is engaged in a struggle for liberation from South African control. In 1983 the United States mounted a diplomatic campaign to obtain a UN-sponsored peace in Namibia in parallel with a withdrawal of Cuban troops stationed in Angola. *The New York Times* noted that, "the linkage with a Cuban withdrawal has been a major demand by both South Africa and the United States."[49]

The "linkage" that most Africans are more likely to make is between U.S. and South African policies. Given the nature of the South African regime, which is anathema even to the United States' African "friends," the implications of such a linkage for the United States in Africa are not difficult to see. The general political mood in most African states is more accurately reflected in this "communist" view:

> One can safely say that the presence of Cuban troops in Angola does not suit anyone, including Cuba and Angola. It is equally certain that South Africa and the United States in particular want Cuban troops to leave Angolan territory. . . . [But] the fact remains that both these countries refuse to offer Angola guarantees that her independence and territorial integrity will be respected. This means that the problem is not so much the presence of Cuban troops as the incumbent government and socio-political system in Angola. . . . At the same time the presence of Cuban troops in Angola is a pretext for continuing the illegal occupation of Namibia. Just as an independent and socialist Angola is not to the liking of [South Africa] so her Western allies resent the idea of an independent Namibia with a government formed by SWAPO, the only legitimate representative of the Namibian people.[50]

If the terminology in reference to SWAPO sounds familiar, it is because there are similarities between the situations in southern Africa and the Middle East, and in the U.S. policy attitudes toward both SWAPO and the PLO.[51]

An essential component of the U.S. anti-communist strategy is the militarization of its allies and clients in Africa. This has tended not only to have a destabilizing effect on regional politics but also to internationalize them. Sudanese-Egyptian claims of Libyan subversion in Chad, the Sudan and elsewhere were readily perceived in Washington as synonymous with Soviet threats. The Reagan administration was sensitive enough to President Numayri's allegations of "imminent" Soviet-backed Libyan and Ethiopian "invasions," to speed up arms deliveries to the Sudan. The inevitable cycle of escalation in Chad and the Horn of Africa tended to transform these local and regional conflicts into yet other pawns in the East–West confrontation.

Testimony delivered to the Committee on Africa of the United States House of Representatives in October 1981, noted that:

> What is at stake here is not just the future of Chad as a political entity, but the stability of the entire northeastern region of the continent, and parts of the Middle East. While there is a rough symmetry in the mutual defense agreements concluded between Egypt and the Sudan on the one hand, and Libya, Ethiopia and South Yemen on the other, the additional symmetry of their East-West connections carries serious implications from the standpoint of regional geopolitics. Given the extent of misperception on the part of both Soviet and U.S. policymakers, and the extent to which these are deliberately encouraged by their respective clients, is there any reason to assume that a localized fight between factions may not eventually result in a wider, and far more serious confrontation across national boundaries?[52]

In the Sudan's case, it was apparent that the regime was tempted to invoke and overplay the communist (Libyan-Ethiopian-Soviet) bogey as a leverage for getting more aid from the United States. As this writer noted elsewhere, "The Sudan's excessive reliance on the Egyptian-American alliance might provoke and not deter the hostility of its pro-Soviet neighbours. More seriously, it could encourage and not diffuse subversion from within by anti-Egyptian and anti-American groups."[53]

Image Formation and U.S. Policy

Anti-Americanism is not only a function of how and why people in the Third World perceive the ideology, policies, and actions of the United States. It is also a reflection of how Americans view other societies and the impact of, and reaction to, this vision in the outside world. In a sense, the United States has been reliving, since the Second World War, a new form of isolationism—the isolationism of its own "bigness" which, paradoxically, drives it to seek to reshape the world in its own ways without sufficient knowledge of the cosmos or any profound understanding of the complex issues involved.

This failure, or indifference, to understand the political, cultural and socioeconomic realities of other societies may explain why the actuality of U.S. relations with most countries in the Third World, foe and friend alike, has been manifestly a thorny set of problems. U.S. public views, to the extent that they are coherently articulated, on highly sensitive issues in Africa (e.g. white minority-rule) and in the Arab world (e.g., the Arab–Israeli conflict), are often based on inaccurate information, inadequate analysis, unabashed bias, and dubious morality.

In the United States, as elsewhere, sociocultural and economic influences play a determining role in fashioning the value system of individuals and groups, and the personal disposition and orientation of policymakers. The sociologist view that sociocultural factors have a pervading impact on man's perception of political reality, applies equally to Americans:

> [These] factors. . .help to shape the cognitive orientation of the community and the individuals within that community, that is, their feeling of attachment, involvement or rejection of political objects and beliefs; and their evaluative orientation, that is, their judgements and opinions about other opinions and beliefs which usually involve applying value standards to political object and events. In other words, the decision-makers in any community always act in accordance with their perception of reality, not in response to reality itself. Reality is seldom as objective as it seems, or rather as it is made to seem. Reality and its image are not always congruous. Worse still, images are often a distortion of, a deviation from, or simply a misconstruction of reality.[54]

Distorted images can give different shades to reality to the point of being "an impediment to communication."

To most Americans, Africa is still, literally, a "dark continent." Educated Africans find this peculiar lack of knowledge incomprehensible in the, supposedly, most highly educated nation in the world, possessing the most effective media apparatus anywhere. The image of Africa in the U.S. media is that of a continent of "abject poverty, rampant corruption, tribal enmity, uncontrolled population growth."[55] What Africans find offensive is not the generalized image as such, but the fact that the Western role in creating and perpetuating African problems is rarely acknowledged and is sometimes indignantly denied. The spread of authoritarian regimes in Africa has tended to create an implicit—and sometimes explicit—assumption in the West that Africans are "congenitally" incapable of maintaining moderate, "democratic," civilian rule. What is not as readily assumed is the complicity of the West and the United States in installing or supporting most of these repressive regimes. The economic and military achievements of white South Africa are often cited as the major exception to the continent's litany of failure, but what is left unexplained is the human cost of *apartheid* and the West's willing collaboration in making these "achievements" possible in the first place.[56]

U.S. administrations seem to regard Africa as "a vast arena of conflict with the Soviet Union, in which victory is likely to go to the side that arms its friends and co-opts them in the East–West struggle."[57] The attitude of some U.S. public figures and scholars toward Africa has been demeaningly patronizing, if not outrightly hostile. Daniel Moynihan's reaction to Afro-Asian criticisms of the U.S. in the U.N. was to advocate for the Third World an economic version of his celebrated notion of "benign neglect"—a notion which, incidentally, many African intellectuals would have welcomed if only in view of continued U.S. interventionism. Kenneth Adelman argued that Africa's "sorry record" on political and civil freedom made the idea of introducing majority rule in southern Africa "excessively naive" and might "lead to even harsher restrictions on civil liberty." Adelman even objected to the adoption of indigenous solutions to African problems claiming that "it is one thing to claim (with a good measure of truth) that Africa *will not* soon adopt Western values but quite another to say that Africa *should not* adopt them and further that the United States should not even promote its goals."[58]

Africa's perennial problems are real enough. But U.S. perceptions of the African experience reflect, at best, a kind of "cultural chauvinism" that assumes the universal validity and applications of U.S. values. As Coker has noted, "in the end, the Africans will have to trust their own traditions and fight shy of the nostrums peddled by American academics and politicians who have spent the better part of a generation denying them self-respect in the name of their own understanding of progress and freedom."[59]

If the image of the African in U.S. eyes is blurred, through ignorance or indifference, to the point of obscurity, that of the Arab has been distorted and collectivized to the point of absurdity. From an Arab perspective, what adds insult to injury is that the dehumanization of the Arabs and Muslims in general is, more often than not, intentionally propagated by the U.S. mass media, U.S. public figures, and U.S. scholars.

Since the oil crisis of 1973, the old stereotype of the Arab as a camel-riding and sensuous nomad *à la Valentino*, has been updated and transformed into a caricature of the lascivious *sheik* with unlimited supplies of petrodollars. The image of the "incompetent" Arab of 1967, in U.S. popular culture (as well as in the policy-planner's world) assumed, after

1973, a menacing dimension as one who, without any moral justification, was holding the "free world" to "ransom." (Many Arabs have not failed to note that when the United States uses its national resources as a leverage in its foreign policy, such as tying foreign aid to pro-U.S. voting records in the UN, this is considered a legitimate exercise in the fine arts of "diplomacy.")

To deal with "Arab blackmail," contingency plans and military exercises were undertaken in preparation for the invasion and occupation of Arab oil-fields to remove the "Arab stranglehold" on the West. In the U.S. public mind and mass media, little attention was given to the fact that the principal beneficiaries of the 1973–74 oil embargo and the subsequent rises in oil prices were *not* the Arabs but the Western oil companies and a small ruling Arab elite.

According to Edward Said, three things have contributed to making even the simplest perceptions of the Arabs and Muslims into a highly politicized, almost raucous matter:

> One, the history of popular anti-Arab and anti-Islamic prejudice in the West, which is immediately reflected in the history of Orientalism; two, the struggle between the Arabs and Israeli Zionism, and its effects upon American Jews as well as upon both the liberal culture and the population at large; three, the almost total absence of any cultural position making it possible either to identify with or dispassionately to discuss the Arabs or Islam. Furthermore, it hardly needs saying that because the Middle East is now so identified with Great Power politics, oil economics, and the simple-minded dichotomy of freedom-loving, democratic Israel and evil, totalitarian, and terroristic Arabs, the chances of anything like a clear view of what one talks about in talking about the Near East are depressingly small.[60]

The simplistic, crude and often cruel images of Arabs and Islam are disseminated in U.S. society through the mass media, school textbooks, and the writings of U.S. scholars, particularly and somewhat surprisingly, the so-called "area specialists." The mass media influenced public perceptions through the superficial presentation of the Middle East situation and through the often imbalanced coverage of events in the area, especially the Arab-Israeli conflict.

There were, obviously, exceptions to the general rule, and in recent years attempts were made to adopt a more evenhanded approach. Some U.S. journalists criticized what they considered U.S.-Middle East policy that did not serve U.S. interests. But even these exceptional few incurred the wrath of Zionist pressure groups, often in terms of the blanket charge of anti-Semitism. From an Arab perspective, the biased anti-Arab tilt of the media as a whole only confirms the unrelenting U.S. hostility toward the Arabs, their history and their culture. From an objective U.S. perspective, this could only be detrimental to U.S. interests in the Arab world and could have more serious implications for the U.S. position in one of the most critical foreign-policy areas. According to Harold R. Piety, "the average American has a grossly distorted, simplistic view of the Middle East, and this inclines him toward support for a dangerous and destructive national policy in that part of the world. The American press bears a major responsibility for this state of affairs."[61]

Indeed, the U.S. mass media increasingly intruded into foreign policy matters that were normally the preserve of political decision-makers and career diplomats. A case in point is the celebrated "media diplomacy" of Sádát's visit to Jerusalem in 1977 and, from an Arab viewpoint, all the disastrous consequences of that controversial move.[62]

The anti-Arab tradition and practice of the U.S. media have, predictably, fueled the anti-American attitude in the Arab media. This anti-Americanism is a natural reaction to U.S. policy in the Middle East which relates to the Arabs in a very vital and immediate way. The Arab media, in all its diverse political shades and ideological motivations, and regardless of whether or not it is government-controlled, is primarily and consistently preoccupied with the Palestinian problem and the Arab-Israeli conflict. Thus, the predominantly negative U.S. image reflected in the Arab media emanates largely from U.S. behavior and is symptomatic of the U.S.-Arab relationship. "Statements lacking an evenhanded position and made by American governmental leaders, whether of the executive or legislative branch, feed this image, as do the similarly partial commentaries and editorials that appear in the various U.S. media."[63]

Besides the mass media, Americans are exposed to other cultures and people through textbooks. The findings of some studies and surveys, conducted before and after 1975, on the presentation of the Arabs and Islam in the social sciences textbooks used in the United States, revealed the presence of inaccurate, misleading and incomplete statements (that lead to wrong impressions) and omissions of important facts about the Arabs and their history. Textbooks overemphasized the negative nature of Arab nationalism (to which U.S. difficulties in the Middle East were attributed), and the presentation of the Arab-Israeli conflict showed a bias toward the Israeli point of view. Islam was misrepresented as a "warlike" religion in which women occupied a position of servitude. Most textbooks used the terms Arab and Muslim interchangeably. In short, Arab culture and history were frequently measured by Western standards and were characterized by negative stereotyping.[64]

The dismal implications of this situation go beyond the adverse effects of the limited components of civic literacy in the U.S. school system and the related distorted image formation at a young and impressionable age. What is more at stake is the crucial role of the level of knowledge in the process of political comprehension and behavior, and the impact of the lack of cross-cultural understanding on the quality of relations between nations. Luther Evans noted that the presentations as "facts" of unqualified, unbalanced and inaccurate statements can be "the seed to a crop of misunderstanding, hate and contempt among natives and towards other ways of life."[65]

Even U.S. academic writings on the Arab world are, in large measure, an example of how a learned perspective can support the caricatures propagated in the popular culture. Edward Said examined some of the writings by U.S. scholars and area specialists, and noted that the main things reproduced were "a certain cultural hostility and a sense based not so much on philology as on 'expertise.' " He pointed out the singular avoidance of Arab literature in contemporary U.S. studies on the Near East and argued that, "the net effect of this remarkable omission in modern American awareness of the Arab or Islamic Orient is to keep the region and its people conceptually emasculated, reduced to 'attitudes,' 'trends,' statistics: in short dehumanized."[66] It is worthwhile to remember that some U.S. scholars and experts often act as political advisers and economic consultants, and sometimes even policymakers, in government and business.

Thus, at almost all levels, the stereotype image of the Arab in the United States is largely one of a negative value. The "Arab" is fixed in a web of prejudices and misconceptions born out of ignorance. In the words of Hazlitt, "prejudice is the child of ignorance."[67] Prejudices, willfully preferred or not, have, in turn, the potential capacity of breeding counter-prejudices. In this sense, Arab anti-Americanism can also be seen as a reactive mechanism to the prejudicial attitudes and policies that seem to doom the Arab to a U.S. ordained destiny from which there is, apparently, no easy escape.

CONCLUSION

There is a correlation between perception and preference that tended to reinforce anti-American sentiment in a variety of related forms. The rejection of capitalism and the adoption of socialism or Marxism in African and Arab states was usually based on perceptions of the unacceptability of the former and the appeal of the latter. It also evoked ideological justifications for the preference. These ideological assertions, which became more vocal in cases where socialist performance had failed to measure up to socialist ideals, often emphasized the limitations of the alternative capitalist model (e.g., the dangers of incorporation into the international capitalist system dominated by the United States).

When the preference for socialism aroused U.S. hostility and interventionism, either directly or by proxy or through destabilization, the anti-American sentiment and rhetoric of socialist leaders and groups was correspondingly intensified. Where U.S. interventionism or pressures succeeded in precipitating a change from a socialist-oriented development model to a free-market economy, the focal point of anti-Americanism tended to shift from the ruling elite to those political and social groups who had little to gain and much to lose (economically as well as culturally and politically) from a capitalist-intensive system and the "Americanization" process that it almost inevitably entailed.

After gaining independence, Arabs and Africans sought to be left alone; but the intrusion of Great Power politics meant, in effect, that they would not be allowed to shape their own destiny. The Arab world, in particular, was caught in what Ajami called "the eye of the storm":

> One power (the United States) is drawn there by economic needs and by all those psychological motivations that drive powerful entities to try to create a world in their image. For the other power (the USSR), there is the desire to break out of what it sees as a hemmed-in position at a time when it may have come to feel that the world owes it more respect than it has hitherto been accorded. The ambitions, fears, and pressures outsiders bring to bear on a tense region are immense and likely to continue.[68]

From the beginning, U.S. policy, in the Arab world and Africa, was clouded and constrained by the "undifferentiated globalism" of its approach. Central to this approach was the U.S. anti-communist fixation and its corollary that radical revolutions—invariably depicted as Marxist or pro-communist—had to be condemned, contained and defeated. According to George Ball, U.S. policymakers were "preoccupied to the point of obsession with the question 'how,' but there was little patience with the question 'why.' " As the United States blundered into a series of military and political *culs de sac*, it encountered only disappointment and frustration.[69] Not surprisingly, anti-Americansim became a major aspect of radical nationalism in Arab and African countries.

Indeed the record of U.S. policy in the Third World had been one of missed opportunity and self-inflicted humiliation. Instead of coming to terms with the Mosaddigs, the Nasirs and the Castros of the 1950s, the United States sought to destroy them and, inevitably, found itself in confrontation with the Ayatollahs, the Qaddafis and the *Fidelismos* of the present.

By contrast, the Soviet Union, whose world role was, paradoxically, even more complicated by the sometimes mutually contradictory claims of state interest and communist ideology, had a more clear and realistic vision of the world situation. The leadership in the Kremlin might have spent some sleepless nights when local communists were ruthlessly persecuted by pro-Soviet regimes as was the case of Egyptian communists in the late 1950s and Sudanese communists in the early 1970s. But, more often than not, ideological niceties were not allowed to obscure the policy objectives of Soviet interests or to cast policy approaches in rigid dogma. Thus, while the United States continued to view the outside world in "white" and "black," the Soviets were prepared to regard it in different shades of "grey." In Africa and the Arab world, the United States seemed insistent in pursuing a policy of "those who are not with us are against us" (dating back to Dulles' "immoralism" of nonalignment). The Soviets, on the other hand, tended subtly to cultivate the approach of "those who are not against us are with us" (dating back to Khrushchev's acceptance of nonalignment and of the "national roads" to socialism).

This situation was obviously to the advantage of the Soviet Union. The Soviets certainly did some bungling of their own (as in Egypt and the Sudan in the early 1970s) and had to face some difficult choices (as between Iraq and Iran and between Ethiopia and Somalia, in the late 1970s). But for the most part, all they had to do was to watch U.S. blunders and pick up the pieces. The Soviet presence in Africa and the Arab world came not through "invasion" but by "invitation."[70]

In the final analysis, anti-Americanism, like many other "antis," is both an attribute of, and a reaction to, power and the threats and fears, real or imagined, implicit in power. In the case of the United States, the exercise of power can be seen not only in terms of its "arrogance" but also of its "ignorance." The Shah of Iran remarked in 1976 that his real opposition was himself[71]—a self-revealing appraisal whose self-destructive implications he himself might not have realized or fully comprehended. The same is true, in a sense, of the United States. While not necessarily being "a nation of sheep," Americans can certainly be, to use yet another American-coined phrase, their "own worst enemy."

NOTES

1. Cited in G.T. Hollayday, *Anti-Americanism in the German Novel, 1841-1862* (Berne, Switzerland, 1977) p. 11. Hallayday's explanation of this anti-American phenomenon is partly that, "European conservatives had attacked America even before the nineteenth century because it was acclaimed by liberals as a model for the Old World. One of the reasons for the intensity of antagonism toward America in the two decades prior to the Civil War was the fact that the conservatives were now joined by disillusioned liberals." p. 159. In the context of the contemporary Third World these premises are reversed: it is the liberal-leftist groups who are anti-American, while the conservatives are pro-American, albeit with some suspicions of U.S. liberalism.

2. Quoted in Thomas B. Morgan, *The Anti-Americans* (Michael Joseph Ltd.; London, 1967), p. 8.

3. J.M. and M.J. Cohen, *The Penguin Dictionary of Modern Quotations* (Penguin, Harmondworth, 1971). The remark is also attributed to Bernard Shaw in other sources.

4. Anti-Americanism differered from the anti-British counterpart, for example, in that the latter sentiment, generated by the physical presence and control of colonies, tended to recede with the end of colonialism as it did, in fact, in the case of the United States itself vis-à-vis the British.

5. Edgar Z. Friedenberg (ed.) *The Anti-American Generation* (Transaction Inc., USA, 1971), p. 15.

6. It is important to note that this anti-Americanism was essentially directed against the U.S. system and society and not against the American people as such. Indeed, most of the educated elite in Third World countries tended to sympathize with the young U.S. militants whose anti-Establishment views reflected, in some cases, their own sentiments toward their own military and/or authoritarian regimes. It did not seem much of a coincidence that the most repressive of these were invariably supported by the U.S. government. On both counts, anti-Americanism was reinforced.

7. *Return to the Source: Selected Speeches by Amilcar Cabral.* Edited by Africa Information Service (Monthly Review Press; New York and London, 1973), p. 12.

8. This, obviously, need not imply that anti-American regimes in Africa and the Arab world are necessarily less authoritarian but only that the structure of their political organization and their ideological orientation derive from different sources and motivations that are considered or proclaimed to be "authentic" (e.g., Tanzania under Nyerere).

9. Maxine Molyneux and Fred Halliday, "Marxism, the Third World and the Middle East," *MERIP Reports* No. 120 (New York, January 1984), p. 18.

10. "Marxism's introduction into the Third World has come through a variety of channels.... [But] much blood was spilt to keep communists from power.... The repressions in Iran, Iraq, and the Sudan comprise the most notable Middle Eastern chapters in this murderous history." *Ibid.*, p. 20.

11. See Morgan, *op. cit.*

12. Hilary Ng'weno, cited in *Ibid.*, p. 183.

13. Molyneux and Halliday, *op. cit.*, p. 20. According to the writers, "Marxism in the Third World has therefore found itself with conflict on two fronts: an overt struggle against capitalist and imperialist domination, and a hidden struggle against those who seek to appropriate revolutionary phraseology for their own purposes. These cramped political and intellectual circumstances have limited Marxist achievements today, de spite its impressive geographical spread."

14. See Patrick Seale, *The Struggle for Syria: a Study of post-War Arab Politics* (Oxford University Press, 1965). Seale offers an interesting explanation of the origins of Arab nationalism that later influenced the ideological orientation of the radical nationalist movements. In the Arab East under Ottoman control, Arabism became an important source and function of identification against a Muslim colonizer, while in Egypt, Islam provided the means of identification against a Christian-Western domination.

15. For a comprehensive analysis of Arab politics in the 1958–70 period, see Malcolm Kerr, *The Arab Cold War: Gamal Abd al-Nasir and His Rivals* (Oxford University Press, 1971).

16. As an ideology, Nasirism was an amalgamation of socialist principles, Arabism, and Islamism within a framework of Marxist terminology. The Islamic aspects of Násir's "Arab socialism" was partly a genuine debate into the socialist content of Islam, *Ishtirak-iyat al-Islam*, and partly a pragmatic element to give legitimacy and acceptance to the notion of socialism in an essentially conservative Muslim society. Haykal argues that in Násir's day, Islam was never seen as an obstacle to socialism; on the contrary, strong sympathy was felt with the saying attributed to the Prophet: "There are three things which belong to society as a whole and which cannot be claimed by an individual—fire, grass and water," a principle which according to Haykal "by many centuries anticipated the doctrine of the nationalization of the means of production." Mohamed Heikal, *Autumn of Fury: The Assassination of Sadat* (Random House, Inc., New York, 1983), p. 129.

17. Richard Falk, "Comparative Protection of Human Rights in Capitalist and Socialist Third World Countries," *Universal Human Rights*, Vol. 1, No. 2, April-June 1979.

18. Christopher Coker, "Neo-conservatism and Africa: Some Common American Fallacies," *Third World Quarterly*, Vol. 5, No. 2 (London), April, 1983.

19. *Ibid.* In Africa, "rapid urbanization has hastened the process of detribalization, but this has created an entirely new set of problems. Attracted by the often spurious promise of wealth in Africa's burgeoning cities, hundreds of thousands of Africans have deserted their native villages.... Many African sociologists see the phenomenon as a primary cause of social disintegration; young Africans discard tribal values and disciplines for an urban-centered culture of Coca-Cola and transistor radios. For many Africans there is a growing awareness that tribal life was the source of tradition, of social and spiritual values." *Time* (New York) January 16, 1984.

20. Ray Vicker, "Tycoon Khalil Osman Builds a Conglomerate with Oil-Money Help," *The Wall Street Journal*, August 5, 1975. Cited in John Waterbury, *The Sudan in Quest of a Surplus*. The American Universities Field Staff, Hanover, Northeast African Series, Vol. XXI, No. 10.

21. Ghali Shoukri, *Egypt: Portrait of a President* (Zed Press, London, 1981).

22. Heikal, *op. cit.*, pp. 90–91.

23. Saad al-Din Ibrahim "Hakūmat Zil Amrikiyya fi al-Qahira" (An American Shadow Government in Cairo) *Al-Ahram al-lqtisadi*, No. 717 (Cairo, October, 1982).

24. David Hirst and Irene Beeson, *Sadat* (Faber & Faber, London, 1981).

25. *North–South: A Programme of Survival. Report of the Independent Commission on International Development Issues* (Pan; London, 1980), p. 269.

26. See Fehmi Saddy, "The Fallacy of Interdependence: The New Face of Dependence." Draft paper for *The XVIII Annual Convention of the International Studies Association*. St. Louis, Missouri, USA, February 16–20, 1977.

27. Quoted in Teresa Hayter, *The Creation of World Poverty* (Pluto Press, London, 1981), p. 11.

28. A Jack Anderson report in *The Washington Post* revealed that the Reagan administration had embarked on yet another secret mission by sending to the Sudan a counterinsurgency team to develop plans for protecting Chevron's oil facilities in southern Sudan against an "insurgent threat." The report, based on a "highly sensitive State Department cable," observes that "while Congress and the public are being kept in the dark, Chevron isn't." *The Washington Post*, October 19, 1983. Since then the anti-Americanism of the rebel movement, because of increasing U.S. military support to the Sudanese government, has extended to Chevron. Following attacks on its installations and personnel, Chevron was forced to suspend all its operations in February 1984.

29. Hayter, *op. cit.*, p. 109.

30. See Timothy M. Shaw, "Debates About Africa's Future: The Brandt, World Bank and Lagos Plan Blueprints." *Third World Quarterly, op. cit.*

31. Falk, *op. cit.* Emphasis in the original.

32. Samir Amin, "Expansion or Crisis of Capitalism," *Third World Quarterly, op. cit.*

33. Samir Amin, *La nation arabe: nationalisme et luttes de classes* (Editions de minuit, Paris, 1976), p. 148.

34. See Frantz Fanon, *The Wretched of the Earth* (Harmondsworth, Penguin Books, 1967).

35. John L.S. Girling, *America and the Third World: Revolution and Intervention* (Routledge & Kegal Paul, London, 1980), p. 218.

36. According to Haykal, Násir also told the Americans that "If I went and told my people that the British status here is going to be changed from occupiers to partners by a change of flag, they would laugh at me.... If I stop leading my people as a nationalist then the communists are going to lead them." *The Cairo Documents* (Doubleday & Co., New York, 1973), pp. 40–41.

37. It is difficult to exaggerate the degree to which Arabs and Africans suspect and fear the pervasive activities of the CIA. These suspicions and fears, given the U.S. global record, are not, of course, simply a case of mass paranoia.

38. Muhammad H. Haykal, *Nahnu wa-Amrika* (We and America) (Cairo, 1968), pp. 5–6.

39. *Al-Ah ram* (Cairo), March 17, 1967.

40. Fouad Ajami, *The Arab Predicament: Arab Political Thought and Practice Since 1969* (Cambridge University Press, 1981), p. 170.

41. Shoukri, *op. cit.*

42. Heikal, *Autumn of Fury*, p. 276. According to another Egyptian writer, "the success of the socialist forces associated with the Soviet Union, and the pro-Soviet and anti-American stance of others, is a matter imposed by the nature of the phase of the struggle against the American-backed Zionist threat. If the U.S. can contribute to the solution of the Palestinian problem on a just and acceptable basis, then there will be no communist danger in the region." Ri'fat al-Shaykh, *Amrika wa al-'Alaqat al-Dawaliyya* (America and International Relations) (Cairo, 1979), p. 181.

43. Haykal remarks, with a note of bitterness, that Sádát's offer of asylum to the Shah was "applauded in the West as an act of generosity, particularly by those countries like America and Britain which had all along been the Shah's staunchest supporters but which had no intention of letting humanity get in the way of the interests of state." *Ibid.*

44. *Ibid.*, p. 170.

45. Book review by this writer of Hirst and Beeson *op. cit.*, in *Third World Quarterly*, Vol. 5 No. 2 (London) April, 1983.

46. Heikal, *op. cit.*, p. 268.

47. *Time* (Atlantic Edition, Amsterdam), October 19, 1981.

48. Girling, *op. cit.*, p. 15.

49. *The New York Times*, March 12, 1984.

50. Mihailo V. Stevovic, "Angola: Eight Years of Independence," *Review of International Affairs*, Vol. XXXV (Belgrade), February 5, 1984.

51. For an analysis of the settler-colonial nature of Israel and its South African connection see Maxime Rodinson, *Israel: A Colonial Settler State?* (New York, 1973); and Richard P. Stevens and Abdelwahab M. Elmessiri, *Israel and South Africa: The Progression of a Relationship* (New World Press, New York, 1976).

52. Cited in Mohammad B. Hamid, "The 'Finlandization' of Sudan's Foreign Policy: Sudanese-Egyptian Relations since the Camp David Accords." *Journal of Arab Affairs*, Vol. 2, No. 2 (Fresno, California) Spring 1983.

53. *Ibid.*

54. Mansour Khalid, *The Socio-Cultural Determinants of Arab Diplomacy.* Selections from Sudanese Literature (2) (Washington, D.C.) n.d., p. 2.

55. *Time* (New York) January 16, 1984.

56. *Ibid.*

57. Coker, *op. cit.*, p. 283.

58. Cited in *ibid.*, p. 291. Adelman even manages to invoke a kind of frivolous cultural determinism to support his case. "Traditional African religions," he explains, "are entirely devoid of notions such as 'fate' or 'the forces of history' marching towards progress and redemption (Christianity) or prosperity and liberation (Marxism). In the traditional African religious scheme an injury, death or calamity can be explained only in direct personal terms as stemming from individuals or ancestral ill-will. This mind could lead some Africans to track the evils of Ian Smith or *apartheid* not to chance or historical forces but to direct personal ill-will stemming from the West."

59. *Ibid.*, p. 299.

60. Edward W. Said, *Orientalism* (Pantheon Books, New York, 1977), pp. 26–27. Said

maintains that "no person academically involved with the Near East—no Orientalist, that is—has ever in the United States culturally and politically identified himself whole-heartedly with the Arabs; certainly there have been identifications on some level, but they have never taken an 'acceptable' form as has liberal American identification with Zionism, and all too frequently they have been radically flawed by their association either with discredited political and economic interests (oil company and State Department Arabists, for example) or with religion." p. 27.

61. Harold R. Piety, "Bias on American Editorial Pages" in Edmund Ghareeb (ed.), *Split Vision: The Portrayal of Arabs in the American Media* (American-Arab Affairs Council, Washington, D.C. 1983), p. 142.

62. See Montague Kern, *Television and Middle East Diplomacy: President Carter's Fall 1977 Peace Initiative* CCAS Occasional Papers series, Georgetown University (Washington, D.C. 1983).

63. Adnan Abu Odeh, "The American Image in the Arab Mass Media" in Ghareeb, *op. cit.* Some of the principal features of the factual elements that have created and continue to maintain the anti-American image in the Arab media are: U.S. policy toward the Palestinian question is partial and biased; the U.S. is endangering its own interests in the whole region in favor of one small and aggressive state, Israel; the U.S. is impotent when it comes to dealing with Israel; the U.S. is imperialistic in its approach to the Middle East, seeking hegemony and exploiting the regions's resources; and the U.S. does not keep faith with its Arab friends. pp. 358–59.

64. For surveys on the shockingly limited knowledge of international issues among U.S. students, and the inaccurate information disseminated in U.S. schools, see Samir Ahmad Jarrar, "The Treatment of Arabs in U.S. Social Studies Textbooks: Research Findings and Recommendation" in *ibid.*, pp. 381–90; Ayad Al-Qazzaz, "Sorat al-Watan al-Arabi Fi al-Madaris al-Thanwiya al-Amrikiya" (The Image of the Arab Homeland in American Secondary Schools) in *Al-Siyasa al-Amrikiya wa al-Arab* (American Policy and the Arabs) by a group of Arab scholars (Beirut, 1982), pp. 233–49; and Frank D. Klassen and Howard B. Leavitt, *Teacher Education and Global Perspective*, ERIC Clearinghouse on Teacher Education, American Association for Teacher Education (Washington, D.C. 1982). The last survey found "weaknesses in such fundamental areas as geography . . . pervasive ignorance of the Middle East and Africa . . . Lack of knowledge about Western Europe and misunderstanding of some key aspects of American history and government." p. 13.

65. Cited in Ayad Al-Qazzas, "Image Formation and Textbooks" in Ghareeb *op. cit.*, p. 370.

66. Said, *op. cit.*, p. 291.

67. Quoted in M. Khalid, *op. cit.*, p. 13.

68. Ajami, *op. cit.*, p. 21.

69. George W. Ball, Edward J. Derwinski and Philip J. Geyelin, *United States Policy in the Middle East*, CCAS Reports (Georgetown University, April, 1984), p. 1.

70. It hardly needs saying that for the Soviets also, "presence" in a Third World environment can be a hazardous undertaking, as in Afghanistan, and may lead to humiliating "expulsions," as was the case in Egypt, the Sudan and Somalia.

71. *Le Monde* (Paris) October 1, 1976.

6

Anti-Americanism in Turkey

Ahmet Evin

"Everybody is crazy about American products. They love to have nylon panties and dacron skirts. Blouses and blue jeans on girls. Well, it is not that I don't get angry at our leaders. A battleship called the Missouri had come. I was doing my military service then, as a driver of the regiment. Our troops welcomed the American sailors on land and sea. The governor gave a speech. Flowers and wreaths all over the place; flags displayed everywhere. They had I don't know how many rounds of gun salute. For a whole week people queued up and paid a quarter in order to see the battleship. While they paid a quarter each, the officials had the whore houses painted and spruced up. They had the girls examined and declared the area off limits to natives so that only American sailors could enter. Well, sir, I get very angry at things like this."[1]

Thus speaks Kerim, the chauffeur of the wealthy businessman Melih Dalyan, in Fakir Baykurt's novel *Amerikan Sargisi* (American Bandage: 1967), while he is driving his employer to a meeting at the USAID Mission. His tirade is triggered no less by the fact that they have been driving through the fashionable part of Ankara where the U.S. presence is highly visible than by his perception that Melih Bey, like all others belonging to the richer echelons of the entrepreneurial classes in Turkey, is sympathetic to Americans, and hence, by extension, is a "collaborator." Kerim resents the fact that vacant apartments smack in the middle of Turkey's capital city have signs in English, "For rent" and "To let," obviously for the benefit of Americans whose presence has driven the prices in the rental market to a level beyond the reach of even upper-class Turks. For who could afford to live in that fashionable district of the embassy now but foreigners and those "collaborators" who are engaged in the imperialistic activities of international trade?

Kerim's attitude reflects accurately the type of anti-Americanism that manifested itself among urban lower and lower-middle classes in the 1960s. It is an attitude that was to a large extent shaped by the perception that Americans had emerged as the real masters of the country. This association with the upper echelons of the business community, the political establishment, and even the bureaucracy was commonly taken as a proof of an undesirably high degree of U.S. influence in the country. After the Marshall Plan (1947) and in the wake of Turkey's joining the Atlantic Alliance (1952), the American presence increased substantially.[2] This presence was all the more visible in the capital, a city which did not have a cosmopolitan tradition and retained a smalltown atmosphere through the 1960s.[3] In such an environment, the average American, with appearance and manners notably different from those of the local population, and unable to utter a word of Turkish, would naturally stand out. Though Turks did not expect foreigners to know Turkish, the resident Americans were not tourists after all; the persistence of a language barrier could be interpreted as a symptom of an unwillingness on the part of the Americans to interact with Turks of their own class.

More importantly, it was the economic status of Americans that kept them visibly apart from the local population. By virtue of being rich, they could afford a higher standard of life in Turkey than even the Turks who ranked higher than them on the social or professional ladder. As such they were seen as a group who was gradually displacing, spatially as well as socially, the indigenous elites. The growth in Turkey of a new capitalist class whose members often displayed an inclination to possess American consumer goods served to heighten these fears. Labelled as "American lackeys," these nouveaux riches, too, began displacing the traditional bureaucratic elite in the elegant residential quarters and expensive restaurants.

To large segments of conservative urban lower classes, these shifts in the composition of the upper classes (particularly the emerging redefinition of upper class in terms of wealth rather than official position) signified a social and moral deterioration.[4] The reticent, distant and somewhat taciturn bureaucratic elite had been relegated to a secondary place, while the outgoing, convivial and often permissive foreigner and the indigenous speculator had come to a position of influence. Their lifestyle and values, viewed as being somewhat degenerate, provided a much-emulated model at the top that pointed to the loss of propriety and morality. They possessed the best pieces of real estate and impressive automobiles; they possessed women, and they had influence. Their influence in government circles aroused suspicions; did they possess Turkey in a similar fashion as they possessed her women?

But even more ominous was the fact that these Americans were in Turkey in an official capacity. They belonged to the military, the diplomatic corps, bilateral agencies, and various missions. Hence their presence as well as their influence bore unmistakable signs of a kind of colonial domination. Had they indeed bought the country or were they simply in the process of controlling the state? The latter alternative would meet national indignation, but the former would make the conspiracy theory complete. The "collaborators" would neatly fit the category of brokers in this deal, the "lackeys" who sell the nation's resources much in the same way as a pimp would sell a prostitute. *Satilmislar* ("the ones that are sold," ironically referring to capitalists) became a radical left slogan in the 1960s.

One is not certain if such an elaborate rationale underlying the urban lower-class manifestation of anti-Americanism could have originated in shanty-towns. The U.S. term, "military-industrial complex" was much bandied about in this context, and that term could not have gained currency in Turkey without the mediation of educated interpreters. But to hold fifth column manipulators solely responsible for the rise of anti-Americanism among the urban masses in Turkey would be tantamount to presenting yet another conspiracy theory. Evidence suggests that radical theoreticians made use of resentments that existed among people in articulating a coherent argument against U.S. involvement in Turkey.[5] The type of resentment Kerim the driver feels stems from personal experience and reflects, above all, the frustration of an individual having a wounded pride. This feeling is not even anti-American in its embryonic form, but eventually translates into such, precisely because the aliens who dominate the scene, and thus remind the have-nots of their poverty or insignificance, happen to be Americans. Channeling frustration and resentments to focus on aliens is a universal phenomenon, but how much more gratifying it is to nurture one's frustrations so that one can blame a larger group of conspirators.

Melih Dalyan, the businessman with a degree from Michigan whose fortunes rise in proportion to the hard currency credit provided by the United States, understands very well why he might be included among the objects of his driver's resentment. He perceives the delicacy of their relationship, and the imminent possibility that the correct relationship between the generous employer and a loyal employee would turn into one tainted by such resentments: "His eyes were on the mirror, looking at me as if I were responsible for closing up the whore houses." He then replies to the driver's tirade, "Well, then, whose fault is it? A big American ship comes. What is wrong with that? But why does the governor have to make a formal speech? Why all these flowers and wreaths? Why do people pay a quarter and queue up? Why all this painting and closing up of the whore houses? Isn't that the crux of the matter?"[6]

Melih Bey, lacking none of the amenities that Americans may have in Michigan or Istanbul and having an expatriate U.S. woman as a mistress in Ankara as well, is totally rational about the situation. If there is anything embarrassing related to the U.S. presence, it is the Turkish officialdom who behave in a fashion becoming Lilliputians. People like Melih Bey cannot but harbor scorn for the officialdom whose asinine servility compromises national pride. The Americans are not the responsible party and hence the feelings of rage have to be deflected: he ends the conversation by admonishing, "Don't be angry at Johnnies. All human beings are human beings, Johnnies, too."[7] In fact, the Melih Bey type is not devoid of pride, national or otherwise, but his is the kind of pride that is not so fragile in the absence of a feeling of insecurity. Just because he can deal with Americans on his own turf as well as theirs, he would not perceive them as being dangerous. The scene that follows describes him having lunch with the AID Mission Chief Boger, a social friend. Smoke from Boger's pipe disturbs him, but what irritates him most is the fact that Boger is insensitive to the fact his pipe may be disturbing his companion. Melih simply retaliates by chain smoking cigarettes and blowing the smoke in Boger's direction, but the latter does not even catch on. The "thick-skinned American" is a frequently encountered image among elite circles abroad. Though it is a convenient prop to heap scorn upon, the sarcastic anti-Americanism of the upper class salons has had in fact very little to do with the manifestation of an anti-American ideology that nearly took the shape of a political movement in itself.

The bulk of Baykurt's novel dwells on a third category of anti-Americanism, that of the Turkish peasant's reaction to a project administered by Americans in a village and ultimately to Americans as a group. As such the book emerges as a case study of how anti-American attitudes are hatched and how they take shape and grow in a community that has been totally devoid of any engagement in ideological or even national issues. The description of this very process in a context free of political overtones yields some valuable clues toward understanding the dynamics of the phenomenon itself. It must be pointed out that the book itself was not written in a political vacuum, since Baykurt is one of the leading leftist writers in Turkey. But it must also be remembered that the novelist himself comes from a rural background and has served as a teacher in Anatolia. He has an insight into the mind of the Turkish peasant, whose world view he captures and accurately conveys without imposing any of his own intellectual categories on the characters he creates.

Briefly, the plot revolves around the disastrous implementation of a pilot project. The USAID Mission has funds and is mandated to undertake developmental activities in Turkey, but the experts realize that spreading the funds too thinly by starting up too many projects would not serve the purposes of public relations, especially in view of the mounting criticism in Turkey that American aid is not enough. A pilot project for rural development appears to be the best way to proceed. Accordingly, a village near the capital is chosen as the site and a large group consisting of Turkish officials and U.S. experts pays a visit there to identify the needs of the villagers and begin implementing the project.

The very first problem is to convince the villagers that the undertaking is for their benefit. They are suspicious particularly because high-ranking Turkish officials are involved in the presentation and the peasants cannot bring themselves to believe that the state can be so generous toward them. Their suspicions are further aroused because nobody has a clear idea of what is to be done. Because all such projects have to be designed to promote self-help schemes, the Americans are anxious to learn what the villagers want most. The villagers in turn suspect a hidden agenda and want to learn what lies behind abstract rhetoric promising them funds, machinery and vehicles. Like most peasants they are conservative and hence do not really wish to have any changes introduced in their village, especially at the behest of outsiders. Yet they are also curious about the promised aid and certainly do not wish to miss a possible good chance. Having internalized the dictum, "There's no free lunch," through dealing with government agents for generations, they comically offer to help the Americans by giving them free food and lodging.

The impasse is finally broken when one shrewd peasant tells the visitors that what the villagers want most is to level a hill that obstructs the morning sun thereby impeding the fast growth of produce. This, of course, would be a way to get rid of the outsiders by demanding of them an impossible task. The AID people however, are very happy to hear a suggestion and jump at the idea thinking that it would convince the villagers of both their seriousness of purpose and the extent of their technical resources. What follows is a number of unfortunate and farcical mistakes on the technical and the cultural side. The land gained from the mountain leveled is designed as a pineapple orchard, but is cordoned off and protected by a guard who prevents villagers from having access to the orchard placed on their own land. It later turns out that such vigilance in guarding the orchard had been necessitated solely by the desire to keep the dying trees a secret from the villagers and to avoid embarrassment. Like the pineapple trees, cattle and poultry brought from the United States cannot adapt to the climate and die. The experiment meets with total failure when a delegation consisting of the usual mix of Turkish and U.S. officials pays a visit to the village only to find the villagers attempting to create a hill where the old one used to stand.

In this somewhat satirical treatment is shown the gradual shift in the attitude of the villagers toward the United States. Their disappointment is certainly an important factor. However, what aggravates them is not the presence or involvement of Americans, but the constant lectures on the greatness of America by a retired Turkish general appointed to oversee the efforts. If America is so great, think the villagers, why should that be stressed in such a way as to make them look insignificant and powerless in their own village. Furthermore, with the resulting failure the United States loses credibility in their eyes. It is interesting, however, that there develops no animosity toward individual Americans; in fact, the villagers come to treat a young expert working with them as one of their own. They dislike, on the other hand, all the goods and materials the Americans have given them and begin reacting unfavorably to official symbols of America. A telling incident is the adverse reaction of one of the villagers to a bandage that has the insignia of USAID. So exasperated is he with the failure of American products that he discards the bandage and flees from the hospital where he was treated.

A fictional narrative of the kind discussed approaches the question of U.S. involvement from within the Turkish cultural context and in so doing offers a glimpse into the attitudes of certain segments of the society that a distanced outsider would be at a loss to evaluate. It clearly establishes certain categories under which anti-Americanism can be considered, and points to the contrast between rural and urban environments. In the village the U.S. involvement leads to a negative reaction only because an experiment fails. Individual Americans are treated as guests and are not considered as sinister agents of an evil force. Even if some of the more conservative villagers have misgivings and fears lest the women should begin imitating the "scanty" attire and outgoing manners of U.S. women, these do not become major issues.

However, a significant and permanent U.S. presence could be expected to lead inevitably to a cultural confrontation, for rural collectivities, in Anatolia as well as most other places in the world, happen to be protective of their local value culture. In the case of Turkey, a further point must be raised that attitudes in different villages around the country would differ significantly from one another on the scale of traditionalism as well as religious conservatism, and that responses to the codes governing the behavior of outsiders would accordingly vary.[8] Nevertheless, in any of these traditionalist communities the acceptance of outsiders is facilitated in proportion to the understanding that the differing codes of aliens do not pose a threat to the local moral order. It seems, therefore, safe to make the generalization that inward looking, apolitical communities are unlikely to develop anti-Americanism as a phenomenon distinctly different from the usual suspiciousness about all outsiders.

The attitude of a representative type belonging to the urban lower class is, however, significantly different. Kerim, the driver, is not only resentful of the U.S. presence but is inclined to view Americans collectively as a force dominating Turkey. It has to be taken into account that the driver does not come from a background that is different from that of the villagers. He is a representative, par excellence, of the first generation migrants from the village to urban shanty-towns. Can the difference of his attitude be attributed to the sui generis cultural milieu of the shanty-town? Does urban poverty, by virtue of its immediate and pronounced contrast with the lifestyle of the urban rich, politically sensitize and polarize people? If so, how does anti-Americanism come into the picture, if the object of envy is the Turkish bourgeoisie? All these questions ultimately lead us to a central one: is anti-Americanism basically a political rather than a cultural phenomenon whose rise is somehow correlated to communication and social mobilization?

It is with these questions in mind that it may be appropriate here to summarize some significant phases of Turkish political life during which the issue of anti-Americanism came to be a major question. Historically, Turkey's relations with the United States were of secondary importance until after World War II. The Marshall Plan aid was welcomed as much for its political value as its economic contribution. At the end of the war, the Soviet Union, representing the historical Russian menace for Turkey, refused to renew the 1925 Treaty of Friendship. For the Turkish government, the military aid agreement of 1947 meant a major step toward defending the country from external threat. It also marked the beginning of tensions and frustrations that have plagued Turkish-U.S. relations since.

The major issue of contention was the congressional demand for the right to supervise, restrict and terminate the administration of the aid. As George Harris has pointed out, "If there was one sensitive nerve in the Turkish body politic, it was according privileges to foreigners. Supervision implied control, and this in turn implied abandoning sovereignty."[9] While on the one hand the Turkish governments of the late 1940s and 1950s strove to enter into closer military cooperation with the United States, on the other hand they found themselves in a position to fight for greater latitude in the interpretation and administration of grants.

Unlike the common heritage of today's Third World countries, Turkey did not have a colonial past. Except for a brief period of occupation after World War I, it had never been a dependency but a colonial power itself. The Turkish sensitivity toward foreign interference stemmed from the fact that towards the end, the Ottoman Empire had fallen under European economic control and had been forced to give concessions to the extent of mortgaging the national resources and admitting special privileges to foreign nationals. It could be said that the Turks ultimately never forgave themselves for the loss of the empire. The ensuing nation-building program of the republic fostered a pride of Turkishness but was unable to erase from the collective memory the failure that put an end to all hopes of reviving the glory of an imperial past.

Another inheritance from the Ottoman era was the importance attached to public opinion. Unlike their predecessors, the nineteenth century Ottoman reformers had been successful precisely because they had paid attention to education and mobilizing public opinion. The tradition of political journalism established by the Ottoman reformist elite had continued in Turkey with the journalist assuming the role of translating abstract political issues for the benefit of the public. By the 1950s, issues such as the national will, independence, external threat and foreign interference had taken shape in the public consciousness. It was in such an ambience that the United States presence in Turkey rapidly increased following Turkey's accession to NATO in 1953. A decade or so later the number of American officials and dependents residing in Turkey would rise to 24,000.[10]

As would be expected, it was particularly the military presence that led to a number of problems. Unlike businessmen who reside abroad for furthering their own interest and unlike diplomats whose careers take them to foreign countries, the military, especially the lower ranks, have a more difficult time adjusting to different cultural environments, which usually have little appeal to them. The fact that U.S. servicemen stayed in their compounds, ate and drank the victuals supplied to them from abroad, and showed little interest in participating in the local social life became a major cause of resentment. Such resentment is noticeable in the wealthy Germany of the 1980s; in the underdeveloped Turkey of the 1950s this behavior, in itself, became a matter of serious concern, for it hurt the national pride. One critic called these compounds "little Americas," and the fact that Americans huddled together in such compounds was interpreted as stemming from their arrogance combined with a feeling of disgust for anything local.[11] Spurning Turkish hospitality was a sin that could not be forgiven, and it became a major factor in the shaping of the image of "the ugly American."

In this situation, offenses caused by individual Americans were magnified, generalized and interpreted as examples illustrative of U.S. arrogance. The Status of Forces Agreement granting certain rights to Americans based in Turkey exacerbated the situation. According to this agreement, Turkey would surrender the jurisdiction to the United States of any offense committed by U.S. military personnel while on duty.[12] The Turkish public considered this as being tantamount to waiving sovereign rights, and as a result, even minor incidents reported in the press took ominous proportions in people's minds. In the initial stages, therefore, an embryonic form of anti-Americanism came to exist in Turkey chiefly as a result of the U.S. military presence, stipulations attached to the agreements governing that presence, and cultural conflicts stemming from it. The stage was set for an increased manifestation of the phenomenon when further catalysts were added into the process.

In the radicalized Turkey of the 1960s and 1970s two such catalysts served to fuel largely latent feelings of hostility. One was the way in which the United States became a party in the Cyprus dispute. When in 1964 Turkey threatened to intervene in the wake of the Cypriot decision to establish general conscription for the Greek Cypriot defense forces, President Johnson wrote a letter of warning to avert a possible war between

Greece and Turkey. This famous letter, which has come to be known as the Johnson letter, gave rise to nationwide feelings of outrage even among people who would have disapproved of a military adventure. First, the letter was considered insulting, especially because it was, in the opinion of many Turks, too strongly worded. It was, moreover, addressed to Inönü, the elder statesman then serving as prime minister. Certain elite circles were scandalized by the undiplomatic bluntness of a "crass Texan." As such it served to reinforce the notion that Americans were basically arrogant. Second, the letter stated that "your NATO allies have not had a chance to consider whether they have an obligation to protect Turkey against the Soviet Union if Turkey takes a step which results in Soviet intervention without the full consent and understanding of its NATO allies."[13] In the eyes of many, this portion of the letter validated the leftist claims that the United States was not a dependable ally and its military agreements were so designed as to serve only U.S. defense interests; that is, Turkey would be sacrificed after the United States made use of Turkey's resources to divert Soviet forces and thus weaken any Soviet offensive in Northern Europe. Third, the statement "that the United States cannot agree to the use of any United States supplied equipment," pointed to the U.S. control of Turkish military capability and hence was viewed as being tantamount to U.S. interference with Turkish sovereign rights.

The Johnson letter established a mode of thinking in Turkey that profoundly affected Turkish perceptions of the United States. Later pressures from Washington, such as the Nixon administration's efforts to make the Turkish government ban poppy cultivation and the arms embargo in the wake of the Turkish occupation of Northern Cyprus in 1974 served as footnotes to reinforce a negative image of the United States in the public opinion. This is somewhat ironic because the latter two interventions entailed more than a mere warning which the Johnson letter did, and they aimed to force the Turkish government to make significant policy changes. Perhaps 1964 was Turkey's first experience with realpolitik vis-à-vis a superpower, that came as a shock. But a more likely explanation of the bitter reaction against the Johnson letter is the fact that by the end of the 1960s Turkey had become politically so polarized that there was little room to further intensify sharply delineated attitudes. By then, the United States had proven itself to the nationalist and Islamic right as well as to the radical left to be an undependable ally, and worse, an imperialist power which sought world domination by practicing extraterritorial law.

In a highly politicized society such as Turkey was in the 1960s and 1970s all major issues are bound to be related to domestic political dynamics, and are variously and relentlessly interpreted and redefined at different locations on the ideological map. Something so broad yet so universal as the criticism of the intruding outsider could serve various purposes and convincingly, too. Approached in this fashion, anti-Americanism could be said to be a prop or a metaphor rather than a governing ideology. It can be the manifestation of frustrations stemming from a variety of causes. It can also be used as a convenient means to validate ideological arguments. More likely, as has been argued, it stems from responses to particular events that are then magnified both in proportion to the U.S. presence and involvement in a country and in respect to the political developments at work there.

To give a somewhat hackneyed example, few people who knew anything about Iran could have been surprised to find an undercurrent of anti-Americanism in that country from the time of Mosaddeq through the reign of the Shah. The United States was held responsible for the overthrow of the Mosaddeq regime and was suspected to be the chief actor behind the scenes. External intervention against a government committed to nationalization of resources could only be dubbed as imperialistic. The reaction against the alleged U.S. interference in Iran's domestic politics, exacerbated by the widespread corruption among the upper echelons believed to be close to the Americans, was bound to elicit a negative response from a variety of groups including the intelligentsia. But the existing attitude towards the United States was reshaped and magnified by Khomeini whose crusade against the "Great Satan" was designed in no small measure to achieve solidarity for nation-building purposes utilizing sansculottes. In Turkey, anti-Americanism could not have been utilized for such nefarious ends despite the wishes of a small group of radical revolutionaries of the Baader-Meinhof type; it simply became a fashionable pursuit. In the words of a keen observer, "It would be no exaggeration to say that it became a prevalently fashionable attitude to be anti-American and blame the Americans for everything."[14]

Anti-Americanism was indeed employed by different groups belonging to diametrically opposite sides of the ideological spectrum. The intellectual left, unsurprisingly, focused on the economic side of the issue, blaming the United States for the growing foreign dependency of the Turkish economy, whereas, in fact, the real problem was the import substitution model of industrialization which was promoted and defended by the liberals, social democrats and moderate leftists themselves.[15] A great deal of noise was also made accusing U.S. multinationals of many nefarious deeds, such as conspiring to control the Turkish economy, but the economy was in fact suffering from periodic crises brought on by hard currency shortages, which in turn could be blamed on economic nationalism restricting the inflow of much needed foreign investment. Anti-Americanism, in this respect, had indeed become a prop, with the U.S. business establishment being blamed for the misdeeds committed by the Turkish capitalist whose interests were best served by the captive market created as a result of the economic policies so vigorously depended on by the left. The nationalist right, on their part, would not neglect to capitalize on an attitude that had become so fashionable as to gain a wide currency among the intellectuals. What better way was there for them to legitimize their rabid nationalism than by giving the appearance of impartiality? They coined the slogan "neither America nor Russia," and blamed the United States for subverting the national will by providing an example of effete liberalism. Another voice of complaint from the right was raised by the Islamic National Salvation Party followers who viewed any close ties with the West as being inimical to the preservation of indigenous values and public morals, but their objection failed to attract much attention.

The domestic political scene that facilitated the nurturing of anti-American attitudes was to a large extent influenced by the changes in the social and demographic map. In the fifty years between 1930 and 1980 the rural-urban ratio reversed itself.[16] The opportunity space in extended urban areas became commensurately narrower, especially in the aftermath of the economic crisis following the energy price hikes. Rural areas, in turn, continued to suffer from the chronic undercapitalization of the agricultural sector. In the meantime networks of communication, particularly the establishment of the national television network, helped to bring current political debates to the attention of the masses. Social and economic frustrations could now be blamed on specific governmental policies and protest could take the form of coherent political action. Critical attitudes toward and accusations against the United States that had been raging among the informed and elite circles could then trickle down to the masses and become a part of mass protest movements.

The issue of anti-Americanism also became inextricably involved in the intraelite rivalry in Turkey. As mentioned earlier, the power of the traditional elite consisting of civil bureaucracy and the upper echelons of the military was eroded with the rise of a wealthy class of industrialists. In the 1950s the policies of the government hastened the redistribution of resources and power by keeping the public sector salaries low in real terms. The establishment, in the form of a military-intellectual coalition, reacted to what they perceived to be a politician-capitalist conspiracy to erode the status of the traditional elite and to bring parvenus to a position of power. The ensuing military intervention in 1960 restored the power of civil bureaucracy and put the intellectuals in an influential position by appointing many university professors to governmental agencies and by constitutionalizing the special independent status of the universities.

But also at work was a process of de-elitization among the civil service ranks. With the establishment of large industrial companies, private banks and ultimately multinationals, civil service began losing the appeal it had for young cadres entering the professional workforce. The net effect was a fracture and then distancing between the lower and upper echelons of civil bureaucracy. The upper echelons had status and retained their elite position so as not to be so resentful of the emerging capitalist class. The young professionals, consisting of the brighter new graduates of universities, constituted a bridge between the remnants of the traditional elite and the industrialists. It was among these three groups that anti-Americanism manifested itself in the form of gentle but biting salon sarcasm. The de-elitized lower bureaucracy, however, was embittered and disappointed that their education and position in government service did not bring to them the social and economic benefits they had anticipated. They did become resentful of the industrialists, professionals, and entrepreneurs. Members of this group, whether they ultimately chose to sympathize with the right- or left-wing of the ideological spectrum, perceived a creeping and debilitating Americanism among the rich and the successful whom they dubbed as "collaborators."

The foregoing discussion points to the fact that, by virtue of not being a typical Third World country, Turkey has had an experience of anti-Americanism that does not fully fit the typology developed by Rubinstein and Smith.[17] I would even venture to say that anti-Americanism in Turkey never became an issue in itself, but was exploited to the advantage of various groups, legitimate and illegitimate, radical or conservative. Furthermore, it could be fairly stated that no Turkish government would help foster anti-American movements even though the political parties represented in the government, ironically, would often make use of anti-American slogans for electioneering purposes. Official disagreements with U.S. policies would not be voiced in a hostile fashion but would be registered through appropriate diplomatic channels.

The decision-makers and those belonging to the top echelons of the bureaucracy have proven, time and again, their professionalism and the responsible way in which the foreign business of the state is conducted. Prime Minister Anönü's measured response to the famous Johnson letter is a good example of how any hostility is avoided.[18]

Yet the foregoing does not point to a total absence of issue-oriented anti-Americanism. Critical even hostile reactions to United States policies have in the past arisen in informed, if not elite, circles, but in the Turkish case they would soon spread among the people and become an issue in the public opinion. As such, reactions to any U.S. policy that was viewed as being contradictory to Turkish national interests became a concern in the public opinion, but no violent protest movements utilizing such dissatisfactions were orchestrated by the elites. Ideological anti-Americanism, on the other hand, was certainly formulated by the radical fringe of the intellectuals, only some of whom belonged to the elite. But the influence of this group did not extend upward toward the government but downward toward revolutionary organizations. The radical revolutionaries of the left and to a lesser extent those of the right received those ideological formulations and used them as a legitimizing framework to plot their political action. The result was that by the end of the 1970s Turkey was plunged into a chaotic situation, engulfed in terrorism carried out by armed extremists of all camps. Unpleasant as the situation was, it did not lead to a mobilization among the elite or the masses along revolutionary lines, though it posed a threat to the country as a whole by increasing the tensions between legitimate sympathizers of the right- and the left-wing causes. Finally, instrumental anti-Americanism has no more place in Turkey than it does in any other country belonging to the Western alliance. In the wake of the Iranian revolution many outsiders began questioning the political stability of Turkey. Their doubts and fears were increased because of the rising violence in Turkey at the end of the 1970s. Implied was a fear of a revolutionary regime that would bring Turkey into the antiwesternist orbit. Recent developments have shown how different the Turkish situation was compared to that of Iran. Although extremist organizations encouraged ideological polarization and the attendant violence stemming largely from socioeconomic frustrations in Turkey, their efforts were not focused on creating a cultural xenophobia. More importantly, it is difficult to imagine a regime in Turkey that would actively try to unleash more movements. In this context it must be remembered that the revived traditions of statecraft dictated extreme caution in dealing with urban masses. The Ottoman ruling elite, for example, would always carefully avoid seeking the support of the potentially disruptive forces among urban masses.[19]

It is difficult to predict whether there will be a revival of any substantial anti-American sentiment in Turkey. As long as there is no serious policy conflict in the international scene between Turkey and the United States, a widespread reaction to the U.S. global role is not likely to occur in the Turkish public opinion. Among intellectuals, however, U.S. economic policies will remain a central subject of debate and criticism. If, for example, the continued high interest rates triggered by the U.S. deficit begin to affect Turkey's developmental efforts seriously, then it would not be surprising to hear voices raised in protest. But the type of anti-Americanism witnessed among the intellectuals has the properties of a heated debate rather than the makings of a dangerous political action. External evaluation of the United States in such quarters may even be beneficial.

NOTES

1. Fakir Baykurt, *Amerikan Sargisi*, 2nd ed. (Ankara: Bilgi, 1969), pp. 26–27.

2. The Marshall Plan was proclaimed in June 1947 and the aid agreement was signed in Ankara on July 12, 1947. Turkey officially joined NATO on February 18, 1952 "after a compromise was devised to create a separate South European Command under an American general," in retrospect somewhat ironically "at the insistence of the Turkish government, which was opposed to a separate Middle East command assigned to a British general." Cf. George S. Harris, *Troubled Alliance* (Washington, D.C. and California: AEI and Hoover Institution, 1972), pp. 43–44.

3. Ankara had a population of only 289,000 in 1950, increasing to 650,000 in 1960.

4. Traditionally Turkey did not have a "bourgeois" class. The suspicion whereby "intermediate classes" were viewed is mentioned in Serif Mardin, "Turkey: the Transformation of an Economic Code," in Ergun Özbudun and Aydin Ulusan, eds., *The Political Economy of Income Distribution in Turkey* (New York and London: Holmes and Meier, 1980), pp. 43–45.

5. In addition to politically engaged literary works, there appeared in the 1960s a large number of interpretive works that dealt with U.S. presence and involvement in Turkey. By far the most comprehensive one is by Nevzat Üstün, *Türkiye 'deki Amerika* (*The American in Turkey*), 3 vols. (Istanbul, 1967–69), which conveys the broad range of accusations against Americans living in Turkey. Treatments linking the U.S. military presence in Turkey to the U.S.'s global economic ambitions constituted another major genre of studies critical of the United States; cf. Türkkaya Ataör, *Amerika, NATO ve Türkiye*, 2nd ed. (Ankara, 1969). A concise treatment of the increasing activism among the leftist intelligentsia is to be found in David Barchard, "The Intellectual Background to Radical Protest in Turkey in the 1960s," in William M. Hale, ed., *Aspects of Modern Turkey* (London and New York: Bowker, 1976), especially pp. 27–34.

6. Baykurt, p. 27.

7. *Ibid.*

8. For local value culture in Turkey, cf. Ahmet Evin, "Communitarian Structures and Social Change," in A. Evin, ed., *Modern Turkey: Continuity and Change* (Opladen: Leske and Budrich, 1984), pp. 18–23.

9. Harris, p. 27.

10. *Ibid.*, p. 167.

11. Cf. Jacob M. Landau, *Radical Politics in Modern Turkey* (Leiden: Brill, 1974), p. 28.

12. Cf. Harris, pp. 57–60.

13. The text of the letter was published in *The Middle East Journal* 20 (1966), 386–88.

14. Cf. Landau, p. 27.

15. A concise treatment of foreign dependency is to be found in Henri Barkey, "Crises of the Turkish Political Economy," in Ahmet Evin, ed. *Modern Turkey*, pp. 47–63. For domestic political views, cf. Ergun Özbudun, "Income Distribution as an Issue in Turkish Politics," in Özbudun and Ulusan, eds., *The Political Economy*, pp. 55–82.

16. By 1980, half the population became urban, cf. Michael N. Danielson and Rusen Keles, "Urbanization," in Özbudun and Ulusan, op. cit., pp. 269–309.

17. See Chapter I, *supra*.

18. Cf. *The Middle East Journal* 20 (1966), 388–93.

19. Serif Mardin, "Ideology and Religion in the Turkish Revolution," *International Journal of Middle East Studies* 2 (1971), 197–211.

7

Anti-Americanism in South Asia: A Symbolic Artifact

Ainslie Embree

Many knowledgeable people, including both Americans and South Asians, deny that anti-Americanism exists in the subcontinent to the extent that would make it a meaningful subject for scholarly discussion. Where it does exist, they argue, it tends to be among small groups who are not representative of either the majority of the people or of those who exercise power and influence within the society. Anti-Americanism is seen as the product of easily identifiable ideological commitments that are not a significant component of the national consensus. The evidence used for the denial of anti-Americanism as a serious factor in social or political life is quickly marshaled: easy personal relations between the peoples of the different countries of the subcontinent and those of the United States; the relative accessibility to South Asian countries to scholars for academic research; the attraction of the United States for South Asians for academic study and careers; the popularity of U.S. culture, especially in its most readily accessible forms, such as music, clothing styles, and films; and, of course, the pronouncements of South Asian politicians of desire for friendship with the United States. Along these lines, it is not very difficult to make a fairly persuasive denial of anti-Americanism as a significant force in South Asia, as it undoubtedly is, for example, in Iran.

There are, however, many careful observers, both in the United States and in the South Asian countries, who present a very different analysis, arguing that anti-Americanism is a dominant mode of expression in the political cultures of a number of South Asian countries. They discount the significance of the popularity of the United States for emigration and higher education as evidence of rational economic choices. The receptivity of South Asians to popular U.S. culture can be read, they argue, as an aspect of the universalizing of culture, or of its homogenization, in the modern world. The ready acceptance of what we may identify as "American" culture is, simply, a response to modernity which, somewhat by historic accident, speaks with a U.S. accent in South Asia. They point instead to the indubitable reality of other reactions to the United States. The burning of the U.S. embassy in Pakistan in 1979 and the destruction of the U.S. libraries in a number of Pakistani cities, then and at earlier periods, are regarded as more accurate indices of popular and, indeed, of government opinion. The continual public attacks on U.S. policies that characterize much of Indian journalism and Indian academic life provide a counterweight to the appeal of the United States for fulfillment of personal career goals. Criticism of U.S. policies is not confined to private channels; Indian officials including the Prime Minister and the Foreign Secretary find occasion to criticize U.S. policy in a fashion that their U.S. counterparts would reserve only for nations that were clearly defined as implacable opponents. One gets the impression that outside the members of the scholarly community who have a professional interest in India, a fairly consistent reading is that in India, and perhaps most South Asian countries, there is an almost automatic anti-Americanism.

Here, passing reference must be made to an intriguing element in the situation: the very different attitude toward the Soviet Union and the United States. This aspect of political life will be referred to in this chapter as it has been in the Rubinstein-Smith paper, but a statistic that may not be altogether accurate points to a significant difference. In India, there are two Indo-American Friendship societies; there are about 1500 Indo-Soviet Friendship societies.

It is always tempting to say that both polar positions—the one that denies anti-Americanism in South Asia and the one that affirms it—are wrong, and that the truth is found somewhere in between. I do not think, however, that this is a useful analysis of a complex issue.

Instead of saying that the polar positions are wrong, I think it is nearer the truth to say that both are right in their analysis insofar as what they are reporting is present in the social and political experience of the South Asian countries. Of the two analyses, however, the one that is most significant is that which emphasizes the reality of anti-Americanism.

The factors emphasized by observers who do not find anti-Americanism an important element in South Asia are not those that ·on balance contribute greatly to policy formation or to the decision-making process. Personal relationships, a liking for the cultural artifacts of another society, recognition of a country's educational achievements and of their pragmatic value in career advancement, all those realities that are certainly present in South Asian attitudes toward the United States, are neutral agents, available as background when a government seeks to create an *entente cordiale*; but anti-Americanism is a more active force, more amenable to a variety of uses. "As a political instrument for manipulating public opinion," as Rubinstein and Smith have pointed out in their essay, "anti-Americanism has been a godsend to Third World regimes." But it has been in South Asia a godsent instrument—or devilsent—depending upon your point of view, to more than just the ruling regimes. It has proved at least as useful to opposition parties as to the ruling regime and it has been used with great effect by groups within universities, for example, to achieve their goals, as well as in the more formal political arenas.

The usages of anti-Americanism in South Asia parallel in some curious ways the role of anti-communism in the United States. On one level, anti-Americanism can be used, as was anti-communism, to appeal to a mob with all sorts of fears and passions; anti-Americanism can be used to get a mob to burn the American library, just as anti-communism could be used by McCarthy. But as Nathan Glazer has pointed out in a recent article, anti-communism could become central to intellectuals, not because they shared the passions of the mob, but because they saw, in a way that the McCarthyites did not, that the Soviet Union represented a radical threat to their understanding of freedom.[1] In some such fashion, anti-Americanism for South Asian intellectuals comes to represent opposition to forces that they regard as destructive of their national hopes and aspirations. It is this aspect of anti-Americanism in South Asia that seems to me to be of particular interest, from the scholarly point of view of a concern with either intellectual history or the political process.

To put it another way, anti-Americanism has become for many people of the South Asian countries a symbolic representation for aspects of the relationship of their countries with each other, with the international political and economic order, including the rivalry of the two superpowers, and, of very great importance, a symbolic representation of their understanding of their own culture and their place in it. When one speaks in these terms, there is, I suppose an implicit recognition that one is speaking of the literate, newspaper-reading public; more precisely of the professional classes, politicians, teachers, journalists, lawyers, civil servants. They are, of course, differentiated from the great mass of the people, but they articulate with symbols the feelings and aspirations of the masses to a far greater degree than we may realize. Raymond Firth has remarked that "Man does not live by symbols alone, but man orders and interprets his reality by symbols, and even reconstructs it,"[2] and it is the use of anti-Americanism as an aid to the ordering and interpreting the reality of national life in South Asia that is of particular interest. I do not wish to suggest that it is the most important symbolic artifact used in this fashion, but only that it has a more significant role than has generally been recognized. A symbol has been defined as something used "to index meanings that are not inherent in, nor discernible, from the object itself,"[3] and this seems to describe quite accurately the function of anti-Americanism in South Asia. It is an indicator of attitudes toward the United States and evaluations of U.S. policies in quite different terms from those that appear on the surface. A few years ago, for example, a group of legislators in Uttar Pradesh denounced a U.S. anthropologist for defaming Indian womanhood, by noting, in a book written years before, that polyandry was an accepted social practice among certain groups in Tehri-Garhwal. On the surface level, the charge was a comic absurdity, but on other levels it was resonant with the resentments at what Indians have regarded as Western distortions of their culture. *Mother India* is a forgotten title among Americans; it is not among Indians. Anti-Americanism becomes a kind of prism that refracts in unexpected ways resentments and hostilities that historically have little to do with the United States.

Not long ago, a colleague and I taught a course for which the reading list, somewhat unintentionally, illustrates the sources of some of those resentments. We called the course "India in the Western Historical Imagination," and the readings were drawn largely from travellers' accounts, memoirs, and generalized interpretations by Westerners of South Asian civilization. Some of the accounts express a deep sympathy for Indian culture; many are stridently critical, epitomized in the famous passage in which Karl Marx spoke of Indian life "exhibiting its degradation in the fact that man, the sovereign of nature, fell down on his knees in adoration of Hanuman, the monkey and Sabbala, the cow."[4]

For Marx as for a host of others, India served the important function in the Western historical imagination of defining the West over against Asia; it has become the *Other* that the West used to understand itself. Whether Westerners praised India for its spirituality and its high creative achievements, sought it for its wealth, or denigrated it for what seemed barbarous and inhuman customs, its value was in relation to the West. India, Hegel remarked, "as a Land of Desire forms an essential element in general history. From the ancient times downwards, all nations have directed their wishes and longings to gaining access to this land of marvels." As a result of this interest in India, the English became lords of the land on behalf of all Europeans since, Hegel continued, "it is the necessary fate of Asiatic Empires to be subjected to Europeans."[5] I am not suggesting that people who are anti-American have been moved to become so by passages such as this, but Hegel speaks for an attitude deeply rooted in Western perceptions of India.

It is not fanciful to suggest that modern South Asians are rejecting the role assigned to them by the West of being the Other, the Land of Desire being used by the West to define itself. I am not thinking here primarily of the historic reality of economic and political exploitation by the imperial powers, which is an element in anti-Americanism, but the more indefinable sense that the United States is the legatee, not so much of Western imperialism as of the Western interpretation of Indian, and by extension, of all South Asian cultures.

This may not seem either sensible or fair, for it is an obvious anachronism to locate the United States among the imperial exploiters of South Asia; but if anti-Americanism is a symbolic artifact, it is an expression of the reality of the relationship with the United States. Two points made in the Rubinstein-Smith chapter are worth stressing in this connection. One is that we must start with the history, cultural values, and political systems of the various South Asian countries in order to understand both the origins and content of their anti-Americanism. This is, in fact, a very complex task and, if done with anything like the rigor the issue requires, would be a major task of cultural reconstruction. All that can be attempted here is to note some specific aspects of anti-Americanism where this understanding seems to be of special importance. What must be kept in mind is that much of the writing on South Asia, both past and present, does in fact endeavor to explain contemporary attitudes, including anti-Americanism, by reference to religion, culture, and the values of the elites. Perhaps the best of such recent books, because of the elegance of their literary style, are those by V.S. Naipaul. *Journey Among Believers* gives special attention to Islam in its South Asian context as a heuristic device for explaining Pakistani attitudes, and he has treated Hinduism in an even more devastating way in *India: A Wounded*

Civilization. The flaw in such works is not the attempt to relate contemporary attitudes to religious and cultural values, which is a necessary procedure, but a misreading of the data of historical experience.

The second general point to be made in assessing the nature of anti-Americanism as a symbolic expression is that it is a reaction to signals and meanings that are not always those that are readily identified in discourse. Many of these responses, to complicate matters further, are products of the previous factor, a nation's own cultural values and history. An example that comes to mind is the opposition that was voiced to the Peace Corps in India. Very frequently the volunteers were characterized as CIA agents, and not just by those who had a strong ideological commitment against the United States. The truth is that the whole concept of the Peace Corps, of sending young and unskilled Americans on a much-publicized mission to offer help was offensive to the national pride of many Indians. It was easier to use a well-known and appealing symbol of U.S. interference in another country's affairs, the CIA, than to articulate a perfectly rational grievance.

The illustration from the history of the Peace Corps is a reminder that the form and content of anti-Americanism may differ very considerably among the six countries of South Asia (Pakistan, India, Nepal, Bhutan, Bangladesh, Sri Lanka), since in some of them, contrary to Indian example, the Peace Corps still exists. Generalizations about anti-Americanism of the kind made above are applicable, with modifications, to all six countries (although Bhutan would probably not supply much data even to a zealous researcher); but then disparities between them are so great that attention would have to be given to them individually for a comprehensive study of the nature and origins of anti-Americanism in South Asia. Since this is manifestly impossible, given the limitations of both knowledge and space, a brief sketch must suffice of anti-Americanism at different periods in regard to a few issues in India and Pakistan. In doing so, the "typology of anti-Americanism," as delineated in the Rubinstein-Smith chapter, will be kept in mind, as will the general observations noted above on anti-Americanism as symbolic of values and attitudes deeply rooted in the cultures of both countries and the response, very largely on the basis of this cultural understanding, to the values and policies of the United States.

It is often suggested that when India became independent in 1947 a fund of goodwill existed between the two countries and that it was only gradually that U.S. policies led to the growth of anti-Americanism in India. This is not an altogether accurate reading. The United States had not impinged much on India before 1947, despite the great sympathy for the nationalist movement that existed among a number of groups in the United States, particularly liberal church people, but strains developed very soon between the two countries. The first important symptom of anti-American feeling was an example of what the Rubinstein-Smith chapter has called "issue-oriented anti-Americanism." This had to do with the actions of the United States in the United Nations debate on Kashmir in 1948. To Nehru, it appeared that the Americans were backing the Pakistanis in order to appease the Muslim world, which had been angered by their policies in regard to Palestine. The United States, he wrote to Mrs. Pandit, had "played a dirty role."[6] Nehru's private evaluation in the years that followed became widespread in the India media.

For Indo-U.S. relations, the Kashmir negotiations set the stage almost as much as they did for Indo-Pakistan relations, and issue-oriented anti-Americanism soon merged with what the conference paper has called ideological and instrumental anti-Americanism. In letters to his confidants, Nehru characterized Americans as "immature in their political thinking," noting that "especially in their dealings with Asia, they show a lack of understanding which is surprising."[7] Later he was to say that Americans are "more hysterical as a people than almost any others except the Bengalis"; in contrast, the Russians "remain calm and collected."[8]

In the early years of independence, Indians still thought of Great Britain as a great power and were inclined to see the Americans as following an anti-Indian lead at British instigation; but very soon, the burden of the evils of imperialism were shifted to the Americans. Long before independence, Indian nationalists had accused Great Britain of favoring Muslim interests at the expense of Hindu, or, as they would have said, of larger Indian concerns, and partition was seen as the final fruit of this policy of divide and conquer. The Kashmir issue led to the charge of pro-Muslim leanings being transferred to the United States. The more secular, or at least more sophisticated, were careful to speak of the United States as being pro-Pakistan, rather than pro-Muslim, but it is difficult to escape the conclusion that an appeal was being made to very deep antipathies rooted in religion, race, and culture. The United States begins to emerge as a power inimical to the values and interests of India.

In the development of anti-Americanism in India as a symbol for India's fears, aspirations, and insecurities, the role of two individuals, one American and one Indian, may be mentioned. In a crucial period, John

Foster Dulles epitomized for Indians the U.S. attempt to weaken India, for anything that strengthened Pakistan was understood to be directed against India. Dulles's denunciation of nonalignment as hypocritical and immoral was only a confirmation of a new imperialism that sought conquest through both military and financial aid to weaker countries. The other actor on the world stage at this period who helped to give anti-Americanism special content was Krishna Menon. A close study of this enigmatic figure would, I am convinced, show that he was not, as now suggested, expressing his own idiosyncratic views, but that his popularity stemmed from his faithful reflection of an anti-Americanism that was an essential component in the social and political attitudes of modern India. The acerbic arrogance that repelled Americans, especially the professional diplomats and politicians, was read by Indians as a timely statement of India's importance on the world scene, an assertion of principles of justice and morality that had long been trampled upon by the West in its dealing with the rest of the world. During this period, there does not appear to have been any disagreement between Menon and Nehru on substantive issues; the difference was in style and mode of discourse, and, for Indians, Menon's style put India center stage, where it belonged by right of culture and achievement.

This is the point of a comment Nehru made after he had returned from his first visit to the United States. Nehru apparently had taken at face value many of the effusive speeches of welcome that had been made, and, as his biographer points out, he was "human enough to be piqued" when he discovered that visiting statesmen from other countries were greeted in much the same style. "I must say," he wrote to his sister, "that the Americans are either very naive or singularly lacking in intelligence. They go through the identical routine whether it is Nehru or the Shah of Iran or Liaquat Ali. . . . Having been trained in a school of more restrained language and action, I am afraid I do not appreciate this kind of thing."[9] Two elements in the anti-Americanism of India come through here. One is annoyance that India is equated with lesser countries, especially Pakistan. The other element may seem trivial, but in fact appears to be of considerable importance in giving content to anti-Americanism. When he spoke of being trained in a school of more restrained language, what he was referring to, of course, was not the national heritage of India, but the British inheritance. It is one of the ironies of history that when Indians speak of the vulgarity and hysteria of Americans, of their immaturity and lack of diplomatic finesse, they are claiming as their own a style that the British had for generations impressed upon them as the one that distinguished and legitimized them as a ruling class, in contrast to the inferiority of Indians themselves.

What is involved in this kind of reaction in India to U.S. politics and culture is an important, but not often noticed, result of the imperial experience. Perhaps one of the most persistent legacies of successful imperial rule is that when indigenous elites come to power they bring with them an admiration for the values and attitudes of their former rulers. A not inconsiderable factor in Indian anti-Americanism is a reflection of British attitudes toward the United States, the curious compound of social snobbery toward the vulgarians and of Fabian socialist criticism of U.S. capitalism.

What the Kashmir issue makes clear, however, at least by hindsight, is that there were genuine differences in national interests between the United States and India. The Rubinstein-Smith paper speaks of major areas of disagreement between the Third World and the U.S., but disagreement may be too weak a word to describe the actual situation. What was involved then and since was, very often, a genuine clash of national interests, with both India and the United States pursuing policies with conflicting goals. One might argue that the United States is too ready to set forth its policy goals in a fashion that stresses confrontation and conflict, but it can also be argued that India's unwillingness to see that U.S. and Indian national interests may come in conflict has led to greater misunderstanding on her part than was necessary.

This was something of what Dean Acheson had in mind when he said that Nehru was one of the most difficult men with whom he ever had to deal.[10] In the pre-Independence period, the history of the tortuous negotiations between the Indian National Congress, the British Government, and Jinnah were often marked by the unwillingness of the Congress to see that all parties had legitimate interests, and that, this being the case, compromise was necessary. On the same model in Indo-U.S. relations, India has often seemed to be unable to recognize that the United States as a great power has legitimate global interests which she must pursue, and that at times these intrude into the region that India is inclined to consider her proper sphere of interest. This is an important aspect of the Indian concern with U.S. relations with Pakistan. The United States has seldom made clear that she recognizes India's legitimate national interests, and this has undoubtedly exacerbated the mood of anti-Americanism.

That there has been a genuine clash of national interests is apparent even from a cursory listing of some of the major issues in the relations between the United States and India in the post-Independence period. While the ill-feeling engendered by the Kashmir dispute did not cause the later problems, most of the basic elements that gave form and substance to anti-Americanism were present. In this connection, it is important to keep in mind that just as the Kashmir dispute had very great relevance for India's identity as a nation, so did many of the other issues to a greater or lesser degree.

Goa provided an example where foreign policy merging with a domestic issue made anti-Americanism almost synonymous with patriotism. Its denunciation of the takeover of Goa put the United States in direct opposition to all shades of Indian political opinion, which had been vociferous in demanding the end of Portuguese rule in the subcontinent. Goa was the most Europeanized segment of the subcontinent, with a Christian population, created, it was widely believed, by the methods of the Inquisition. For the rest of the world, the takeover of Goa appeared to be a fairly simple case of territorial aggression; for Indians it was an assertion of nationhood and culture. As friendly commentators noted, "The necessity of state demanded the ultimate incorporation of Portuguese territories into India: A corporate morality superior to law, and based in this case on the axiom that nationalism must prevail over colonialism, governed India's action."[11]

One of the odder aspects of Indo-U.S. relations concerns what may be called the China question. In the early 1950s, when U.S. policy opposed the recognition of the new government of China, Indian politicians and publicists excoriated the United States for its hostility to the Chinese Communists. *Hindi-Chinni bhai-bhai* was contrasted with U.S. policy which, it was alleged, was aimed at continuing the Western domination of Asia. Both ideological and instrumental anti-Americanism colored Indian rhetoric. Then the great shift took place: the India–China War altered the perspective from which India viewed her Himalayan neighbor. What the Indians had urged in the 1950s became a reality in the 1970s with the new U.S. opening to China. But now, U.S. friendship with China was seen by Indians as a threat to India, and much anti-Americanism in the 1970s saw the new China policy as deliberately aimed at India by the United States.

Discussion of anti-Americanism and the China question leads inevitably to U.S. and Indian relations with the Soviet Union. On the issue of whether or not anti-Americanism in India is actually fostered by the Soviet Union, the answer must surely be "of course," and left at that. But to the question of how important Soviet initiative is in creating anti-Americanism, the answer is both ambiguous and tentative. Certainly the

Soviets cannot be given credit for its pervasiveness, which as I have tried to argue, has to be seen in the context of the Indian cultural and historical experience. Perhaps the most useful approach to the subject is through a few rather schematic observations. The first is that, from the Indian side, there is little recognition that U.S. attitudes toward the Soviet Union are not based on a simple-minded anti-communism, despite the publicity given in high places to the concept of an empire of evil. Much opposition toward the Soviet Union on the part of the United States is to be understood in terms of great power rivalry, which would exist if both shared identical economic and political systems, as was the case with European rivalries in the nineteenth century. Second, among Indian intellectuals of either the left or right there is very little sense of the Soviet political system as a radical threat to human freedom, as one finds in both Europe and the United States. Even when this is recognized in India's intellectual circles, it is not regarded as a matter of ultimate concern. For these reasons, Indian politicians and intellectuals, including Nehru and Mrs. Gandhi, have misunderstood the U.S. reaction to the Soviet Union. Indians see no inconsistency in belaboring the United States for its friendship with the squalid dictators of Central America while stressing their own friendship with the Soviet Union. No significant segment of Indian intellectuals has ever questioned their government's commitment to the Soviet Union, in terms of political morality, as have U.S. intellectuals about their government's support of dictators.

Anti-Americanism in India, when it has a Soviet referent, is remarkably free from ambiguity and self-doubt. The Soviet Union has usually sided with India in matters that were of great moment to India; India has sided with the Soviet Union in matters of concern to them. John Foster Dulles, as we have noted, is a stereotypical figure in anti-Americanism, especially for his insistence that those who were not for us are against us, but Nehru enunciated the same principle when he declared, in relation to Goa, that support of India is the "acid test by which we can judge the policies of other countries."[12] The United States has time and again failed the acid test, while the Soviets have taken it with ease. When this is added to immense Soviet military and economic cooperation, it is not difficult to understand why the Soviet Union is perceived as more friendly toward India and more of a force for world peace than is the United States. The Soviets, as Indians have not failed to point out, do not have a base in the Indian Ocean comparable to Diego Garcia.

Many points of strain in Indo-U.S. relations have led to anti-

Americanism, but even in cataloguing them one is driven back to the conclusion that they are made to serve a persistent and pervasive anti-Americanism rather than causing it. Economic aid, for example, in the years when it was at its height, was a fertile source of anti-American sentiment. This was partly because of the dependency relationship which it created, but it was also because there was always the suspicion that the aid was intended to force India to move in directions that were not in her own best interests. The dispute over the Bokaro steel mill is an example of an issue where the Indian perception was that for ideological reasons the United States refused to help the growth of the public sector. Much the same kind of reading was given to U.S. opposition to IMF loans in the 1980s. On another level, serious and thoughtful Indian commentators have seen the U.S. refusals to supply nuclear fuel to India as a desire to prevent India's economic development.

Any discussion of anti-Americanism in India would be incomplete without at least a reference to the same phenomenon in Pakistan, if, for no other reason, than so much of it in India has been justified because of the alleged U.S. assistance to Pakistan. One might expect, if one were familiar only with Indian sources, that Pakistanis would be pro-American, but there have been far more dramatic examples of anti-Americanism in Pakistan than in India, including the burning of the embassies and the destruction of the American U.S.I.S. libraries. Pakistan has also been far less welcoming to such academic enterprises as the Fulbright program than has India. On the other hand, perhaps because the press is much more controlled, there is less continuous public expression of anti-Americanism. There is, however, an undercurrent that is fairly open and it is possible to identify certain general characteristics.

A common theme of anti-Americanism in Pakistan is that the country and its leaders have been betrayed by the Americans, often in the service of Indian interests. The violence against U.S. property may have been, in the terms of the Rubinstein-Smith paper, instrumental, that is, used by the regime for its own ends, but it was also an expression of popular frustration and anger. Such moments occurred after the India–China war, when the United States seemed to be proffering help to India that could be used against Pakistan. The 1965 war between India and Pakistan led to deeper anti-American feeling, for once more the United States appeared to have betrayed Pakistan by cutting off military assistance.

An important feature of anti-Americanism in Pakistan was demonstrated on both occasions, when criticism of the United States was turned against the military regime. The charge was made by Ayub's opponents that he betrayed Pakistan to serve U.S. interests. This charge was made even more vociferously after the 1972 Bangladesh succession, when U.S. failure to honor its commitments was seen as one of the major reasons for the debacle in the eastern wing of the country.

Under the present regime, since the attacks by the mobs on the embassy and the American libraries in 1979, anti-Americanism has not been particularly overt, but there are indications that it is playing a quite potent role in current politics. Opposition groups, especially in the universities, are sharply critical of the United States for what they regard as the bolstering up of a corrupt and tyrannical regime, and it is conceivable that this could link up with other sources of discontent that have an anti-American focus. One of these is the flood of Afghan refugees and the problems that have attended the guerrilla war in Afghanistan. Opposition groups argue that the war in Afghanistan serves only U.S. interests, and that the Zia regime is forced, because of its dependency on the United States, to acquiesce. From a rather different direction, advocates of a more rigorous program of Islamization point with admiration to the success of the Khomeini regime in ending U.S. domination of Iran. Another source of discontent is with U.S. policy in the Middle East, which seems not only to be against the interests of Islamic countries, but to threaten the prosperity of the Gulf countries with their demand for Palestinian labor and skills. To a quite remarkable degree, the economic well-being of Pakistan depends upon a fragile political and economic arrangement that U.S. policies might destroy.

It is not difficult to equate all that is corrupt and un-Islamic with U.S. influence in Pakistan. It is possible that anti-Americanism in Pakistan, although guarded in its expression, might fit into the category of what the Rubinstein-Smith paper has categorized as a revolutionary variant. Nationalism, Islam, and a yearning for political freedom, may find in anti-Americanism a useful instrument.

In conclusion, we turn to the question that has been behind our discussion: Does anti-Americanism matter? A preliminary observation must be, I think, that it does matter, and that it matters more to the people of South Asia, particularly the people of India and Pakistan, than it does to the United States. I stress this because there is a tendency to suppose, both in the United States and abroad, that anti-Americanism is our problem, something about which we should be concerned, and about which we should take action. But anti-Americanism should be of concern to the South Asian countries (indeed to all countries) because as it becomes pervasive in a society it can force a nation in directions in which, in its own self-interest, it should not go. Anti-Americanism can foreclose options, just at the moment when national leadership should have the flexibility to make decisions based on the nation's self-interest and not have to make decisions based on a distorted view of reality. One suspects that the present Indian leadership is aware of the dangers of the anti-Americanism that it has sometimes tacitly encouraged.

Anti-Americanism should be of concern to the United States for the same reason because in our dealings with other peoples our opportunities for constructive action are limited if our overtures are suspect before they are made. Beyond this pragmatic consideration is a broader one that was enunciated long ago: a decent respect for the opinion of mankind. Not to respect the opinions of mankind surely implies a lack of respect for our own values and institutions. If anti-Americanism is grounded in a correct perception of our policies, and if those policies are based on a regional understanding of our national self-interest, then we can at least endeavor to explain our reasoning. If, on the other hand, anti-Americanism is based on erroneous readings of our purposes, or deliberate distortions, respect for ourselves and for the opinion of mankind requires that we give serious attention to the anatomy of one of the most significant political phenomena of our time.

NOTES

1. *The New York Times Book Review*, February 26, 1984.
2. Charles D. Elder and Roger W. Cobb, *The Political Uses of Symbols* (New York: Longman, 1983), p. 28.
3. *Ibid.*
4. Karl Marx, "The British Rule in India," *New York Daily Tribune*, June 25, 1853.
5. Georg Hegel, *Philosophy of History*.
6. *Quoted in* S. Gopal, *Jawaharlal Nehru* (Cambridge: Harvard University Press, 1979) vol. 2, pp. 27–28.
7. *Ibid.*, p. 63.
8. *Ibid.*, p. 101.
9. *Ibid.*, p. 63.
10. *Ibid.*, p. 60.
11. Charles H. Heimsath and Surjit Mansingh, *A Diplomatic History of Modern India* (Bombay: Allied Publishers, 1971), p. 331.
12. Quoted in Heimsath and Mansingh, *Ibid.*, p. 328.

8

Anti-Americanism in Southeast Asia: The Malaysian Case

Robert C. Horn

The study of anti-Americanism in a country such as Malaysia might seem in some ways to be of limited intrinsic interest or academic value. After all, Malaysia is a small country, containing a population of only about 14 or 15 million people living in less than 130,000 square miles of territory (only slightly larger than the U.S. state of New Mexico). It is located in Southeast Asia, a region the United States has been at best ambivalent toward since the end of the Vietnam war (and perhaps earlier). A member of the regional organization ASEAN, the Association of Southeast Asian Nations, Malaysia has clearly been perceived by Washington as the least significant of the five member countries: the U.S. has deep historical ties to the Philippines as well as important military facilities at Clark air base and Subic naval base; long-standing military relations have existed with Thailand and currently it is the "front-line" state next to Vietnam-dominated Kampuchea; Indonesia has long been viewed as the future dominant power in the region because of its size and rich resources; and Singapore stands as one of the world's leading commercial centers and a development "success story." Malaysia, not surprisingly, ranks as the lowest of these five in quantity of U.S. aid received and in trade conducted.

For its part, too, the foreign economic and political policies of successive Malaysian administrations have seemed to eschew a more substantial relationship with the United States. Although 16 percent of the country's foreign trade is with the United States, significantly more is conducted with Japan—23 percent—and with the Pacific region (exclusive of the U.S. and Japan)—28 percent. Recent statements by Malaysia's Prime Minister, Datuk Seri Mahathir Mohamad, who took office in July 1981, have indicated the relatively low ranking of the United States in Kuala Lumpur's foreign policy priorities: first is ASEAN, then the Islamic world, East Asia, the nonaligned movement, the British Commonwealth, and only then "the West."

Within this context, what can be the contribution of a study of anti-Americanism in Malaysia? It is the main hypothesis of the chapter that there is a direct correlation between the degree of U.S. involvement in a Third World country, the magnitude of the relationship, and the degree of anti-Americanism. Relatedly, it is the argument of the chapter that it is precisely the modest nature of U.S.-Malaysian relations that can provide useful data for crosscultural analysis of similarities and differences in the phenomenon of anti-Americanism in the Third World. It is only through examining a case of a more limited nature that we can attempt, in juxtaposition to cases of a greater degree of anti-Americanism, to define the limits and the "periphery" of the concept itself.

In addition, it must be recognized at this point, and will be discussed below, that important ties exist between the two countries. The United States buys large quantities of Malaysian rubber and tin and the two share mutual, if somewhat differing concerns about the situation in neighboring Indochina, the Soviet naval build-up in Asia, China's future behavior, the United States' regional and global role, as well as a variety of other political and economic issues. Prime Minister Mahathir's visit to the United States in January of 1984 illustrated the existence of these and other ties and issues that keep the two countries in closer contact than might first appear.

Before moving to an examination of the nature of anti-Americanism which exists in Malaysia and in Malaysian policy, an attempt will be made to assess the domestic environment: that is, the internal political, economic, and social context which inevitably and critically affects Malaysia's perceptions and behavior. Next, the chapter will analyze the anti-Americanism which can be observed and relate it to this environment. This anti-Americanism in the Malaysian case does indeed, as Rubinstein and Smith have addressed in their chapter, range "from suspicion and resentment to disdain and hostility toward the government, policy, culture, and society of the United States."[1] The chapter will seek to determine what factors create it and define it. What different forms does anti-Americanism take and what are the causes of these different forms? It is only after these discussions that the chapter will attempt to evaluate the implication for U.S. interests and to assess what light may have been shed on anti-Americanism as a concept.

A number of disclaimers are in order before proceeding. First, it must be pointed out that this analysis is largely impressionistic. There is a lack of studies of U.S.-Malaysian relations and, in fact, no in-depth examination exists of their relationship for the 1970s, much less the 1980s.[2] The material presented here has been gathered in the "field" while the author was a Visiting Fulbright Professor in Malaysia in 1983–84. The data were gleaned from newspapers and other media as well as interviews and discussions with a wide variety of Malaysians, Americans, and others. Consequently also, the analysis here focuses primarily on the current and very recent aspects of the relationship. Finally, there is little generalizing from the Malaysian experience to that of Southeast Asia as a whole; as enticing as that might be, the diversity in this region is such that facile generalizations and comparisons are risky and often highly misleading, and thus to be avoided.[3]

THE MALAYSIAN DOMESTIC CONTEXT

One cannot discuss Malaysia in any context without first addressing the ethnic and religious situation in the country.[4] Malaysia is an ethnically divided society. According to the 1980 census, it is made up of Malays constituting 47.8 percent, Chinese 32.1 percent, Indians 8.6 percent, native communities of Sabah 6.1 percent, other natives 4.7 percent, and others 0.7 percent. This pluralism and the communalism that results from it has been the dominant aspect of the Malaysian domestic environment since independence was achieved in 1957. There are deep cleavages between the groups geographically, economically, and religiously. The Malays, for example, tend to live in the rural areas and to be poorer than the characteristically urban-dwelling non-Malays. Virtually all Malays are also Muslim while very few non-Malays profess the Islamic faith. These various differences exploded in racial riots in Malaysia in 1969 and led to a variety of new policies intended to control the situation more tightly and to improve the conditions underlying the racial antagonism. Among the former, there were new procedures under the Internal Security Act and a ban on discussions that touch on racial matters. Among the latter was the New Economic Policy, or NEP, which is intended to bring the ethnic groups closer economically. For example, a target of 30 percent ownership and control of the corporate sector was set for the Malays and other indigenous people (*bumiputra*, or "sons of the soil") for the year 1990.[5]

Certainly this context is not anti-American per se but it does provide a context in which specific or even generalized grievances can flourish or possibly explode. To the extent that Malays are less "Westernized" or "modernized" they are probably more likely to harbor suspicion or distrust of the United States than their more urban compatriots. The latter may have disagreements with the United States to be sure, but these are less likely to be based on lack of knowledge or understanding. The former group, which is politically dominant, is more likely to have attitudes toward the United States of suspicion and distrust, based on having less in common with the urban, industrialized character of contemporary America. Moreover, language differences add to this perceptual problem. English has been phased out and Bahasa Malaysia, or Malay, has been declared the national language and the medium of instruction in the National Education System. Many non-Malays would prefer to use, and to have their children taught in English. The development of Bahasa, as it is often referred to, as a sophisticated language is part of a current program of the government as is the continuing effort to insure the language's use in parliament, government ministries, and university lecture halls. Thus, there is an increasing "language gap" that often exacerbates cultural differences and this is only aggravated by a conscious official and societal campaign "against" English. (The precise "rub-off" effect of an anti-English campaign on attitudes toward foreign English-speaking countries needs to be explored.)

Finally, the fact that Islam is the official religion of the country points to further serious differences between U.S. values and those of this majority segment of Malaysian society. The Muslim world view is different from and largely antithetical to that of the Christian West. The rise of so-called fundamentalist or militant Islamic groups in the Middle East has had an impact on Muslim attitudes in Malaysia as well, an impact that has reinforced and strengthened differences with the United States. The repercussions of this "revival," especially in foreign policy, have been minimized thus far, however, by skillful governmental actions and policies.[6]

Given this cultural gap between the United States and Malaysia, and particularly Malays, what of the values and attitudes of the elites who have emerged in the political and intellectual system? On this elite level, the gap appears narrower. While many of the differences noted above are present, it needs to be pointed out that Malaysia's political elite, Malay and non-Malay alike, have been almost exclusively educated in English and abroad, attending universities in the United Kingdom, Australia, the United States, and Canada primarily. Indeed, the current Prime Minister, Dr. Mahathir, is the country's first Prime Minister who was *not* educated in the West, but in Singapore; yet he is far more "Western" and consequently "less Malay" than his four predecessors in political style and attitudes. He came into office promising a "clean, efficient, and trustworthy" government and has been a dynamic, open, articulate, and direct leader. His style of campaigning before large public rallies during Malaysia's recent constitutional amendment "crisis" made him look very much like a U.S. candidate out on the hustings. The fact that he is not attached to any of the country's various royal houses makes him closer in outlook to Western elites as well. Finally, there has been a dramatic increase in the number of Malaysian students going to the United States for higher education. This number increased from 7,000 at the beginning of the 1980s to 20,000 in 1983–84. (This number includes the Prime Minister's son.) Forty percent of Malaysian students studying abroad are in the United States making it the host to the largest number by far. Since a large proportion of these future elites sent abroad are Malays, this greatly increased U.S.-Malaysian contact seems likely to at least partially bridge the cultural divide. There seems likely to be a gradual increase in understanding and shared perceptions, if not cultural intimacy, between the elites of the two countries.[7]

How much in common does Malaysia have with U.S. democracy? As above, this too is a mixed picture. On the one hand, Malaysia is a democracy *inter alia* in terms of most personal freedoms, free elections, political leaders leaving office after electoral defeats, and the military being subordinate to civilian control. Compared to the rest of the Third World, and, perhaps more relevantly and importantly, to its regional neighbors Malaysia is indeed remarkable for its degree of democracy and political stability.

On the other hand, the degree of governmental authoritarianism was greatly increased after the 1969 riots. Various laws and constitutional amendments were passed that greatly restricted participation in political parties and activities. Opposition parties to the ruling *Barisan Nasional* (National Front) which is dominated by the United Malays National Organization (UMNO), have been heavily restrained. UMNO continues to be acknowledged as the senior partner in the ruling coalition and there is recurrent friction because of this with its major partners, the Malayan Chinese Party (MCA) and the Malayan Indian Congress (MIC). There is often no public discussion of major issues in the media as the television[8] and radio stations are government operated and the various daily newspapers are owned by member parties of the *Barisan Nasional*. The Western democratic concept of a free and critical press is alien to the Malaysian political system where the press is expected to serve the country's interests as interpreted by the ruling administration.[9]

It must be said that many aspects of this increased authoritarianism have eased somewhat since 1981 under the Mahathir administration. One sign of this slight "democratization" was the 1983 effort by the government to amend the constitution to limit the power of the country's king—elected every five years from among Malaysia's sultans who rule by hereditary right in nine of the country's thirteen states—and make him truly a constitutional monarch. Although this was only partially successful, it seemed a step forward, making the Malaysian political system more similar to Western democratic systems such as that in the United States. Other trappings of tight government control, such as aspects of the Internal Security Act and the controls on the media, will continue to underline differences between Kuala Lumpur and Washington in the domestic political sphere. Yet, as pointed out above, there are fewer differences and more similarities of this kind between the United States and Malaysia than between the U.S. and most other Third World countries. Soviet efforts to capitalize on these differences, for example, seem basically to recognize this situation and have been modest by Soviet standards; Moscow's accomplishments have been still more modest in fostering anti-Americanism in Malaysia. What anti-Americanism that has existed has developed from differing U.S. and Malaysian attitudes toward various issues of mutual concern—with apparent independence from Soviet propaganda or "active measures."

AREAS OF DISAGREEMENT

There are many areas where U.S.-Malaysian differences have arisen and where varying degrees of anti-Americanism have been present. These areas may be broken down into: (1) resentment over American neglect of and lack of knowledge about Malaysia; (2) differences in global and regional policies; (3) sharply divergent views of American economic activity in the Third World; and (4) Malaysian perception of American society. Although there is a good deal of overlap between these areas, they can be usefully separated for analytical purposes as long as the interrelationships between them are kept in mind.

U.S. Neglect

Charges of U.S. neglect and ignorance of Malaysia have been a recurrent theme of political administrations in Kuala Lumpur. Certainly ignorance among the general U.S. public is well substantiated. In a recent set of surveys taken nationally the evidence of lack of knowledge about Malaysia was striking.[10] For example, on a question regarding to what degree respondents held favorable or unfavorable attitudes toward about 17 Asian countries, including all five of the ASEAN states, Malaysia ranked the highest of all in the category of "Do Not Know." On a question asking how much the respondent knew about different countries Malaysia led all Asian countries in the "Nothing at All" category. Consistently, Malaysia was also first in the "Do Not Know" column on questions regarding respondents' impressions of standards of living among Asian countries, political stability, and quality of products. Malaysia certainly had a more positive image in the minds of this sample of U.S. opinion than did, say, Vietnam, North Korea, or the Soviet Union, but what was notable relative to the non-Communist states of Asia was the substantial body of ignorance in the United States about the country.

It is not difficult for Malaysians, the elites as well as the masses, to link this lack of knowledge about Malaysia among Americans in general to an ignorance on the part of elites and, specifically, U.S. administrations. It is but a short step from that to accusations of U.S. arrogance and insensitivity toward Malaysia and its interests. As one political reporter wrote in the *New Straits Times*, Malaysia's major English-language daily, "the Washington establishment seems to have misinterpreted Malaysia's historical desire for low-profile ties with the U.S. as giving them the right to put Malaysia on low-priority."[11] Malaysia is a friend of the U.S., he went on, neither an ally nor an enemy:

> Herein may lie the root of the problem; Washington finds it much easier to deal with allies and well-defined enemies.
>
> But their "good-guy" versus "bad-guy" policymaking guidebook apparently does not contain any guidelines on how to deal with good friends who are not allies.

Washington officials must find it very difficult to fathom a country which is strongly anti-communist domestically, stiffly opposes Vietnamese and Soviet communist designs in Southeast Asia and yet openly attacks American policies on economic matters.

These themes have often emerged in bilateral meetings between Malaysian and U.S. leaders. When Deputy Prime Minister Datuk Musa Hitam visited the United States in October 1983, for example, he articulated similar feelings to the Council on Foreign Relations in New York. He told members of the Council at a two-hour luncheon meeting that Malaysia would "like to think that you think Malaysia is important to you. But we don't get that impression."[12] He went on to discuss the realities of interdependence in the contemporary world and to expound rather eloquently on Malaysia's economic and political progress. Washington has made some effort to respond to these Malaysian perceptions. Vice-President George Bush, for instance, tried to reassure Musa that the United States in no sense took Malaysia for granted. The administration's appointment of Thomas Shoesmith as the new ambassador to Malaysia in October 1983 was perceived in Kuala Lumpur as being a highly significant gesture that indicated that "Washington now attaches greater importance to its relationship with Malaysia...."[13] Shoesmith was seen to be President Reagan's top diplomat on East Asia—he had been serving as Deputy Assistant Secretary of State for East Asia and the Pacific since 1981 and had served in U.S. missions in Japan, South Korea, and Hong Kong—and a knowledgeable "old Asia hand."

Despite these signs of increased sensitivity to Malaysia's needs and concerns, there were continuing indications that this remained a problem in the bilateral relationship. In Prime Minister Mahathir's January 1984 visit there were press reports in Malaysia that the country was considered as "no news" by the U.S. media which was also accused of displaying a great ignorance about Malaysia.[14] On more than one occasion, Dr. Mahathir reiterated the theme that although Malaysia was a small country, that should not mean it can be taken for granted, and he pledged to make Malaysia's voice heard in world affairs. He reserved his greatest criticism in this regard for the U.S. press. On his return to Kuala Lumpur, he elaborated on the "obstacles mounted" to his trip's objectives by the "biased foreign media":

Their reports on Malaysia have never been true. It appears that there are certain quarters who purposely concentrate on the bad sides of things.

For instance, just before I left Malaysia on my visits [he also went to Canada, France, and Switzerland in addition to the U.S.], American journalists sought an interview with me. They said it was to enable them to have a better understanding of me because in the U.S., one's personality was very important.

I granted them an hour's interview but when the report appeared in the U.S., none of the things said in the interview was in print.

It gave me the impression that they were not interested in hearing our views.[15]

A pledge by President Reagan to establish closer understanding and cooperation with Malaysia was viewed by Mahathir as a major gain but it seems clear that this area of disagreement is not going to disappear suddenly.

Global and Regional Policy

A number of mostly subtle issues have emerged between the United States and Malaysia in the area of noneconomic U.S. global policy and, relatedly, regional policy. The differences in their respective perceptions of the Middle East are certainly among the least subtle. Being a Muslim state, Malaysia is a strong supporter of the Arab states and of Palestinian rights and has regularly made known its opposition to Washington's support for Israel. More broadly, Malaysia has also resisted the U.S. inclination to categorize states as either allies or enemies by remaining an active member of the nonaligned movement while maintaining friendship with the United States. Kuala Lumpur has also demurred from and cautiously argued against what it sees as Washington's continuing tendency to emphasize military solutions to delicate and complex global issues. Related to this, Malaysia also dissents from what it has long seen as the United States' fixation on the Soviet Union. To the Mahathir administration this U.S. tendency to see the Soviet Union as at the root of all threats to U.S. interests or the cause of all the various conflicts around the globe is not only wrong but also costly in terms of consequent inappropriate U.S. policies. The U.S. focus is seen to be on the Cold War and the arms race rather than on the possibility of some kind of detente and arms control. There is, however, certainly some ambiguity here: on the one hand, the Malaysians are pleased that the Reagan administration seems more committed to the defense of U.S. interests globally—including in Southeast Asia—while, on the other, they are worried that the President's fixation on the Soviet Union runs the risk of dissipating U.S. will and power in some conflict with the Soviets that is of marginal importance at best. Moreover, Malaysia is concerned lest Reagan's hostility toward the Soviet Union preclude the kind of contacts necessary between the two superpowers if there is to be any hope of a settlement of such issues as Afghanistan and, particularly, Kampuchea.

Indeed, it is when these differences in world view are applied to the regional level, such as regarding Kampuchea, that they become far more significant. This is also when the ambiguities become more pronounced, if still largely hidden from public view. Basically, there is a difference in perception of the threat to the security of the non-Communist states of Southeast Asia. The U.S. position since the Vietnamese invasion of Kampuchea in 1978 has been that the threat to the region came from the Soviet Union operating through its client state, Vietnam. And Washington has seemingly missed no opportunity to point that out to the states of the region. Secretary of Defense Caspar Weinberger made a five-nation tour through Asia—including Singapore, Thailand, and Indonesia—in August–September 1982 to promise U.S. military support to Asia in the face of the "increasing Soviet threat through Vietnam...."[16] A little over a year later, Assistant Secretary of Defense Richard Armitage was warning the *Bangkok Post* correspondent in Washington that Southeast Asians should be wary of the "dramatic expansion" of Soviet military power in the region, the "clear evidence" of Vietnam's expansionist designs, and Moscow's "single-minded dedication to hegemony."[17]

Malaysia certainly shares a degree of this concern with growing Soviet naval power in Asia and with the future intentions of Vietnam. Kuala Lumpur also stands by the ASEAN position—which is supported by both the United States and the People's Republic of China—that calls for a Vietnamese withdrawal from Kampuchea as the first step in the process of normalization in Indochina. Nevertheless, one gets a clear if implicit sense that Malaysia perceives the longer-term situation in the region rather differently. Fundamentally, Kuala Lumpur perceives China as a greater worry to its security over the long haul than either the Soviet Union or Vietnam. This is primarily a result of historical and internal factors: Beijing's past support for the Communist Party of Malaya

(CPM) during its insurrection in Malaya's "Emergency" period (1948-1960), Beijing's continuing refusal to completely jettison party-to-party relations with the CPM in favor of exclusive state-to-state relations,[18] and, of course, the multi-ethnic nature of the Malaysian state. The PRC's willingness to aggressively attempt "to teach Vietnam a lesson," while perhaps beneficial in checking Vietnam, was unsettling to Malaysia in its evidence of China's willingness to use force beyond its borders.

This U.S.-Malaysian difference of opinion concerning the source of the major threat to the region has other ramifications as well. The most important is the suspicion with which Kuala Lumpur views the Sino-U.S. relationship. The Malaysians have been uneasy with any indications of a Sino-U.S. "strategic partnership" and have worried that Washington was being naive in its dealings with Beijing. Particularly anxiety-producing for Kuala Lumpur have been the indications that significant U.S. technological, economic, and particularly military assistance would be made available to the People's Republic.

Finally, there is some difference in the two views of the future overall strategic picture in the region. Malaysia has long espoused a "Zone of Peace, Freedom and Neutrality" (ZOPFAN) for Southeast Asia which would apparently mean the exclusion of all big powers from the region. However, given the growing Soviet presence especially in the Pacific and the longer-term concern with China, Malaysia has been more interested in a continuing U.S. commitment to the region, at minimum as a balance to the two other powers. The general decline of U.S. involvement in the aftermath of its withdrawal from Vietnam has been of great concern to Malaysia. Thus, additional ambiguities: circumstances have brought U.S. and Malaysian policies in this aspect closer together, not in rhetoric but in substance.

U.S. Economic Policy

It is in the area of U.S. economic activity in the Third World that Malaysian-U.S. differences have been the most pronounced, that Kuala Lumpur has been the most outspoken, and that anti-Americanism has been the most evident. Malaysia's disagreements with the U.S. have ranged from Washington's overall approach to the Third World, to its behavior in various international organizations, to specific bilateral differences, such as over U.S. tin sales.

Malaysia's most candid enunciation of its dissatisfaction with U.S. attitudes toward the Third World came during Prime Minister Mahathir's visit to Washington. In his address to the Washington Foreign Policy Association, Mahathir was particularly "free and frank," as the local Malaysian press had it. Although Malaysians and other Southeast Asians who are accustomed to Mahathir's direct style were not surprised by the forceful and blunt nature of his remarks, apparently the U.S. State Department was and it so admitted privately.[19] In his wide-ranging address on "The Problems and Expectations of the Third World" the Prime Minister accused the United States, and specifically the Reagan administration, of not paying enough attention to the "legitimate aspirations" of the Third World nations. Washington, he said, "often supports vested interests and opposes much-needed reforms that would bring relief to many small Third World countries." U.S. opposition to international economic and monetary reforms aimed at aiding the developing countries helped to stifle the development efforts of those states. He went on to cite U.S. opposition to various tenets of the New International Economic Order, lack of cooperation in multilateral trade negotiations, manipulation of raw material stockpiles, and the closing of Western markets to Third World manufactured goods by high tariffs and other forms of protectionism.

> Between the managed commodity markets in the developed countries—which are sometimes not averse to selling stolen products—and the threats posed by stockpiles, it is all a raw material producer can do to survive.
>
> There is no choice for the developing countries but to exploit their low labor cost and availability of raw materials and go into manufacturing.
>
> But immediately they run up against an obstacle.[20]

This obstacle, he pointed out, was protectionism and was unfair not only to the developing countries but also to the consumers in the developed, "protected" state who have to pay a higher price just to "maintain a production facility that is no longer economical." "It is truly unfortunate," he concluded "that a great country like the United States all too often stands on the opposite side against small Third World countries."[21]

Malaysia has likewise taken the United States to task for its attitude toward international economic organizations. Kuala Lumpur has particularly criticized Washington's refusal to sign the Law of the Sea treaty, its announced decision to leave UNESCO by the end of 1984, and of course the Reagan administration's cut in funds to the International Development Association, the "soft-loan" window of the World Bank. U.S. behavior on these issues and in other organizations such as GATT and the IMF are viewed by Malaysia as mechanisms that the U.S. has successfully manipulated in order to avoid dealing with the legitimate concerns of the poorer countries.

It is, of course, direct bilateral issues that create the greatest danger to Malaysian interests. For example, Malaysia wants more trade with the United States, particularly the further opening of U.S. markets to Malaysian textiles and new manufactures. Kuala Lumpur worries about current and potential protectionist measures against its commodities. It calls for more active U.S. governmental encouragement of private U.S. investment in Malaysia, a theme raised by Mahathir in Washington and reiterated by Musa when U.S. Deputy Secretary of State Kenneth Dam visited Malaysia one month later.[22] Most symptomatic of these various economic issues between the two countries, issues that cause serious strains of anti-Americanism, is the problem of tin. Malaysia has long been the world's leading producer of tin and in recent years friction with Washington has escalated as the U.S. periodically sold the metal from its large stockpile. This problem has become more acute as the worldwide price for tin has dropped. Malaysia's argument has been that it needs and deserves at least a warning from the United States, if not consultations, before the General Services Administration (GSA) releases tin for sale because of the major impact this has on the world market which in turn has an inordinate impact on the Malaysian domestic economy. Mahathir has in the past described such sales as "an act that is not becoming of a nation, many, many times richer than Malaysia."[23] Even the threat of U.S. sales, argue the Malaysians, can seriously weaken the price support measures, which include severe production cutbacks in Malaysia, established by the International Tin Council in an effort to stabilize the commodity's prices. After lengthy negotiations, some consultative machinery was set up in 1983 and, on his visit, Mahathir was given further assurances that the United States would not release any surplus tin in the future without consulting Malaysia. Whether this will actually remove this major source of anti-Americanism in Malaysian attitudes, or whether tin sales will continue to exemplify, in Malaysia's perception, U.S. arrogance and insensitivity, remains to be seen.

Perceptions of U.S. Society

Malaysian perceptions of the United States, its society and culture, are ambivalent in the extreme. On the one hand, there are the cultural ties as seen in language—which is, of course, declining—and in such things as student exchanges. There is an appreciation of the advantages and conveniences in U.S. life, an admiration for the benefits of "consumerism." U.S. films and videos are extremely popular in the country as are U.S. television programs. It would seem, for example, that hardly any Malaysian with access to a television set would miss an episode of "Dallas," even though the program was shown (its run just concluded) quite late in the evening, and discussions of recent episodes among Malaysians were often exhaustively detailed. If imitation is indeed the sincerest form of flattery, then Radio Television Malaysia's creation of its own homespun version of "Dallas," called "P.J.," furnishes further evidence of this perception of the United States.

However, U.S. society both attracts and repels. While there is admiration and certainly envy of U.S. affluence there is also a revulsion toward what this culture seems to represent. U.S. values threaten the corrosion of Malaysian values and institutions. In a country striving to establish a *national* identity, a single *Malaysian* identity as opposed to several communal ones, this danger is real and not insignificant. This worries many Malaysians, certainly the government leadership. Many are concerned about the threat presented to Malaysian art forms and institutions by U.S. "culture" as portrayed in such programs as "Dallas." There has been negative reaction to the program and even to the local spinoff.

The current administration's "Look East" policy speaks volumes about these attitudes toward the United States. It is the policy of the Mahathir government to look to Japan and South Korea rather than to the West and specifically the United States for an economic and cultural model. It is in those Asian states, the Prime Minister argues, where there can be found examples of the work ethic which Malaysia needs to emulate. The U.S., in comparison, is seen as corrupt, dissolute, immoral.

There is little anti-Americanism in Malaysia stemming from the fear that the United States stands for change in general, change that would threaten traditional authority relationships. The government itself is bent on changing such aspects of Malaysian society as can be seen from its effort to trim the sails of the king and sultans. The regime itself is largely a "westernizing," in the sense of modernizing, one and welcomes this aspect of what the United States represents. Even the fundamental Islamic groups seem more concerned with the general U.S. threat to Muslim values than with the threat of change to the traditional system. After all, most of them are not entirely pleased with the traditional relationships either, although they foresee a different end result of the process of change than does Mahathir.

MANIFESTATIONS AND TYPOLOGY

As can be seen, anti-Americanism in Malaysia focuses on a rather wide spectrum of differences, from those of world view to specific policies to culture and society. These differences, this anti-Americanism, have been manifested almost exclusively in the attitudes of individuals, elites and some groups and, particularly, in speeches, writings, and news reporting. During the latter 1960s regular demonstrations against U.S. policy in Vietnam were held, the U.S.I.S. library in Kuala Lumpur was wrecked several times, as were other "representatives of U.S. imperialism"—such as the First National City Bank of New York, which happened to have the misfortune of being on the ground floor of a building one of whose tenants was the American embassy, and anti-American riots took place in major cities including Kuala Lumpur—where a youth was killed in front of the U.S.I.S. library on the occasion of Lyndon Johnson's visit in 1966—Penang, Malacca, and Ipoh. These manifestations of anti-Americanism have almost entirely disappeared since the end of U.S. involvement in the Vietnam conflict.

It is also notable that virtually all of the anti-Americanism we have observed in contemporary Malaysian attitudes and policies has been of the issue-oriented type. Most of this seems to represent basic differences between two states each pursuing its own respective national interests. This seems normal, unavoidable, and not surprising. What exacerbates it, of course, is Malaysia's perception of the U.S. "style" of pursuing its own interests. The United States is seen as heavy-handed, insensitive, and often arrogant. Ultimately, what is difficult for a small country like Malaysia, facing a large and powerful country like the United States, is the sense that Washington treats it like a pawn, either in the global struggle against the Soviet Union or simply in its generalized pursuit of its economic interests. An editorial in the *New Straits Times* on the occasion of President Reagan's announcement that he would run for a second term, seemed to sum up well this frustration of dealing with the U.S. colossus:

> As Ronald Reagan once more seeks the mandate of his people—a mandate he should receive without much difficulty—we are once again left to ponder the curious injustice that prevents us from voting in the

presidential elections of a nation which has so much control over our own destinies, but to which our voices sound as no more than faint squeaks on the far horizon.[24]

A second type of anti-Americanism that is found in the Malaysian case, although not nearly as prominently as the first, is one that might be called instrumental anti-Americanism. To a certain extent, but to much less an extent than seen in so many other countries in the Third World (and also in the first and second worlds, for that matter), the Malaysian government has manipulated disagreements with or hostility toward the United States to serve its own ends. Anti-Americanism, for example, has certainly been used as a way of playing up Malaysian nationalism. There are repeated exhortations from the government to the masses calling for a united, hard-working, dedicated Malaysia as a prerequisite to standing up to the power of the U.S. giant. Anti-Americanism on various issues, especially having to do with North–South economic ones, has also been used to polish Malaysia's credentials as a member-in-good-standing of the nonaligned movement. Since Malaysia has military ties with the West—it is part of the Five-Power Defense Arrangement with Australia, New Zealand, Singapore, and Britain, has a Mirage squadron from the Royal Australian Air Force stationed in Butterworth on the peninsula's West coast, and receives U.S. military assistance—the enunciation of differences with the United States on other issues is highly significant to Malaysia's nonaligned status. Moreover, anti-Americanism has been useful to the regime as a tool for neutralizing domestic opposition on the left and somewhat paradoxically, on the far right (primarily the Muslim fundamentalist groups). The government in Kuala Lumpur has, however, been cautious in this and has largely avoided going to the extreme of utilizing the United States as a scapegoat for internal problems. Washington's periodic tin sales have at times been blamed for all the woes affecting Malaysia's tin industry but neither this nor other possible issues fixing blame for problems on the United States as an external target have been pursued in any sustained way.

The other types of anti-Americanism, ideological and revolutionary, have not been significant categories of the phenomenon since the end of the Vietnam war. The Communist Party of Malaya attempts to picture the United States as the world's arch-villain but this seems to have very little impact on Malaysian attitudes. Militant Islamic groups, perhaps taking their cue from Iran—and some Malaysians, making the Haj to Mecca, were discovered to have pro-Khomeini literature in their suitcases, for example—also try to characterize the United States in this light. The government and the currently dominant elites have been much more persuaded that the Soviet Union, through its naval expansion, and China, through its cultural influence and geographical proximity, present the greater threat to Malaysia. Other than these militant groups on the left and right of the spectrum, then, and of course the "ideological" rejection by many Malaysians of the values that U.S. society seems to represent, the roots of anti-Americanism in Malaysia seem to reflect little of the ideological or revolutionary character seen in many other countries of the Third World.

IMPLICATIONS FOR AMERICAN POLICY

The issue-areas, manifestations, and types of anti-Americanism discussed in this chapter must be considered in the context of the basically positive nature of the U.S.-Malaysian relationship. Most of the differences between the two are issue-specific and represent mainly legitimate and largely inevitable differences between two states very different from one another in size, power, location, history, and culture. Malaysia's strenuous efforts to make its voice heard are a perfectly normal approach for a small state to take in such an asymmetrical relationship. The strength of the relationship seems to lie in the recognition that these differences of perspective are legitimate, can be talked about, and ought not to overshadow the broad areas of agreement and cooperation.

There are other factors that help to explain this nature and degree of anti-Americanism in Malaysia and which consequently have important implications for both U.S. and Malaysian interests and policies. For one, Malaysia has had no shortage of other useful "scapegoats," or external targets of dissatisfaction, should it need them. The British have played that role, most notably in the "Buy British Last" campaign that Mahathir initiated in 1981 and has only eased up on recently. Japan is a candidate for the future as Tokyo's economic profile continues to grow. It is no secret that certain aspects of the Japanese "style" create a great deal of antagonism in Southeast Asia and this has exploded in the past, for instance in Indonesia. Malaysian suspicions of China, held especially strongly by Malays, are grounded in the historical fact of Beijing's support for the CPM and in its continued refusal to sever all ties. Finally, fears of the Soviet Union exist, sometimes vague—for example, Soviet naval expansion and intentions in or via Vietnam—and sometimes more specific—as in the spy scandals involving Soviet diplomats which pop up rather regularly in the region, including in Malaysia. The emotional Malaysian reaction to the Soviet role in the Korean airline disaster in the fall of 1983, on the governmental and elite levels, showed the potential for "anti-Sovietism." Actions included boycotts of Soviet ships in Malaysia's two major ports in Klang and Penang, a fire in the Aeroflot office in Kuala Lumpur, and the burning of an effigy of Soviet leader Andropov.[25] What all of this adds up to, at minimum, is that Malaysia recognizes that among all the major powers the United States is "the least unwelcome."[26]

The current limited political strength of the militant, or revivalist, Muslim groups also helps to account for the relatively low level of anti-Americanism observed. Should the political clout of these groups increase significantly, one would expect the nature and degree of anti-Americanism to escalate. Should the world economy enter another recession, anti-Americanism would probably rise as well. Even in this recent recession, however, U.S.-Malaysian relations did not suffer any drastic increase in strain and, in fact, Malaysia weathered the recession quite well. The country's stable economy and impressively and consistently high growth rates over the last decade mean that economic models other than the present capitalist one hold little or no appeal at present (and into the foreseeable future). Moreover, Kuala Lumpur recognizes that it needs various things from the United States such as a protective security environment, trade, aid, and investment. Finally, given all of these factors, there is virtually no role for Soviet propaganda in contemporary Malaysia. There is no Soviet oriented elite and little in the way of fertile ground for a Soviet-fed campaign of anti-Americanism.

On the whole, the limited degree of anti-Americanism in Malaysia may be also a result of the limited role of the United States in the country. Washington has kept, apparently deliberately, a relatively "low profile" in Malaysia. There seems to be a recognition in both Kuala Lumpur and in Washington of the value of this kind of relationship. The critical test may be whether the United States can pay more attention to Malaysia's legitimate concerns and give it more support, which the Malaysians call for, without becoming overbearing and exacerbating the anti-Americanism to the point that these attitudes overwhelm the improvement in relations in any particular area. Perhaps the current relationship is close to as good as it can be, for both sides.

NOTES

1. Alvin Rubinstein and Donald E. Smith, "Anti-Americanism: Anatomy of a Phenomenon," chapter one, p. 1.

2. For the earlier period, see Pamela Sodhy, *Passage of Empire: United States-Malayan Relations to 1966*, Ph.D. Dissertation, Cornell University, 1982; and James W. Gould, *The United States and Malaysia* (Cambridge: Harvard University Press, 1969).

3. A particular useful complement to this study, for example, would be an equally in-depth one of anti-Americanism in the Philippines.

4. Much of the following discussion is based on Michael Ong, "Malaysia: Sense of Change and Urgency," *Current Affairs Bulletin* (Australia), November 1983, pp. 23-31.

5. By the early 1980s, *bumiputra* control had increased from 4.3 percent to 12.4 percent. Non-Malay ownership has increased from 34.0 percent to 40.1 percent and foreign ownership declined from 61.7 percent to 47.5 percent.

6. See the discussion in Simon Barraclough, "Managing the Challenges of Islamic Revival in Malaysia," *Asian Survey*, August 1983, pp. 958-75.

7. See Rubinstein and Smith, *op. cit.*, pp. 7-8.

8. There are currently two television stations but a third, which is to be privately operated, is to begin broadcasting perhaps as early as June 1984. It is unlikely that this station will diverge far from the pattern of the other two in political matters.

9. An interesting example of how alien an uncontrolled press is to the Malaysian elite can be seen in the reaction to a negative story in a London daily in February 1984; see *New Straits Times* (Kuala Lumpur), February 22, 23, 25, 1984. Mahathir's position is that there must be "close relations" between the government and the mass media; see, for example, *Far Eastern Economic Review*, December 22, 1983, pp. 16-17.

10. See William Watts, *The United States and Asia. Changing Attitudes and Policies* (Lexington, Mass: Lexington Books, 1982), pp. 4, 12, 21, 42, 45.

11. M.A. Razman in the issue of July 29, 1983.

12. *New Straits Times*, October 13, 1983.

13. *Ibid.*, October 14, 1983. The paper's headline writer went so far as to claim: "Malaysia-U.S. ties back on track."

14. For example, see *ibid.*, January 20, 1984.

15. *Ibid.*, February 1, 1984. Emphasis added.

16. See *South China Morning Post* (Hong Kong), September 2, 1982.

17. See *New Straits Times*, October 10, 1983.

18. That this remains an issue is evidenced by reports of the discussion between the Malaysian leadership and the visiting Chinese Foreign Minister, Wu Xueqian; see *New Straits Times*, February 29, 1984. See also *South China Morning Post*, February 27, 1984.

19. See *Asiaweek*, February 3, 1984, p. 9; and *Straits Times* (Singapore), January 22, 1984.

20. *New Straits Times*, January 18, 1984.

21. *Straits Times*, January 22, 1984.

22. See *New Straits Times*, February 29, 1984.

23. See *Far Eastern Economic Review*, January 19, 1984, p. 19.

24. *New Straits Times*, February 1, 1984.

25. The Parliament did reject an opposition motion to formally condemn the Soviet Union as well as demand a public apology and full reparations; see *ibid.*, October 12, 1983.

26. See the discussion in Chin Kin Wah, "A New Assertiveness in Malaysian Foreign Policy," in Huynh Kim Khanh, ed: *Southeast Asian Affairs 1982* (Singapore: Institute of Southeast Asian Studies, 1982), p. 274.

9

Anti-Americanism in Africa:
The Constraints of Globalism

Harvey Glickman

This chapter argues that manifest expressions of anti-American attitudes in African countries[1] are unsustained by large segments of the citizenry over long periods of time and that specific public expressions of anti-Americanism are usually instrumental to the policy goals of elites in or out of power. Nevertheless, the United States is perceived in African elite circles as pursuing interests that frustrate the goals of African dignity and material progress, such as its policy toward South Africa and policies of trade, credit and investment in relation to Africa's ailing economies. In North Africa the United States' determined and extensive support of Israel presents an additional problem for perceptions of the United States. Deep, active and persistent anti-Americanism usually requires cultural coherence or political strength, beyond the present resource or command of black African states, although puritanical Islam as currently observed in Libya foreshadows possible shifts in states of large Muslim populations. Because the power base of most African governments remains narrow and changeable, and because coping with Africa's economic and political problems requires U.S. and/or Western help, constructive relations between the United States and African states are not totally ruled out by expressions of opposition to U.S. policies by African elites; yet so great is the present gap between Africa's perceived needs and the U.S. response that a climate of comfort and intimacy seems ruled out for the foreseeable future.

AMBIGUITIES OF EVIDENCE

Discussions of opinions and attitudes in Africa are greatly constrained by Africa's pervasive underdevelopment—in this case, the underdevelopment of institutions of political communication. The density and complexity of communication reflects political resources, which are largely confined to Africa's small political and economic elite. While there are suggestions of differences between mass and elite opinion, the overwhelming evidence is drawn from what a small number of well-off people are prepared to say.

Institutions of political communication in Africa are dominated by government; thus, there is no sure way of discerning differences between official and unofficial points of view. A few African countries (e.g., Nigeria, Kenya, Senegal) have the resources and intermittently permit the expression of nonofficial viewpoints in matters of high policy. The meager data from opinion polls regarding attitudes toward the United States come from such places. The starting point for consideration of anti-Americanism in Africa is therefore the extremely narrow base of information about political opinion in general in African countries. If the processes of politics are weak and concentrated, we must be extremely tentative about the scope of the phenomenon of anti-Americanism.

It is also difficult to be certain about the depth of political attitudes, or more precisely, the effect of attitudes on decisions. This is especially true in the realm of foreign policy, where governments have more freedom in acting and in explaining their actions than in domestic policy. Probably because African governments are weakly and discontinuously connected to their societies, official reversals of position can occur without decisive domestic repercussions, at least immediately. Somalia and Egypt shifting sides in relation to the East–West struggle in Africa seem cases in point. Official diplomatic positions reflect the *realpolitik* considerations of a small circle of government officials, rather than underlying attitudes of a larger population. It would be difficult to discern any causative role for anti- or pro-American attitudes in the populace in such sudden switches of position.

Official statements are reversible without changes of government, but more typically, governments change rather abruptly in Africa and these produce sudden shifts in rhetoric and sometimes in policy. The Ethiopian coup in 1974 illustrates the quick collapse of a center of pro-American attitudes and policy. The rise of a Marxist military regime split established elites, creating important issues of differences between old and new leadership, civilian vs. military, bureaucrats vs. politicians. Expressed anti-American opinion in Ghana at the present time seems susceptible to such an analysis.

Africa as a continent provides many more opportunities for expression of anti-American sentiments than other parts of the Third World, simply by dint of the multiplication of official arenas. It would be misleading to merely count heads (or votes) in order to generalize about Africa compared to other regions. Moreover, in places where votes are added, such as the United Nations, the African delegations make a real effort to reach common positions before voting, thus masking differences in depth of feeling on many matters.[2]

Despite the mercurial quality of evidence and our reliance on the public statements of official leaders, the United States cannot, however, ignore perceptions of U.S. aims and activities on the part of African leaders that, if persistent, undermine possibilities for future fruitful cooperation.

COUNTER META-FACTUALS

To begin understanding the phenomenon of anti-Americanism, it might be useful to turn the question over and ask what would be the reasons for African leaders to display pro-American sentiments in today's world? Compared to Western European countries, the United States has had little historical involvement with Africa, except as a destination for the millions taken from the continent as slaves. Clearly the treatment of blacks in the United States is a major issue in defining the character of the United States for African leaders. Recognition of the promise of the U.S. system was evident in the founding meeting of the Organization of African Unity in 1963, when "deep concern" about "racial discrimination" against Afro-Americans was voiced, but was followed by "appreciation for the efforts of the Federal Government of the USA to put an end to these intolerable practices...."[3]

The struggle for independence in Africa saw African nationalists draw some inspiration from the U.S. anticolonial rebellion and its leaders.[4] But once independence is won and Africans achieve seats of power, what would pro-Americanism look like? From the 1960s to the present, the United States in Africa appears as the guarantor of Western capitalism, taking on the obligation to guide the development of Africa toward prosperity. Pro-Americanism in Africa would reflect a Kennedyesque partnership in modernization, in which the U.S. government underwrote African governments in their planning and financing economic diversification and growth. Pro-Americanism in Africa responded to the United States' early advertisements of its active interest in shaping Africa's independent development.[5] To state matters this way suggests a thesis of "let-down" as a context for the growth of anti-American sentiments in Africa, a product of a betrayal of expectations rather than a perception of malevolent force.

As well, such psychologically tinged speculations permit another reversal of perspective. In view of the United States' self-defined role of global leadership, its attempts to create a new and expanded connection to Africa at the time of the emergence of new states there inevitably clashes with the exercise of global responsibilities. A let-down is working on *American* notions of anti-Americanism. We are victimized by our own inflated expectations of gratitude for our exertions on behalf of the security of African states.

On the other hand, Americans feel undeserving of high-pitched abuse, as for instance in the OAU meeting of 1981, where the United States was condemned for its "unholy alliance" with South Africa, its "baseless hostility toward Angola," and its effort "to misrepresent the nature of the colonial conflict in Namibia as one of global strategic consideration."[6] We ask for the same consideration of political complexities as the OAU demands when faced with criticism of their failure, for example, to condemn Libya's invasion of Chad.

While gleeful reactions on the part of African diplomats to defeats of American positions in the UN are discomfiting, much of the politics of international meetings involve the manipulation of symbols. In Africa the United States cannot match the commitment of the Soviet Union to the notion of liberation of Africa from white rule. As Raymond Copson observes, "The United States has no single, popular policy to counter the Soviet advantage on the southern Africa issue. Policy toward this region is indeed the most troublesome aspect of U.S. relations with Africa."[7] Recently, within southern Africa, black African leaders have openly recognized the critical role of the United States in forwarding the ultimate aim of independence of Namibia via working for interlocked intermediate aims of the disengagement of Angolan and South African armed forces. Such accommodation to power realities has come about without announced changes in elite attitudes toward the United States.[8]

THE DEVELOPMENT OF AFRICAN PERCEPTIONS OF THE U.S. ROLE IN AFRICA

In reflecting on the salience of anti-Americanism in Africa, based largely on the expression of official opinion and commentary, it seems clear that worry over victimization is a key factor. "The Second Scramble" was the phrase used by President Julius Nyerere of Tanzania in the early 1960s to describe the predatory interests of both the United States and the Soviet Union in regard to the prize of Africa. This was a more imaginative concern with imperialism as the era of formal colonialism was coming to an end than the often-voiced concern for neocolonialism of former colonial powers.

Nevertheless, the United States is identified with the West and with capitalism. Coupled with the assumed designs of a superpower, this creates a type of double jeopardy for the United States. Although less is heard these days of Africa's natural affinity to communalism, there remains considerable sympathy among intellectuals for socialism as a social system and as a blueprint for centrally directed economic development. As the world's chief nonsocialist power, overtures by the United States are liable to suspicion of hidden exploitation, not because that is the intention of the U.S. government, but because that is the way that capitalism is supposed to work.[9]

Therefore, as far as attitudes to U.S. policy in general are concerned, in Africa we are suspect as capitalist exploiters and as global superpower strategists.[10] African leaders agree that protecting African interests is primary and that they must guard against manipulation in superpower struggles. African leaders, however, divide in their views on the degree of necessary conflict with U.S. capitalism, in accordance with their own development ideologies.[11]

On the other side of the coin of attitudes to the United States in general is the obvious attraction of U.S. culture, especially in its popular varieties. Freedom in politics as well as lifestyle are known and valued by Africans exposed to information about the United States. Polls taken over a decade ago were reporting that the United States was regarded as more popular than all other foreign countries among African students in the United States, with negative attitudes more prevalent among Francophone students than Anglophone students. There was also some correlation of greater negativism at high levels of education.[12] More recent commentary reports that inequalities, race relations, and a meager family life are seen as unattractive aspects of the United States to black Africans. But U.S. prosperity and technological advancement are viewed favorably.[13]

By the time the independence of African territories became an issue in the late 1950s the ambiguous image of America had already formed. On the one hand, the United States supported the end of colonialism as a worldwide trend. On the other hand, the United States did not want to alienate its Western European allies, especially when "premature" independence in the colonies could mean instability and a rise in influence for radical elements. With the Cold War as the organizing principle of U.S. foreign policy from the 1950s, the United States could view Africa, once released from European control, as a battleground between East and West where the main issue was the degree of complementarity of the new states with Western political economy.[14]

Attitudes of Africans reflected the roles assumed by the leaders of African nationalism. In company with the first generation of Afro-Asian leaders of the early 1960s, African leaders were divided by the meaning of "nonalignment" in foreign policy. More Marxian African leaders, such as Nkrumah and Toure, opted for radical nonalignment. In general, they were rather critical of U.S. foreign policy as insufficiently energetic in pressing anticolonialism on the European metropolitan powers. African leaders who were satisfied to retain strong economic links with former colonial rulers tended toward pragmatic nonalignment, pressing the United States to pay more attention to the development needs of Africa.

The reference point for "pro-Americanism" in Africa is the period 1960–62. The Kennedy campaign made Africa part of the new frontier. It was something of a clean slate of newly emerging states on which the United States could record its leadership in aiding modernization in freedom. Kennedy succeeded in depicting Africa as vital to demonstrating what democratic systems could achieve in the less-developed parts of the world.[15]

Between election victory and taking power, as well as immediately afterward, the Kennedy administration attempted to project an active and comprehensive U.S. presence in Africa, especially in newly independent states. In black Africa to this day, the positive side of the United States' official concern for Africa is recalled as a personal involvement of President Kennedy. The Congo crisis, which exploded in July 1960 and which was inherited by the Kennedy administration, permitted the United States to distance itself from European support of the Katanga secession, making concrete the U.S. policy of support for African nationalism. Yet the requirements of strategic anti-communism led to an anti-radical interpretation of African nationalism that has not changed substantially over 20 years of U.S. policy in Africa.[16]

Two other strands of the Africa policy of the New Frontier complete the image. One dealt with support for black African rule in colonies of white settlement, such as Kenya and what was then Rhodesia. The second concerned a rather large and vigorous push for African development, which manifested itself in highly visible assistance to big ticket projects, such as the Volta River Dam and Aluminum Smelter, in Ghana, and grass roots aid in the form of Peace Corps volunteers who swarmed into the African bush. The basis for African attitudes to the United States were then formed by the United States' overall position in the earliest years of independence of Africa's ex-colonies. The United States would support African development and nonalignment, as long as that meant no important connections to the communist powers outside. The United States would support continuing and rapid decolonization unless that collided with the strategic necessities of the Cold War. Thus the United States could not prevent Portugal from using NATO equipment in fighting African guerrillas, nor could it openly press for an end to Portuguese rule in Africa, as long as the Azores bases were treated as a national security matter. If chaos could lead to communism, then the United States would support only orderly progress to majority rule in African states. If nonalignment meant denial of African connections to Communist states, then at least the United States would not insist on actively pro-American positions on the part of African leaders.

The course of the U.S. connection to Zaire since our involvement in the Congo crisis in 1960 reflects the logical implementation of a U.S. policy that views Africa solely in a globalist perspective.[17] The Mobutu coup simply ended feuding among politicians who could not decide on an alternative to the radicals. The United States supported the Mobutu regime against a variety of rebellions in the mid-1960s to keep Zaire from breaking up and especially to keep a large part of it from succumbing to left-wing guerrillas. To that end the United States assumed a role not very different from that of colonial guarantor. By the time of the Stanleyville airdrop in 1964 to rescue white hostages, the United States was supplying transport for Belgian paratroopers, pilots and jets for the Mobutu government, and cooperating with white mercenary battalions. The airdrop occurred while several African leaders thought they were conducting diplomatic negotiations to free the hostages. The furious African reaction recorded at the U.N. after the airdrop surprised Adlai Stevenson, then U.S. representative to the U.N. and a person sympathetic to African opinion. Within the course of a few years, the two faces of U.S. policy in Africa had been revealed.[18]

Perhaps the greatest damage to the U.S. image in Africa resulting from the intimate U.S. involvement in the formative years of the Mobutu regime comes from the role of the CIA.[19] The success of the CIA in finding, installing and protecting Mobutu allows vulnerable leaders in Africa to suspect the CIA as behind all antigovernment activity. Ironically, information about CIA activity emerges from U.S. congressional investigations and the free press of the United States. KGB activities in Africa can only be surmised. Be that as it may, confirmed information about CIA activity elsewhere in Africa continues to surface. U.S. policy continues to depend on covert operations at critical junctures in the creation of postcolonial governments. The Angola civil war at the time of transfer from Portugal in 1974 and 1975 is a case in point.

In the case of Angola the U.S. image went through virtually all phases of a worst-case scenario. CIA involvement, which went back to the early 1960s, wound up supporting the least effective anticolonial movement (FNLA of Roberto) and joined forces with an invasion by South African troops. Cuban troops and Soviet equipment could then be seen by Africans as saving the nationalist successors to Portuguese rule. Angola could be pictured as a scene of Cold War conflict, but the U.S. proxies were the racist South Africans. Any U.S.-installed government in Angola would have appeared as an extension of South African influence.

The United States lost interest in Africa from the mid-1960s to the mid-1970s, as Vietnam and the Middle East rose to the top of the Cold War regional agenda in foreign policy. At the same time, the demise of civilian nationalist governments and their replacement in many of Africa's new states with military regimes underscored the weakness of governments and the instability of political conditions. Economic aid did not seem to have much to do with political development. In turn, political development seemed to mean the destruction of institutions of popular consultation.

The focus of political struggle shifted to Portuguese colonies and to Rhodesia. The United States' strategic ties to Portugal and reliance on Britain to deal with the Unilateral Declaration of Independence by the white settler regime put the United States on the side of resistance to the further extension of African nationalism. At least that is the way it appeared to African leaders by the 1970s.[20]

The United States had more or less abandoned any effort to establish a unique progressive role in Africa, a position that would go beyond Europe's protection of its investments, but which would not forsake the interests of the West in a non-Communist order. It was an era of frustrated expectations on the part of African leaders. The United States was perceived as maintaining capabilities it was unwilling to exercise. In the Kissinger era of foreign policy, the United States did not expect black nationalists to overcome white rule in its settler or colonial variety in southern Africa.[21]

The Carter administration tried to project a more sympathetic image to the Africans. The appointment of Andrew Young as U.S. representative to the U.N. was a clear signal that the United States was going to try to respond in a more sensitive way to the interests of Third World countries. Young himself took a great interest in Africa, stressing that the major U.S. interests in the future lay in black Africa and not in strengthening ties with increasingly troubled South Africa.

In an important sense the United States' Africa policy in the Carter years summarizes the ambiguities of a policy meant to be both responsive to African interests and simultaneously resistant to changes that could be exploited by the Soviet Union. At the same time help from the United States seemed almost irrelevant to the economic shocks of an increasingly hostile world economy. In the Horn of Africa, we stayed with the emperor of Ethiopia for too long and then lost a chance to retain influence with the new military regime by insisting on their adherence to our newly applied standards of respect for human rights. In Rhodesia we were important backers of the British-managed agreement to establish arrangements by which a majority rule government could come to power. But this occurred after twelve years of guerrilla warfare, considerably reducing positive American influence.[22]

The Reagan administration has emphatically placed its Africa policy in the context of strategic competition with the Soviet Union. Many Africans see "contructive engagement" with South Africa as concealed support for the present system; U.S. aid now goes largely to strategically vital spots, such as Egypt, Sudan, Kenya and Somalia. Africa's economic problems are seen as requiring greater doses of private investment.[23]

There is a strain of anti-Americanism in Africa that reacts negatively to actions of the United States that intervene directly in small, poor Third World countries. The prosecution of the war in Vietnam created the image of the U.S. imperialist monster which has been difficult to dissolve. African leaders are particularly quick to see the restoration of colonial and racist connections when the United States projects its military might into weak and non-white countries. The U.S. invasion of Grenada is a case in point. Most African representatives at the U.N. spoke out against the U.S. action. No African states voted with the United States in the resolution deploring U.S. armed intervention; nevertheless seventeen African countries abstained.[24] That suggests that a new and growing differentiation of interests among African states that commentary based on the U.N. fails to capture.

CHANGING PATTERNS OF AFRICAN INTERNATIONAL RELATIONS

It is doubtful that African states will display a general and continent-wide pattern of attitudes toward U.S. policy in the future. African states are splitting up according to subregional interests, which permits African leaders to define positions separable from a continental African interest.[25] Material connections to the Soviet Union are now more significant in a few cases. To a lesser extent, regime type may also define positions taken. Operationally, the U.S. administration may overemphasize anti-Americanism in terms of votes and speeches at the U.N. or in other international agencies. In these places African states in leadership roles tend to feel they must represent a unified continental posture rather than a state position. Such is the justification offered by Zimbabwe in refusing to condemn the downing of the Korean airliner by the Soviet Union. Prime Minister Mugabe claimed he was upholding an African consensus on nonalignment in an international forum.[26] But within African regions African states are not acting out anti-American inclinations.

Cross-pressures are now at work on the attitudes of African leaders. The overall continental attitudes are attenuating. Despite general suspicion of the United States as an imperial power and disappointment with declining U.S. development assistance, real security concerns are emerging within Africa itself, serving to create a climate of receptivity for U.S. or Western support. Although the United States may place African security in the context of threats from the Soviet Union or surrogates such as Cuba, the effects of aggressive initiatives by African states create real fears for certain regimes, which can be reduced by direct or indirect U.S. help.

In Northern and trans-Saharan Africa Libyan intervention in Chad and supposed sponsorship of subversion against Sudan and Egypt mean that security assistance for the latter two countries and support for French intervention against Libya in Chad are no longer regarded as illegitimate U.S. interference, at least by people with stakes in the continued existence of the threatened regimes. In fact, active Libyan intervention elsewhere, e.g., in Uganda on the side of the Amin regime against the Tanzanian invasion, represents clear evidence of subimperialism that can be related to Soviet help.

Growing appreciation of the U.S. role as a great power and the requirements of its interests in that regard may lie behind the collapse of automatic support of liberation/self-determination causes, such as that of Polisario in Western Sahara on the part of African states. Recognition of Polisario as a member "government" of the OAU has split the organization. Morocco has seized and defends part of the former Spanish Sahara against guerrillas who claim nationalist/liberationist credentials. In the past they received help and sanctuary from Algeria. In some circles in Africa, the use of U.S. equipment by the Moroccans is not viewed in the same light today as the use of U.S. equipment by the Portuguese a decade ago.

What is interesting now in the 1980s is that U.S. or Western assertiveness cannot be seen as the sole cause of African conflicts. Morocco and Libya have seized neighboring territories and are not acting as proxies for the West or the East. Both countries have designs for a greater territorial expanse. In this part of Africa local conflicts are bringing in the great powers.[27] Manifestations of anti-Americanism are directly related to which side of the conflict a government inclines.

If Libyan subimperialism has been successfully resisted as a regional power system in the North, that is not the case with regard to South Africa at the other end of the continent. South African troops and South African supported guerrillas have been active in several neighboring states. On the other hand, the African "front line" states in southern Africa have provided training opportunities for the African National Congress, dedicated to overthrowing the South African government. South Africa's overwhelming military might permit it to operate at will in Namibia, which is still administered by South Africa, and to sponsor paramilitary operations by the Mozambique National Resistance against the successor regime to Portuguese colonial rule in Mozambique. While African states in this region may believe that the U.S. is not doing enough to undermine white rule in South Africa, they also recognize that the United States holds the key to a settlement in Namibia that would give local Africans a chance to run their own affairs. As in the

North, intra-African disputes have attracted elements of East–West conflict to the area. Opposition to certain U.S. policies are tempered by the necessity to support U.S. efforts on the side of decolonization.

East Africa and the Horn taken as one region is dominated by its proximity to the Middle East, including Iran, and the simmering conflicts on the Ethiopian borders. Both Kenya and Somalia have military aid agreements with the United States, Somalia the residual legatee of the U.S. departure from Ethiopia. These two countries and Sudan form a platform for U.S. strategic interests in the Middle East. All three countries have to be concerned about the significance of an Afro-Marxist, revolutionary, militarily strong Ethiopia. With Cuban and Soviet help, Ethiopia turned back a Somalian incursion and now occupies a small part of Somalia. The Ethiopian army remains embattled in Eritrea and in parts of non-Amharic Ethiopia against several "liberation fronts" based on locally dominant ethnic groups. Official attitudes toward the United States vary with the connections of present African leaders to the United States and with their perceived need of a U.S. presence to advance their own interests vis-à-vis African neighbors.

A similar analysis could be made in West Africa, although the regional power there, Nigeria, creates a strong presence by its comparatively active economy, which until recently drew workers from a number of neighboring states. Nigeria has asserted a regional role in the Chad conflict, expressing a particular interest in preventing Libyan influence from seeping southward. Nevertheless, Libyan radicalism seems to exert an attraction on other military regimes in the region, such as the Rawlings government in Ghana. That was the scene of an accusation of subversion against the U.S. ambassador himself over a year ago.[28]

In summary, more active roles for African states in African international relations mean that relations with the United States do not reflect continent-wide problems as much as current vectors of power and interest in the several regional subsystems of Africa. Attitudes toward the United States at official levels respond increasingly to security needs of African governments.

THE SIGNIFICANCE OF AFRO-MARXIST AND RADICAL STATES

Levels of officially expressed anti-Americanism would be expected to rise the more leftist the regime. In fact, the most stridently anti-American sentiments regularly emanate from Libya and Libyan representatives in African countries. The source is a combination of Islamic fundamentalism and populist radicalism. U.S. policy will remain basically suspect in North Africa as long as the United States is the chief support for Israel in the Middle East. Unhappiness about the U.S. position on Israel can be overridden partially by complementarities of concrete economic and military interests. Even in the case of Libya, Qaddafi's strident anti-imperialist rhetoric did not prevent him from doing business with U.S. oil companies without harrassing U.S. employees resident in Libya. Nevertheless the depth and durability of anti-Americanism of official Libya is disturbing because it draws on strong cultural trends in Islam today. Insofar as U.S. influence can be depicted as corrupting the cultural identity of Africans, especially Muslim Africans, it will sanctify whatever opposition arises to U.S. policies.

Leftist ideologies among African regimes can be divided into populist socialist and Afro-Marxist.[29] It is difficult to make sharp separations in policy, but differences can be discerned in regard to doctrinal adherence to more explicit Marxism–Leninism and in degree of intimacy with the Soviet Union. (A key sign in reflecting this difference may be in the institutional display of communist symbols and portraits of Marx and Lenin.) Opposition to "American imperialism" becomes an early part of political mobilization inside the country in places like Ethiopia and Mozambique.

Afro-Marxist states represent a potential source of anti-Americanism, if the political development of such regimes reflects the growth of effective vanguard parties with explicit ideologies. As well, Soviet and Cuban help in establishing such regimes in violent struggles against external and internal enemies creates a basis for ties with the Soviet Union. But Soviet assistance cannot create internal political stability or spur economic growth. Afro-Marxist states born in guerrilla struggle remain weak in peripheral rural areas and dependent on the personal control of top leaders. Some states, labeled in recent years by their own leadership as "scientific socialist," are really searching for influence rather than reflecting a connection to socialist states outside Africa. In an important sense all African governments are personal governments; therefore, all discerned inclinations may be temporary.[30] Projected policies justified by doctrine may be more a reflection of personal inclinations of the ruler than the established ideas of the leadership below the top, e.g., Tanzania and Zimbabwe.

It is not clear to what extent signs of anti-Americanism are contingent on current policy, even in leftist states. In the past few years, with the exception of Libya, all of Africa's radical regimes have made overtures to the United States with the object of relaxing tensions, hoping for some sort of U.S. aid or expansion of U.S. markets. Sekou Toure's Guinea may be the representative case in point. During his 26 years of rule, Toure swung from imitating the Maoist cultural revolution to seeking financial involvement with the Rockefeller interests in the United States. In 1979 Toure found he was not invited to a minisummit of left-wing heads of state held in Benin because he was seen to be too closely aligned with the Americans.[31]

"Sauve qui peut" may summarize the perspective of many African leaders in the face of today's harsh realities of political and economic decay. Continuing drought, worldwide recession, the failure of "statist" investment and marketing policies, and spreading personal corruption lead to more benign attitudes toward freer markets and personal incentives. Africa's harsh realities have made the United States more relevant to Africa than ever before. The present ideological disposition of a regime or a particular president does not override growing recognition that the West, and the United States, in particular, commands the economic resources to help Africa pull itself out of its present difficulties. Mugabe of Zimbabwe, who calls himself a Marxist, can offer the theological opinion that "communism is a much holier dogma than capitalism," but he also announces that the United States and Zimbabwe have no differences on policies regarding his country.[32] Mengistu of Ethiopia, who can link U.S. diplomats as "imperialist agents" to a plot against his government, also announces he is open to Western investment. In the same report his foreign minister asks for closer cooperation with the United States.[33] Whatever the underlying attitudes of African leaders to the basis of U.S. economic policy, the United States remains the main source of help in the near future.

While the symbolic links of pan-Africanism remain strong enough in the U.N. to permit common African positions to emerge on many votes in the General Assembly, differing interests have developed in relations between African states. In a number of cases these changes have placed the United States in a more favorable light. Perhaps the most spectacular example is now emerging in southern Africa. Despite much previous criticism, the U.S. policy of "constructive engagement" with South Africa has permitted the United States to emerge as broker between Mozambique and Angola on the one hand and South Africa on the other. Power rather than preference, certainly reluctantly and perhaps temporarily, has overcome previously overt support for the overthrow of the South African system on the part of South Africa's two "leftist" neighbors. A straw in the wind is the commitment of a U.S. mission to monitor the disengagement of Angolan and South African forces in southern Angola. The price of achievement may be increasing direct U.S. involvement in keeping the peace in southern Africa. U.S. officials are now receiving politely favorable receptions in capitals where they were shunned a few years ago.[34]

In northcentral and northwest Africa, the United States has moved to counter Libyan subversion. It is interesting to note that "conspiracies" cited are no longer confined to colonialists and imperialists, but come from other quarters, as observed by the vice-president of the Sudan not long ago.[35] In Africa at present, perhaps the only unmitigated anti-American stance adopted by a government is represented by Libya. The case deserves further investigation as a modular example of one extreme on the spectrum of possibilities of demonstrated anti-Americanism. Hostility to the United States encompasses opposition to U.S. policies as well as the character of U.S. society, for Qaddafi's vision of progress requires a degree of puritanism and communitarianism radically at odds with U.S. capitalist modernization. So deep is Libyan anti-Americanism that Libyan attacks on the United States have run the gamut from verbal abuse through violent demonstrations to military engagement, climaxing in an alleged plot to assassinate President Reagan in 1981.

Libyan anti-Americanism draws strength from revivalist, militant Islam. Thus far its greatest influence has been in Arab and Arabized Africa, rather than among Muslim populations in black Africa. Libyan diplomatic missions regularly propagandize against tthe United States, but the evidence of effective influence remains sparse and largely confined to places geographically close to Libya itself. Although the extent of imitation of Soviet political organization may have gone farthest in Ethiopia, whether it establishes a basis for long-term hostility to the United States remains unclear. In any case, Afro-communism has not created Soviet puppet states where it has appeared in Africa.[36] Even the Ethiopians have expelled Soviet as well as U.S. diplomats. Rather than primarily a cultural trend or an ideological-political trend, anti-Americanism in Africa reflects opposition to perceived U.S. policy inclinations or particular disagreements on policy; and it seems limited to political elites. As such, it is susceptible to policy shifts. At the very least, among better educated Africans, the potential for cooperating with the United States remains strong, compared to other industrial countries.[37]

COPING WITH ANTI-AMERICANISM

Not long ago the Uganda ambassador to the United States could say that Africa and America still know little about one another, for the U.S. system was unique and not easily understood by foreigners.[38] Attitudes to the United States develop constructively as a consequence of knowledge of the United States, as well as the policies of the United States in particular parts of the world. Concern for anti-Americanism in Africa is met in good part by offering windows on an open society. The tour by USIA in February 1984 for 22 African ambassadors is a promising illustration of this principle.

More than a decade ago, a poll of short-term African visitors to the United States revealed race relations as a major negative factor in the visitors' view of the United States.[39] In 1984 a black leader ran for president of the United States. Emphasis on increasing involvement of blacks in the U.S. presidential process is not just a propaganda message helpful to the United States in Africa; it also makes the issue of the U.S. relationship to the Third World a national issue. It is important for African elites to appreciate that a more generous assistance policy toward African countries draws considerable support inside the United States.

Getting the word out and letting others freely observe us are important recommendations for action. But the United States has global responsibilities as a superpower that are sometimes going to override sensitivity to African viewpoints. A concern for combatting anti-Americanism must not be confused with anxiety over why we are not loved. A focus on more effective propaganda can spill over into purely cosmetic matters, emphasizing the worst of image-building in the political process. The United States cannot close its society. Instead, it can glory in its diversity and pluralism, elements of which will be urging views at variance with the U.S. administration's policies at a given moment.

In the final analysis attitudes toward the United States overseas are products of policy, not causes of it. In stating that the United States expects it can have good relations with South Africa as well as black Africa, Assistant Secretary of State Chester Crocker derived his case from an accepted tradition of analysis in international politics.

We have interests in independent African states, in black Africa, that are significant and growing. We also have very important interests in South Africa. It is not going to be our position that we are going to let ourselves be driven to choose between those interests.[40]

If U.S. bilateral relations cannot be divorced from global responsibilities, that does not mean that they must be forced always into an East–West framework and defined only in terms of anti-Soviet priorities. The United States has an enormous global role to play in Africa that only indirectly relates to the Soviet Union, in matters of racial equality and economic development. As long as even favorably disposed African elites believe that U.S. policy is insensitive to their human needs, relations will respond to power necessities rather than possibilities for expanding mutual interests.

NOTES

1. The focus of this chapter is on anti-Americanism in relation to an African environment for U.S. policy. Research centers on black Africa, although the importance of trends in North Africa are noted. Anti-Americanism in South Africa, a phenomenon of some complexity that cuts across racial lines deserves a paper of its own. The author gratefully acknowledges the help of William Kaye, Raymond Hopkins and Richard Greenfield, who are absolved of responsibility for shortcomings in this final version.

2. *Africa News*, November 14, 1983; see also *The New York Times*, March 14, 1984.

3. Claude S. Phillips, *The African Political Dictionary*, Santa Barbara, CA: ABC-Clio Information Services, 1984, 189.

4. For example, Kwame Nkrumah, *Ghana, Autobiography*, London: Nelson, 1959, 20–39.

5. For the high symbolic visibility of Africa in the Kennedy administration, see Arthur Schlesinger, *A Thousand Days, John F. Kennedy in the White House*, Boston: Houghton Mifflin, 1965, 551–84.

6. Phillips, *op. cit.*

7. Raymond Copson, "African Perceptions," in *Soviet Policy and United States Response in the Third World*, report prepared for the Committee on Foreign Affairs, U.S. House of Representatives, by the Congressional Research Service, Library of Congress, Committee Print, 97C, 1S, March 1981, 283.

8. *The New York Times*, February 24, 1984.

9. Ali Mazrui, *African International Relations*, London: Heinemann, 1977, 194f; see also Copson, *op. cit.*

10. Ladun Anise, "African Attitudes toward America," *Issue* (African Studies Association), Fall 1971, 4; also Copson, *op. cit.*

11. See Crawford Young, *Ideology and Development in Africa*, New Haven: Yale University Press, 1982.

12. USIA Research Memorandum, "The U.S. Image in Three English-Speaking African Countries," Nov. 16, 1970, M-31-70; USIA Office of Research and Assessment, "Changes in Attitudes and Impressions Concerning the United States by Selected Groups of Short-term African Grantees," Mar. 31, 1971, R-1-71; USIA Research and Reference Service, "African Student Outlook: A Comparison of Findings at English and French-speaking Universities," August 1965, R-115-65; USIA Office of Research, "Opinion of the U.S. and U.S. Policies in Nairobi between Presidential China and USSR Visits," August 31, 1972, R-36-72: USIA Research Memorandum, "Educated Kenya Opinion on Selected Issues," Mar. 30, 1972, M-25-72. Cf. Walter Skurnick, "Ivoirien Student Perceptions of U.S. Africa Policy," *Journal of Modern African Studies*, v. 17, #3, September 1979, 409–32.

13. Copson, *op. cit.*, 285.

14. For a concise review of the main conceptual themes in U.S. foreign policy toward Africa in the 1950s and into the early 1960s, see Stephen R. Weissman, *American Foreign Policy in the Congo, 1960–64*, Ithaca: Cornell University Press, 1974, 15–114; see also Rupert Emerson, *Africa and United States Policy*, Englewood Cliffs, NJ: Prentice Hall, 1967.

15. See note #8.

16. Weissman, *op. cit.* A lively review of two decades of foreign policy toward Africa emphasizing anti-communism is contained in Henry F. Jackson, *From the Congo to Soweto, U.S. Foreign Policy toward Africa since 1960*, NY: William Morrow, 1982.

17. See the review in Crawford Young, "Zaire: the Unending Crisis," *Foreign Affairs*, v. 57, No. 1, Fall 1978, 169–85.

18. Weissman records this dramatically, *op. cit.*, 211–56.

19. Rene Lemarchand, "The CIA in Africa: How Central? How Intelligent?" also Stephen Weissman, "The CIA and U.S. Policy in Zaire and Angola," in Lemarchand, ed., *American Policy in Southern Africa: the Stakes and the Stance*, Washington, DC: University Press of America, 1978, 341–432.

20. Donald Rothchild, "Engagement and Disengagement in Africa," in Alan M. Jones, Jr., ed., *U.S. Foreign Policy in a Changing World*, NY: David McKay, 1973, 215–40.

21. See *The Kissinger Study of Southern Africa, N.S.S.M. 39*, ed. and introduced by Mohamed A. El-Khawas and Barry Cohen, Westport, CT: Lawrence Hill, 1976.

22. Donald Rothchild, "U.S. Policy Styles in Africa, From Minimal Engagement to Liberal Internationalism," in Kenneth A. Oye, *et al*, eds., *Eagle Entangled: U.S. Foreign Policy in a Complex World*, NY: Longman, 1979, 304–35.

23. "The United States and Africa in the 1980s," address by Secretary of State Shultz, February 15, 1984, Washington, DC: U.S. Department of State, Bureau of Public Affairs, Current Policy No. 549, 1984. See also Brenda Branaman, assisted by Geoffrey Johnson, "South Africa: Issues for U.S. Policy," Issue Brief No. IB 80032, Library of Congress, Congressional Research Service, March 18, 1980, October 18, 1983.

24. *Africa News*, November 14, 1983.

25. For an analysis that emphasizes growing differentiation of interests, see Henry Bienen, "United States Foreign Policy in a Changing Africa," *Political Science Quarterly*, v. 93, #3, Fall 1978, 443–64.

26. *Washington Notes on Africa*, Winter 1984.

27. Colin Legum, "Communal Conflict and International Intervention in Africa," in Legum, *et al.*, *Africa in the 1980s*, NY: McGraw-Hill, 1979, 23–68.

28. See report in *People's Daily Graphic* (Ghana), April 1, 1983, quoted in "Soviet Active Measures," U.S. Department of State, Bureau of Public Affairs, Special Report No. 110, September 1983. A penetrating assessment of Libya's involvement in Chad is contained in Benyamin Neuberger, *Involvement, Invasion and Withdrawal, Qaddafy's Libya and Chad 1969-1981*, Tel Aviv University, Shiloah Center for Middle Eastern and African Studies, Occasional Papers No. 83, Tel Aviv, Israel, May 1982.

29. See note #14.

30. Carl Rosberg and Robert Jackson, *Personal Rule in Black Africa*, Berkeley: University of California Press, 1983. For the uses of socialist ideology, see Kenneth Jowitt, "Scientific Socialist Regimes in Africa," in Carl Rosberg and Thomas Callaghy, eds., *Socialism in Sub-Saharan Africa: A New Assessment*, Institute of International Studies, University of California, Berkeley, 1979, 133-73.

31. John Cartright, *Political Leadership in Africa*, NY: St. Martin's Press, 1983, 209.

32. *Washington Post*, December 15, 1983; see also *IDAF News Notes*, October 1983.

33. *The New York Times*, February 7, 1984.

34. *Christian Science Monitor*, January 20, 1984; *Washington Post*, February 5, 1984.

35. *The New York Times*, March 6, 1984.

36. Cf. David and Marina Ottaway, *Afro-Communism*, NY: Africana, 1981.

37. Scott Thompson, remarks at symposium, "U.S. Policy toward Africa," *Issue* (African Studies Association), Fall/Winter 1982, 24.

38. *Washington Post*, February 10, 1984.

39. USIA Office of Research and Assessment, *op. cit.*, R-1-71, March 31, 1971.

40. Quoted in *Africa Report*, July 1981, 45.

10

Multinational Corporations and Anti-Americanism

Dan Haendel

Anti-Americanism is difficult to define, although it may be generally described as a negative attitude toward the United States in general terms and, on occasion, flares up in overt acts against U.S. entities such as embassies and firms. The near-automatic coupling of such U.S. bodies as the Central Intelligence Agency (CIA) and American Multinational Corporations (MNCs) in the view of many host countries often reflects a Marxist stimulated perception of the United States. The United States is often portrayed as an imperial giant with U.S. MNCs serving as instruments located abroad for controlling its global interests and subjugating developing countries. The triangular relations of MNCs, host countries, and home countries are driven by the differing interests and perspectives of the parties, thereby making the phenomenon of anti-Americanism even more difficult to disentangle.

MNCs generally, and U.S. MNCs in particular, are usually cast as a threat to the ability of its host developing country to control the activities within its boundaries. This may reflect a host country's self-doubt about its capacity to control an MNC. The struggle for control often occurs against the backdrop of the view of MNCs as institutions that plunder the national resources of the host country with the major

The views expressed in this essay are solely those of the author and not necessarily those of the U.S. Department of the Treasury.

benefits accruing primarily to the firm and its home country, and few to the host country.

Rising nationalism in host countries has been manifested in efforts by a number of such developing countries to exercise greater control over and gain a greater share of the benefits from resources generated by MNC activities within their borders. Quite often the most emotional conflicts have centered on natural resources.

The "love–hate" relationship between U.S. MNCs and their host countries is often mirrored by the ambivalent relations between the United States and such countries, especially those of the Third World. Preconceptions and overt acts against U.S. MNCs reveal a deep-seated antipathy toward them, even as developing countries try to lure them to advance their economic development. This antagonism seems to be based both on realistic and conflicting interests intertwined with imaginary fears that can result in harmful consequences.[1]

Prejudice has been defined as "thinking ill of others without sufficient warrant."[2] Interestingly, U.S. MNCs are often feared and viewed as threats even in Third World countries, such as India, where their presence is negligible. The strangeness of and assumptions about the attributes of U.S. MNCs produce an image or stereotype that exaggerates their role in the Third World but may well serve to justify the way such countries relate to these firms.[3] Real grievances are often set against a general climate of anti-Americanism.

Selective perception may serve to sustain a stereotype of U.S. MNCs, a stereotype that may well be based on a kernel of truth. For example, national elites of developing countries tend to view U.S. managers of MNCs in their countries as "aggressive, impatient, tense, brutal, insular, arrogant, and heavy-handed."[4] Furthermore, the stereotype may well serve to turn U.S. MNCs into choice scapegoats for the frustrations of developing countries and their leaders in the event their economic development plans fall short of expectation. Needless to say, the hostility aimed at U.S. MNCs can prompt chronic anxiety on their part as they seek to accommodate themselves to the environment they face.

Conflict and controversy have been hallmarks of the relationship of multinational corporations (MNCs), host countries, and home countries during the past several decades. Much ink has been spilled over the theme *Storm Over the Multinationals*.[5] Often the literature is as emotional and controversial as the phenomenon it is analyzing.[6]

Many writers automatically tend to associate MNCs with U.S. firms. There is a certain appealing symmetry between the perceived attributes, perhaps more accurately described as stereotypes, associated with these two entities and each set of views may well serve to reinforce the other. MNCs are perceived as big, foreign, generators of enormous profits, and exporters of the host country's resources. Americans are often viewed as avaricious, materialistic, alien, and amoral. The marriage of these two sets of characteristics in a U.S. MNC provides an appealing target.

Critics of MNCs often present a stinging indictment of their behavior and impact. MNCs are portrayed as agents of their home governments acting in furtherance of colonialist ambitions, plundering the natural and human resources of the host countries, and raping the host country by remitting to the home country outrageous profits generated by local projects.[7] Alternatively, some critics argue that MNCs do not owe their allegiance to any nation–state and operate only in pursuit of their own interests and insatiable thirst for profits without any consideration for values or social responsibility.

Proponents of the benefits generated by the activities of MNCs point to the contribution they make to the economic growth of the host country. They emphasize the positive affects of MNCs as "socially responsible corporate citizens," who reinvest a large percentage of their profits, develop local managers, and provide services that would not be otherwise available.[8]

Some writers have adopted a more balanced and analytical view of the advantages and disadvantages arising from the operation of such enterprises in host countries. This has given rise to the development of cost/benefit analyses to examine the role of MNCs in a host country. Nonetheless, the realm of the relationship between MNCs and anti-Americanism is largely the zone of emotions.

THE PROFILE OF MNCs

If the characteristics of "bigness," foreign" and profit seekers contribute to a negative perception of and prejudice toward MNCs, as indeed seems to be the case, MNCs would appear to have little leeway in avoiding these labels. MNCs are big, foreign, and profit-motivated by definition, since they tend to be the largest corporations of the largest economies. This bigness and operations across national boundaries lend focus to the image of MNCs as an octopus with tentacles reaching out in different markets, with a global organization that does not take account of host country goals.

The data clearly support the proposition that "bigness" is an attribute of MNCs. The profile of the top 15 U.S.-based MNCs is provided in Table 10.1. Not only are these among the largest U.S. corporations, but the foreign operations constitute a very large percentage, averaging over 50 percent in most cases, of the firm's total. The complexity of such a firm can be seen in General Electric's profile of 400,000 employees in 144 countries producing or servicing 130,000 products with 1980 sales of about $25 billion and earnings of $1.5 billion—about 40 percent from foreign sources.

It is interesting to compare the gross revenues of such MNCs with the GNP of developing countries. Even if this is an imperfect comparison, it is noteworthy that leading U.S. MNCs generate revenues greater than the gross national product of such countries as the Philippines, Peru, and Egypt.

However, since the association between MNCs and U.S. MNCs is often made automatically, it is important to point out that many of the

TABLE 10.1:   Top 15 American MNCs (as of year-end 1982)

	Total Revenue (Millions)	Foreign Revenues As % of Total	Foreign Operating Profits As % of Total	Foreign Assets as % of Total
Exxon	$97,173	71.4%	50.8%	48.0%
Mobil	60,969	62.0	63.8	51.6
Texaco	46,986	66.2	65.0	47.8
Standard Oil of California	34,362	49.3	29.3	37.8
Phibro-Salomon	26,703	62.2	64.7	11.6
Ford Motor	37,067	44.6	—	65.3
IBM	34,364	44.6	37.3	43.4
General Motors	60,026	23.9	—	29.7
Gulf Oil	28,427	40.5	33.3	37.3
Du Pont	33,223	33.3	32.7	24.3
Citicorp	17,814	61.0	62.0	60.4
ITT	21,922	44.8	71.3	34.0
Bank America	14,955	53.8	65.0	45.8
Chase Manhattan	10,171	61.0	70.0	51.2
Dow Chemical	10,618	52.2	40.2	44.5

Source: Adapted from *Forbes,* July 4, 1983, p. 114.

largest MNCs are not American at all. Indeed, as shown in Table 10.2, many of the largest MNCs are European or Japanese, even though many observers often incorrectly identify them as American, an interesting and telling mistake. Furthermore, many Third World-based MNCs have recently risen on the global scene. Nonetheless, as we shall see, quite often the attacks on MNCs are a manifestation of actual grievances, disagreements, or conflicts with U.S. MNCs. In addition, these firms also serve as a convenient vehicle for demonstrating hostility toward the policies of the U.S. government.

The dominance of U.S. MNCs in international business, to include their foreign assets and revenues, is striking and has been estimated at about 60 percent of total MNC activity and as high as 20 percent of total global economic activity.[9] U.S. foreign direct investment abroad grew at a rapid pace during the late 1960s and early 1970s, rising from about $75 billion in 1970, to about $110 billion in 1974 and to $225 billion in 1982.

Interestingly, in 1982, developed countries accounted for about 75

TABLE 10.2: Top 15 Non-American Companies (as of Year-end 1982)

	Revenues (Millions)	Corporate Headquarters
Royal Dutch/ Shell Group	$83,809	Netherlands/U.K.
Mitsubishi	68,721	Japan
Mitsui	68,184	Japan
CITOH	55,863	Japan
Marubeni	52,199	Japan
British Petroleum	51,353	U.K.
Sumitomo	48,389	Japan
Nissho Iwai	34,661	Japan
ENI	27,525	Italy
IRI	24,833	Italy
Unilever	23,134	Netherlands/U.K.
Total	20,040	France
Petroleos Mexicanos	19,624	Mexico
UEBA	19,318	Germany
Petroleo Brasileiro	18,937	Brazil

Source: Adapted from Forbes, July 4, 1983, p. 124.

percent of this investment while developing countries accounted for 25 percent, with Latin America hosting about two-thirds, or $33 billion, of all foreign U.S. direct investment in developing countries. U.S. firms had a rate of return of 8.2 percent in developed countries and 15.8 percent in developing countries. However, the rate of return in Latin America was 7.9 percent whereas in other developing countries it was 30.9 percent. Furthermore, the 62 and 46 percent rate of reinvestment by U.S. firms in 1981 and 1982 in the developing countries has been substantially higher than in the developed countries.[10]

THE RISE OF MNCs

U.S. corporations had relatively simple reasons for their original direct entry into foreign markets. This entry sought, for the most part, to capture markets and avoid tariff barriers. Of course, there are many other reasons for direct foreign investment, including the advantages derived from access to technology, cost differentials, raw material sources, and a favorable regulatory environment.[11]

The dramatic rise in U.S. MNC development and activity occurred primarily in the aftermath of World War II and during the period of Pax Americana. The dominant position of the United States in global affairs was not limited to the political arena; it was also reflected in the international financial system. London was overshadowed by New York as the world's financial center, with the U.S. dollar emerging as the key international currency. The pivotal role of the United States in international finance could be seen in the linchpin role played by the dollar, whose stability provided the security required for the availability of long-term capital. The connection between the diplomatic dimensions of U.S. foreign policy and its international, economic and financial aspects has not always been apparent, notwithstanding such cases as U.S. intervention in Guatemala on behalf of United Fruit or the role of ITT and the CIA regarding Allende in Chile.

U.S. power provided the guarantee for international trade and investment to flourish. Protection for trade routes and access to raw materials such as oil and nonfuel minerals were assured. "As both banker and cop, the U.S. was the guarantor of the postwar global economy."[12]

The degree of control exercised by MNCs in host countries has long been an issue at the forefront of the triangular relationship among MNCs, host countries, and home countries. Such fears are not limited to developing host countries. During the post–World War II period, the

perceived danger on the part of host countries was that U.S. corporations would acquire control of foreign corporations and seriously impinge
on the sovereignty of the host countries, especially their government's
capacity to control domestic economic and political matters.[13]

It is interesting to note that Western Europeans were quite concerned
about U.S. investment in Europe, a reflection of the shift in global power.
Furthermore, since the 1970s many Americans have raised concerns
about the degree of control accruing to Arab states from their corporate
investments in the United States and the way this control will be used.
In short, anti-American sentiment, reflected in fears and negative attitudes toward U.S. investment is by no means limited to developing countries. Nor is the phenomenon of host country penetration limited to developing countries. Indeed, the anti-Arab sentiment reflected in fears
and prejudices toward Arab investment in the United States is an interesting foil to the phenomenon of anti-Americanism and its relationship to activities of U.S. MNCs in the Third World.

Since U.S. MNCs followed the global extension of the U.S. flag, the
U.S. business community's recent concern has grown as it perceives the
folding of the umbrella that protected its interests. On occasion, the U.S.
government intervened either politically or militarily to assure its interests
and those of its business entities. This type of interference toward
manifestations of anti-American sentiment or resentment about the role
or activities of MNCs served to buttress the image of the U.S. government as an oppressive force working at the behest of the U.S.-based
MNCs.

Moreover, many countries, both developed and developing, resented
the global dominance of the United States. There was a lag between the
rise of U.S. power and expansion of U.S. business abroad. The largest
increase in this exposure during the late 1960s and early 1970s coincided
with a period that many point to as the "Retreat of American Power."[14]
The concern of numerous U.S. MNCs is the high and rising percentage of their assets abroad at a time of perceived decline in U.S. global
power. This concern was particularly reflected during the severe anti-
American Iranian upheavals that brought down the Shah's rule.

MNCs AND NATIONALISM

Although the major benefits provided by an MNC include the transfer of such vital factors of production as capital, managerial expertise,
and technology, an MNC is often an agent of change within the host

society. Such effects may be welcomed in certain instances but are more often viewed as overbearing intrusions. The entry of foreign MNCs into the domestic environment of developing countries in the throes of fundamental changes provides an environment of inherent conflict for the relationship. Not only is an MNC perceived as an "outsider," but an MNC with a centralized organizational structure means that the subsidiary located in the host country takes its instructions from the parent corporation in the home country. Although a decentralized structure provides the subsidiary in a host country with greater leeway, it will still be perceived as "foreign" and under the domination of outsiders.

Although nebulous in nature, the importance of the focus of nationalism and national interests as driving forces for the "we" versus "them" attitudes of emerging nation–states should not be underestimated. Nationalism has been described as a state of mind that encompasses a group's sentiment with respect to their common characteristics, traditions, and goals.[15]

Such a state of mind can create extremely strong feelings that may well be irrational and not subject to alteration through a logical reasoning process. By identifying as a "we" and providing their loyalty to the nation–state, citizens of a host country are predisposed to view "foreign" corporations as "they" whose political and economic objectives are either not in harmony with, or even antithetical to, those of the nation–state. Accordingly, the power struggle between an MNC and its host country government revolves around the degree of control each will exercise in their relations. Often the allocation of resources "becomes more of an emotional issue dominated by images of the outsider preying on the property of the we-group than a question which can be thought out fairly logically in terms of economic benefits and obligations."[16] Furthermore, the degree of control a host government exercises over foreign firms stems, in part, from its animosity toward foreign investment.

Some have argued that an MNC must accommodate itself to the host country's environment. Although the focus is often on anti-American feelings aimed at MNCs, during the 1960s U.S. MNCs often rejected joint ventures with local firms. Research into this phenomenon revealed the following: "An inflexible policy against entering any joint-ventures was nearly always a veneer covering basic distrust by United States businessmen, and possibly dislike of non-Americans."[17]

Although expropriations are often the most severe manifestation of anti-American sentiment targeted at U.S. MNCs, numerous other restrictive regulations can also influence the investment climate. In 1962, the U.S. Congress passed the Hickenlooper amendment that requires the termination of U.S. aid to a country that has expropriated U.S. property without providing prompt and adequate compensation. This is another demonstration of the effort of the home country, and the United States in particular, to protect the interests of its firms.

In comparison with historical experiences that included extraterritorial rights granted to foreign firms by host countries, such as China, at the insistence of the home country, to include intervention by military force, the role played by home countries on behalf of their firms has declined markedly. Despite the prevailing view in most developing countries, the United States and other home countries have, for the most part, intervened on behalf of their corporate citizens abroad when they perceived other substantial national interests were at stake. Furthermore, local political leaders have employed anti-foreign investment and anti-MNC oratory as a means of tapping into the anti-foreign sentiment prevalent in many of these countries.

LOOKING INTO ATTITUDES

An analysis of the connection between U.S. MNCs and anti-Americanism requires a focus both on the behavior of these MNCs and the attitudes of the host country. Harsh criticism leveled at MNCs in general, and U.S. MNCs in particular, as well as several instances of outbreaks of severe conflict have motivated their efforts toward becoming good corporate citizens. Nevertheless, some maintain that MNCs are constrained in achieving such goals on the grounds that the MNC–host country relationship is inherently conflictual and because an MNC subsidiary is, at best, unlikely to be viewed as anything better than a resident alien. In short, U.S. MNCs are big, foreign, and seek profits and those factors are sufficient to fuel suspicions, foster jealousies and resentment, and result in a negative, if not hostile, attitude toward these entities.

MNCs have been described as being in a state of siege.[18] However, the question is whether U.S. MNCs have brought this upon themselves by their actions or whether they are innocent victims of unjustified and irrational attacks by their host countries. In short, if U.S. MNCs are hated, have they caused this hatred; if they have, are these firms culpable for causing the general phenomenon of anti-Americanism?

MNCs face a number of contradictory trends in both developed and developing host countries. On the one hand, MNCs have been feared because they are considered to be so big as to defy the ability of host governments to control their behavior which, combined with their perceived alien nature and greed, fosters the notion of *Sovereignty At Bay*.[19] On the other hand, many host governments have often considered MNCs a critical component of their economic development programs and not necessarily difficult to regulate or, indeed, expropriate.

Prophecies of those who thought the nation–state would wither away under the pressures of the economic rationalization brought to the global stage by MNCs have proven to be ill-founded. Nevertheless, the perception of the threat posed by MNCs to the sovereignty of the host nation–state has had a significant and lingering impact on mobilizing opposition to MNCs, with U.S. MNCs the leading culprits. These images have fueled an undercurrent of resentment to their very presence in many countries. Although dormant for the most part, anti-American outbursts have resulted in a number of dramatic confrontations between U.S. MNCs and their host countries, with the U.S. government often called upon to intervene on behalf of the U.S. firm. Ironically, actions taken by the U.S. government on behalf of its firms on a number of occasions have done more than place it in direct conflict with the host government. Such measures reinforce the image of the MNC as an instrument of the U.S. government, whose willingness to intervene in the "domestic" affairs of a host country to protect its business empire exacerbates its negative portrayal.

ATTITUDES TOWARD MNCs

Although attitude surveys regarding U.S. MNCs are sparse, the Conference Board has examined the views of MNC managers and host country national elites.[20] These surveys conclude that the generally negative attitudes toward U.S. MNCs are not as hostile as often portrayed in the academic literature. Nonetheless, it is an environment in flux with a substantial degree of differentiation between the attitudes in developed as opposed to developing countries.

Major findings from surveys of national elites toward U.S. MNCs in such *developed* countries as Canada and Italy suggest the following: 1) they are not viewed as a serious problem, in part because of their contribution to the local economy, and the criticism is often aimed at the host government's failure to develop an adequate regulatory framework for coping with such firms; 2) they are perceived to conform to local laws, and issues such as payment of taxes, repatriation and reinvestment of profits, local use of resources, and the hiring and training of local employees are not considered contentious; and 3) they are urged to integrate more fully into the local economy, contribute more to host country economic development, and adapt more readily to the changing environment they are likely to confront, but are not called upon to withdraw.[21]

Despite the less negative view of U.S. MNCs in developed countries, such countries do have an ambivalent attitude toward U.S. MNCs. This is reflected in data indicating that over half of those elites surveyed in European countries believe that foreign direct investment poses a threat to their business independence. The threat many perceive stems from the international nature of MNCs which is believed to provide them with the ability to violate local laws.

The ambivalence of developed and developing countries' elites toward MNCs is also reflected in the attitude of the U.S. government. To a varying degree, each in its own way seems to have the attitude of "MNCs, you can't live with 'em, and you can't live without 'em." Developed countries seem to appreciate the contribution of MNCs as they also seek to counter the threats to sovereignty they perceive them to present. Developing countries tend to have a starker view of the role of MNCs and their conflicts tend to be more bitter and emotional. As we shall discuss below, this tendency may have a number of causes, such as the dominance and visibility of the MNCs in smaller developing host country economic markets, a colonial legacy, concentration in natural resources, and the notion that "foreign" is equated with imperialism and an alien culture.

THE PERCEPTION OF MNCs
IN DEVELOPING COUNTRIES

The term developing countries cuts across a spectrum of nation–states at different stages of economic development, varying from Bangladesh to Brazil. Most MNC activity is largely confined to the more advanced developing countries, recently labeled the newly industrialized countries. For U.S. MNCs the locus of activity in developing countries has been primarily in Latin America, with the Far East and the Middle East as secondary areas.

In many host developing countries, particularly those with traditional societies, MNCs are viewed as avaricious and the purveyors of change, often contrary to the host country's national interest. Despite this negative view of MNCs, many developing countries, having adopted a strategy of economic development, seek to entice MNCs to locate within their borders as a means of obtaining employment opportunities, the requisite capital, managerial expertise, and technology. The ambivalence toward U.S. MNCs, the specter they are perceived to be, and the explanations often presented are well summarized in the following observation:

"Curiously enough, the MNC is the institution most coveted and most feared by those national leaders who would further economic growth. The fact that the MNCs have neither armies nor guns is not always reassuring. Overbearing political intervention in Chile, as well as the use of large sums of money to win favors from highly placed political and administrative officials in other countries, are events that lead to nightmarish visions of the uses to which economic power can be put. It is then but a short step to the conclusion that the MNC is really the instrument of an imperialist national government, available to do whatever bidding those who carry the flag may demand.

Others will take the same information to support the apocalyptic claim that the world will soon be controlled by a few hundred of the largest MNCs. This particular inference reverses the first, for it returns to the idea that national sovereignties are things of the past and that, unless the further development of the MNCs as private centers of economic power is forestalled and cut back, national governments will everywhere be nothing more than corporate pawns."[22]

The Conference Board's attitude studies concluded that developing countries such as Brazil and Nigeria were not bitterly hostile toward U.S. foreign investors. However, there is a marked degree of greater suspicion and distrust among developing host countries toward MNCs. In addition, developing countries' elites tend to feel that the host country is overly dependent both on the U.S. MNC and its home country, with varying results on the question of whether the host country is in control of its destiny. The issue of control is dramatically portrayed in the struggle over the natural resource industries in host developing countries and may well be emerging in the area of foreign debt repayment.

It is noteworthy that few investment disputes have arisen regarding manufacturing industries. Some argue that manufacturing assets are "inherently immune against nationalization."[23] Nevertheless, both IBM and Coca-Cola struggled with the Indian government regarding the basis for their operations in that country. These companies considered the demands made by India unacceptable and opted to leave. Nevertheless, such episodes appear to be relatively rare.

NATURAL RESOURCES

Foreign investments in natural resources have been the areas of greatest conflict and aroused strong emotions of anti-Americanism in the 1970s. The issue of dependence on certain U.S. mineral and other producers has been particularly acute in Latin American countries. Yet this dependence often stems from national objectives greater than can be achieved by domestic efforts.

Major U.S. involvement in protecting investments of U.S.-based MNCs has stemmed from nationalization disputes, primarily in Latin America, ranging from Mexico's nationalization in 1938 to those of Chile and Peru in the 1970s. A profile of Latin America reveals that the bulk of these nationalizations have occurred in the natural resource, banking, and utilities sectors. U.S. manufacturing investments were nationalized only in the sweeping actions taken by Castro in Cuba and Allende in Chile.[24]

Resource nationalism has been reflected in the oil and nonfuel minerals industries. Both immediate and creeping expropriation of oil and mining projects have become common when host countries seek to control their natural resources. Cognizant of its dependence on critical resources, the United States has sought to ensure access to them, and its actions in support of its firms has put it in conflict with certain countries. However, the trend in the Middle East oil and Latin American oil nonfuel minerals industries has been similar, namely their nationalization.

Third World demands for major changes in the world's distribution of power and resources are reflected in the call for a New International Economic Order (NIEO). These countries tend to regard the United States as a conservative power favoring the maintenance of the status quo and the protection of MNCs. The underlying theme of the demands enshrined in several United Nations General Assembly resolutions is a producer state's "full permanent sovereignty" over "all its wealth, natural resources and economic activities." The Charter of Economic Rights and Duties of States gives each state the right to regulate and exercise authority over foreign investment, to regulate and supervise the activities of transnational corporations within its national jurisdiction, and to nationalize, expropriate or transfer ownership of foreign property.[25]

Many of these demands are significant not so much because of the novelty of the issues but rather because of the intense emotions they aroused. The stated purpose of the NIEO is to advance the goal of world development and international economic cooperation. The uncertainty created by such strident demands, however, has often channeled private foreign investment away from developing countries to developed countries whose investment climates are perceived to be safer by MNCs.

Secretary of State Hull's letter of April 3, 1940, to the Mexican ambassador to the United States clearly and succinctly expressed the U.S. view, which remains the official U.S. position, with respect to expropriation, namely that "the right to expropriate property is coupled with and conditioned on the obligation to make adequate, effective and prompt compensation. The legality of an expropriation is in fact dependent upon the observance of this requirement."[26] However, investment disputes arising from such host country actions as intervention, forced contract negotiations, coerced sales, and confiscatory taxes may not consitute a formal expropriation yet may be expropriatory in effect.

The most contentious provision of the NIEO is the concept of a state's permanent sovereignty over its natural resources coupled with its sole control over all related economic activities and disputes. The NIEO questions such notions as "the inviolability of private property," the "sanctity of private international contracts," and the good faith performance of contractual obligations of states. Although the concept of private ownership was pivotal for foreign investors involved in extractive industries, many present-day concession agreements provide that natural resources are the property of the state, not of the foreign investor. To safeguard its stake in the fixed assets as well as the overall arrangement, the MNC and its home country often insist that the principle of *pacta sunt servanda* should control. A breakdown of the arrangement, however, will often result in disputes over "appropriate compensation."

The politics surrounding the nationalization of Chile's mining industry provides an example of a host country's adoption and implementation of compensation principles and the emotional environment in which the actions occurred. The Chilean 1971 law authorizing the nationalization of private investment did accept the principle of compensation. It provided, however, that the amount of compensation would be measured by the book value of the firm reduced by deductions for excess profits and assets not in good working order.

The deduction of excess profits became the most controversial provision of this compensation formula. This deduction was justified as a means of readjusting an "unconscionable" contract, that is, one unreasonably favorable to one of the parties, reached because of the uneven bargaining position of a host country vis-à-vis a foreign investor at the time it granted the original concession. The perception of such imbalance often stimulates negative perceptions of the home country, with the United States the leading player in Latin America, and prompts host countries to get such firms under the government's control.

Technical and legal arguments over compensation formulas were not the cause of actions taken by U.S. firms located in Chile. They were opposed to the expropriation itself and several, with ITT often accused as the leading villain, took steps to involve the CIA in opposing Allende's measures. The "dependencia" of Chile on Anaconda and Kennecott copper production was enormous, accounting for over one-fourth of Chile's economy, and their taxes constituting about one-half of the government's budget.[27]

Table 10.1 demonstrates a typical firm's investment/return behavior. Depending on the type of industry, the initial investment outlay may not be recouped by the generated profits for a number of years. A mining venture, for example, may not recoup its investment for ten to twenty years. However, as the project matures, the developing country often feels that it is being exploited because of the decrease in benefits it receives. This sense of exploitation is a festering sore of anti-American sentiment.

BANKING: EMERGING RESENTMENT?

During the 1980s foreign banks may usurp the role played by resource companies during the 1960s and 1970s as the primary focus of resentment in the eyes of certain developing countries. Having borrowed vast sums for their development, many countries are experiencing great difficulties repaying their debts.

The domestic political repercussions of the approximately $810 billion year-end 1983 debt burden of such key developing countries as Mexico, Brazil, Argentina, Chile, Venezuela and Nigeria, to mention only a few, have emerged in stark terms. A number of observers are convinced that the increased demands being made by bankers are creating a "political pressure cooker" with an explosive potential of great consequence. Prompted by their self-interest, banks tend to focus rather narrowly on a country's ability to repay its loans, not necessarily on the fall-out that may ensue, even though those events could well reduce the probability that such payments can be made.[28]

Not only have questions been raised about whether the priorities of the banks, especially U.S. banks, are the same as those of the creditor governments, but also whether the demands of banks on debtor countries of importance to such creditor nations as the United States sour the relationship between these countries. As one U.S. diplomat is reported to have framed the problem, even if with a dash of hyperbole:

> If Mexico told the government that hordes of Mexicans will cross the border unless interest payments are cut, the U.S. government might cut those payments. But bankers have ice water in their veins when it comes to such a threat. They couldn't—and shouldn't—care less. [This] narrow view could go against U.S. aims: the cost of more illegal aliens coming into the U.S. may be greater than the cost of some sort of concession on the debt. Bankers won't make that calculation.[29]

The prominent role of foreign banks, especially such U.S. banks as Citibank, Chase Manhattan, Bank of America, and Manufacturers Hanover, who are the major creditors of developing countries, has contributed to a degree of resentment whose implications are likely yet to be determined. Bankers have sought debtor government guarantees for private loans to assure the availability of foreign exchange, leading the State Department official to observe that "it just doesn't look right when they give a businessman money to pay foreign bankers when they don't have the foreign exchange to import food."[30]

More significant, perhaps, is an increasing public awareness in debtor countries of the austerity demands being made by the banks or by the IMF—often, in the popular mind, at the behest of these U.S. banks—to which they attribute their economic difficulties. Often this is reinforced by the perception that these banks are holding back on lending essential foreign exchange. This negative domestic reaction against these foreign banks could result in severe restrictions on their future activities in these countries. Although to date the resentment has not specifically focused on the United States, it has not gone unnoticed that U.S. banks are the key players in the Latin American debt game. It is not a great distance from resentment against banks, to U.S. banks, and then to the United States.

The reduction in the growth rates of developing countries during the early 1980s caused increased unemployment and brought to an abrupt halt much of the economic and social progress achieved by developing countries during the 1970s. Many experts fear that prolonged austerity measures adopted as part of current rescheduling efforts will result in debt repudiation, riots, or even revolution. "Support has been mounting in Brazil for declaring a moratorium forcing a debt renegotiation, including a grace period, longer terms and reduced interest rates."[31]

The chances for the success of austerity programs would appear to require fine tuning to avoid causing social upheaval if the measures are too tough, or a cutback of foreign commercial loans if they are not tough enough.[32]

> If re-entrenchment goes too far, it will probably bring on a revolt and a takeover by a nationalistic regime that would repudiate Brazil's foreign debt. If it doesn't go far enough—as appears likely—foreign banks will find it difficult to put up the money Brazil will need over the next several years. In that case, too, Brazil is probably in for dangerous social turbulence.[33]

As these austerity measures, such as cutting wages, are implemented, they can trigger social and economic dislocations with potentially severe political consequences.

> The government will be hard put to enforce even this more moderate wage law without bringing on grave social unrest. While government officials, the IMF, politicians and businessmen grapple with the targets and statistics of austerity, the Brazilian masses live it. During the past three years, real per capita income in Brazil has fallen more sharply than during the Depression of the 1930's. More than a quarter of Brazil's work force of 49 million is either out of work or "underemployed," meaning that the family head cannot even earn a $66 minimum monthly wage. The slums that millions of Brazilians live in were beginning to improve, but with austerity the construction of sewage systems, hospitals, and schools has come to a standstill. In desperation a traditionally peace-loving and resilient people have taken to crime. Some 230 riots and lootings were reported in September [1983] alone. In a country where hope has been nurtured by an unflappable faith in a superpower future, little hope remains.[34]

The unanswered question is whether the political stability in these countries will hold as the austerity measures induce social and political strains. Whether a revolution or the rise of a demagogue will focus the undercurrent of resentment on foreign banks generally, and U.S. banks specifically, or their home countries, especially the United States, remains to be seen.

THE IMPORTANCE OF THE HOME COUNTRY

For host countries experiencing political and economic turbulence, MNCs generally, and perhaps U.S. MNCs in particular, the home country serves as a convenient whipping boy or scapegoat for all the difficulties, anxieties, and problems confronting the state. One of the major benefits provided by a "Great Satan," such as a U.S. MNC, is that having been tagged with the label, it can be identified as the culprit responsible for any or all of a country's ills. "Because at bottom many of these attacks reflect a prescriptive belief that private property is itself evil and unacceptable, a seemingly formidable ideological foundation for such attacks is readily at hand. This being so, it seems apparent that today it is not the nation–state but rather the multinational corporation that is at bay."[35]

The importance of the behavior and policies of an MNC's home country government in forming the attitude of the host country toward the MNCs is not well documented, although there is some evidence to indicate its significance. It is in this area that the greatest differentiation seems to occur in the behavior of developed versus developing host countries. For example, even when the United States applied its laws and regulations on an extraterritorial basis to branches and subsidiaries of U.S. banks and corporations located abroad in freezing Iranian assets in 1979 and in preventing the transfer of U.S. technology in connection with the Soviet gas pipeline in 1982, few would suggest that there was a significant rise in anti-Americanism in such deeply affected host countries as the United Kingdom, France, and West Germany. There is an inherent conflict in the effort of a subsidiary of a U.S. based corporation to foster good corporate citizenship in the host country when it is subject to potentially conflicting policies, through laws and regulations, of the home country. The key seems to be how such differences are perceived and resolved.

Despite the view of many developing host countries that U.S. firms have an aggressive and imperial style, some leaders of host countries view U.S. MNC behavior as no worse, and many cases better, than that of the U.S. government. Yet commentators appear to agree that being an

American, as opposed to a European MNC, has a number of disadvantages. Many developing host countries presume an active degree of cooperation between the CIA and U.S. MNCs and their involvement in the policies of the host country. Furthermore, behavior often considered unacceptable when performed by U.S. MNCs may be undertaken by their European counterparts without negative repercussions. The negative perception of U.S. MNCs is further reinforced by the charges, often discussed in numerous writings dealing with cases of questionable political activities, such as those of ITT in Chile. As a result "more often than not, diffuse feelings of anti-Americanism abroad most readily and easily come to rest on the most perceptible American institutions located there—the American multinational companies."[36]

Furthermore, jealousy of a U.S. MNC's presence around the globe and success may account for some of the conflicts and hostility that have characterized the relationship between MNCs and their host countries. Fear of foreign domination has been a serious issue with U.S. MNCs accounting for about 80 percent of foreign direct investment in Mexico and about 35 percent in Brazil.[37] The concentration of firms in such countries is particularly apparent, in large part because of the relatively small size of the market. Four firms account for about three-fourths of the market in many products, such as chemicals, machinery, and transportation equipment.

The fall of the Shah of Iran and the rise of Khomeini present an intriguing question about whether the large U.S. presence in Iran contributed to the fervor of the anti-American demonstrations, including the seizure of the U.S. embassy in Teheran on November 4, 1979. At the time of the upheavals, Americans had a substantial presence in Iran, estimated at 40,000 personnel and over 300 corporate offices, although U.S. foreign direct investment only amounted to approximately $700 million.[38] Iran's market lured U.S. multinational firms, but their impact may have had a part in triggering the anti-American sentiment of the Islamic leadership. These ayatollahs opposed the Western influence transmitted by U.S. MNCs, including movies, and sought the eviction of such alien forces—the Great Satan—in order to ensure the establishment of an Islamic state. The suspicion of foreigners and resentment toward their influence upon the society was used to whip nationalist fervor. Although the focus of the massive demonstrations, estimated at crowds of over one million, in Teheran was the U.S. embassy, U.S. corporations were also the targets of attacks.[39]

The intense, massive demonstrations, including the burning of the

U.S. flag and vitriolic rhetoric by Iran's clerics, left little doubt about the virulent anti-Americanism being displayed. Many U.S. firms were forced to evacuate their personnel from Iran during the upheavals. Nevertheless, several major U.S. companies, including General Motors and Gillette, held on to their interest and operations.

From the political-diplomatic confrontations between the United States and Iran during the November 4–13, 1979 period, both sides opened a new economic and financial chapter for the range of conflict on November 14, 1979. Abolhassan Bani-Sadr, at the time Iran's acting foreign minister, had announced the previous day that Iran's Revolutionary Council had decided to withdraw its reserves from U.S. banks and would transfer them to banks in European countries that had not joined the U.S. boycott of Iranian oil. Ostensibly, the President's order freezing Iranian assets was issued in response to the reports regarding Iran's plans to withdraw its funds from U.S. banks. The order froze about $8 billion of Iranian assets with about $4 billion of that amount located in U.S. banks located in Europe. The order was justified in terms of protecting U.S. banks and not as part of an economic warfare plan aimed at Iran. This Iranian case not only represents an emotional outpouring against U.S. diplomatic, military, and business presence in the country, but it also reveals the problems arising from the efforts of a parent corporation and its home government to control its subsidiaries located in host countries, in this case develped countries.

Reportedly the British were angered by the application of the U.S. freeze of Iranian assets to the London branches and subsidiaries of U.S. banks. The British viewed this freeze as an arrogant assertion of U.S. extraterritorial jurisdiction and allegedly threatened to revoke the charters of U.S. banks in London. One Treasury Department official was quite blunt in stating the obvious implication of the regulations: "Our position is that these are U.S. entities and that we can freeze their assets anywhere in the world."[40]

Obviously, the assertion of U.S. jurisdiction over such banks led to strained relations between the United States and host countries of U.S.-controlled banks. As a home country, the United States will, by and large, seek to extend its jurisdiction over its parent corporation's foreign subsidiaries by treating them as an extension of the parent corporation, thereby squarely raising issues of extraterritoriality and sovereignty.[41] Often this runs counter to a host country's assertion of control over an entity within its borders. Therefore, where the directives or policies of these countries are inconsistent, the stage is set for conflict with the host country viewing such actions as an infringement of its sovereignty.

The most celebrated case of such a conflict is *Fruehauf v. Massardy*. In that case the extraterritorial application of Treasury regulations promulgated pursuant to the Trading With the Enemy Act to U.S. subsidiaries abroad resulted in a French rejection of the U.S. effort to exercise jurisdiction within France's borders.

In the Fruehauf case, the U.S. Treasury Department ordered the U.S. company in control of Fruehauf France to cancel a contract for the sale of tractor-trailers to the People's Republic of China (PRC). The French courts upheld the relief requested by the three French directors against the five U.S. directors by granting the appointment of a judicial administrator to execute the contracts and temporarily manage the company. The divergent interests of the host and home countries are obvious in the Fruehauf case. The French government was seeking to improve its relations with the PRC, while the United States was trying to prohibit commerce between a U.S.-controlled subsidiary and the PRC by enforcing the Trading With the Enemy Act. U.S. laws and regulations were making it exceedingly difficult for the French-registered U.S.-controlled subsidiary to be a good corporate citizen of France, the host country.[42]

These types of conflicts may arise, and indeed have arisen, both with developed and developing host countries. The key difference seems to be in the higher level of stridency and rancor when the conflict is between a developed home country and a developing host country, with the United States often involved in such disputes.

A PROFILE OF POLITICAL ACCEPTABILITY

Numerous U.S. MNCs seek to mitigate the hostility they may encounter by comparing their objectives with those of the host country. By doing a cost/benefit analysis of issues such as sources of funds, the value added, new technology imports, local content, and control, a corporation seeks to analyze the impact it will have on the local economy and gauge its profile from the perspective of the host country. In fact, a number of countries have used cost/benefit analysis to decide whether or not to allow multinational corporations to operate within their borders.[43]

The corporation's profile may also help indicate future areas of conflict.[44] Many MNCs adopt strategies to manage risks and maintain their leverage by negotiating the terms of their presence. If a corporation's investment places it in a highly visible, economically dominant position, its sheer size often provides ammunition for an opposition party, thereby turning the corporation's presence into a critical political issue. The nature of the problem of long-term investments abroad has been described as follows: "Once you build a car assembly plant, you're there. It's not just a question of where we should invest next, but it is also a question of whether a government is going to do anything that's going to affect us while we're in a particular country."[45]

Even Canada, a country long viewed as a safe haven for U.S. and other investors, presents foreign companies with an uncertain environment given a revival of economic nationalism. This development to "Canadize" the country's oil and gas industry is reflected in legal restrictions that reduce foreign ownership in Canada's energy sector, and is in part, a reaction to the dominance of U.S. companies in that country. Similar restrictions may be extended to other industries by more stringent application of the Foreign Investment Review Act. The Canadian government has promised to conduct vigorous surveillance of foreign investment and is likely to pressure foreign-based companies on issues such as increasing the local content of their products and conducting more research and development locally.[46]

Gulf Oil's actions in Angola are illustrative of a corporation's effort to adapt to a radical change in government because of the large financial payoff involved. Gulf Oil successfully maintained its operations there despite the emergence of the Marxist government because it correctly assessed that the new regime would honor the terms of a negotiated agreement, in large part because it did not consider itself capable of maintaining oil production. This case is also fascinating because the U.S. government requested that Gulf terminate its operating so as not to generate revenues for the Marxist government. Gulf refused and maintained the operations.[47]

A corporation may make a conscious decision to try to blend into the host country's environment. Singer's corporate policy, for example, is to hire local managers, stay out of local politics, and keep as low a profile as possible.[48] Many manufacturing firms also market their products using a local brand name.

Multinational corporations are increasingly involved in shaping their profile by public relations activities and negotiations about the terms of their operations. Although a substantial amount of such work is under way in the United States, many firms restrict their public affairs activities abroad to avoid accusations of interference in the domestic affairs of a host country in reaction to past political intervention by some U.S. MNCs. Many of these corporations are seeking to improve their image by making a more extensive effort to explain their role and goals. Starting with basics, MNCs seek to explain that making a profit is not a crime, but the fuel for future investment and growth. Many U.S. MNCs have sought to counter the image generated by such works as Richard Barnett and Ronald Muller's *Global Reach*. Highlighting reinvestment and the construction of schools and hospitals is helpful as long as the host government does not feel that such activities impinge on its sphere of responsibility.

U.S. MNCs are aware of the increased ability of host countries to control their actions. Whether this will reduce the degree of anti-Americanism in such countries is not clear. However, many U.S. MNCs now look to direct negotiations with the host government as the most effective way to shape their destiny because future direct intervention on their behalf by the U.S. government is unlikely.

Carl A. Gerstacker, the chairman of Dow Chemical, has described Dow's behavior in Chile as exemplary, "a model of how a multinational company should conduct itself in a developing country," because it provided its best technology. Dow claims to have had outstanding relations with its employees and the business community. "The conclusion is that the very best plans and intentions can come to an unhappy ending when an extremist political government takes over control of a democratic nation with whose previous democratic government you have carefully developed all proper and legal requirements."[49] Another example of a radical change in government occurred in Cuba that resulted in the expulsion of U.S. MNCs without compensation and bitter relations between the United States and Cuba. The sugar-based Cuban economy simply replaced one form of dependence on U.S. companies and the U.S. market with dependence on Soviet aid.

CONCLUSION

The "love–hate" relationship between developing countries and MNCs can be seen in the effort of developing countries to turn to MNCs to raise capital despite the numerous investment disputes that have characterized the relationship. Obviously, the relations of MNCs with host and home governments raise critical issues of control and sovereignty. Conflicts between an MNC and a host country often arise despite its efforts to be a good corporate citizen, perhaps because regardless of its actions it will be regarded as a resident alien. MNCs are often viewed as omnipotent, whose size rivals that of the host country and whose global operations make it less likely to be effectively regulated and whose objectives are often perceived to be in furtherance of those of the home country. Management of the parent company is presumed to make key decisions, thereby resulting in being perceived as agents of colonialism and imperialism.

Differentiation between the general phenomenon of anti-Americanism and hostility toward U.S.-based MNCs is extremely difficult to make, in large part because of the way in which these sets of attitudes and events are intertwined. Nevertheless, an examination of the experiences of U.S.-based companies in different industries in various regions of the world point to a number of tentative conclusions.

First, a negative view of MNCs, and in particular U.S.-based MNCs, is widespread and not limited to developing countries. The basis for such hostile attitudes may well lie in the essence of the MNC-host country relationship whereby a large foreign entity penetrates the domestic polity.

Second, the intensity of the anti-American MNC attitude and hostility is significantly greater in developing than in developed countries. It is not clear, however, whether this difference can be attributed to a developing host country's perceived inability to exert the control that a developed country can exercise over a MNC.

Third, it seems unlikely that MNCs are the cause of anti-Americanism. This phenomenon is prevalent in many countries where the presence of U.S. MNCs is negligible. Furthermore, in a number of countries where U.S. MNCs have a substantial presence anti-Americanism is not a significant issue.

Fourth, U.S. MNCs have served as a catalyst for the expression of nationalist fervor. Efforts have been made by a number of Latin American states to eliminate their "dependencia" by reasserting their control over their natural resources by nationalizing such firms. U.S. MNCs in the extractive industry have been involved in a significant number of investment disputes. The foreign debt problem confronting many key developing countries may shift the resentment aimed at natural resource MNCs during the 1960s and 1970s to foreign banks during the 1980s and 1990s.

Fifth, the difference between developed and developing countries in their attitudes as well as investment disputes with U.S. MNCs may stem from the greater dominance and visibility such firms have in developing economies. Furthermore, U.S. Marines have not landed in a developed country to protect a U.S. investment nor has the U.S. government sought to overturn a government of a developed country because of an investment dispute. The publicity surrounding several such U.S. activities has created the presumption that this is the rule rather than the exception in U.S. relations with such host countries.

Sixth, the most violent outbreaks of anti-Americanism and manifestations of anti-American MNC actions appear to be intertwined and coincide with a radical change in government. In the recent past, such manifestations have occurred in Cuba in 1960, Chile in 1971, and Iran in 1979. U.S. MNCs may serve as a convenient target of resentment during such upheavals.

Seventh, the large presence of a U.S. MNC in a developing country may stimulate changes unwelcomed by traditional segments of the society. In such cases, the U.S. firm may be viewed as a source of the problem and the hostility may also be focused on the home country for exporting such an alien entity. The Ayatollah's Iran may be a case in point. Furthermore, U.S. MNCs may also be identified with an unpopular regime, such as the case of Batista's Cuba.

Eighth, aware of the resentment and hostility they often evoke, U.S. MNCs have sought to explain their role and insure, to the extent possible, that their objectives are in harmony with the goals of the host government. Furthermore, there have been intensified efforts to adopt codes of conduct and other means of regulating the activities of MNCs.

Finally, in seeking to cope with the phenomenon of anti-Americanism and its connection to U.S. MNCs, the U.S. government may find it useful to distinguish between latent anti-Americanism and specific conflicts that swirl around MNCs. Combating anti-Americanism in its latent and diffuse forms may require a public relations effort to change a series of negative stereotypes. Anti-Americanism manifested by host country grievances, whether real or irrational, may also be alleviated by measures designed to resolve them to the satisfaction of the parties.

NOTES

1. Gordon W. Allport, *The Nature of Prejudice*, Garden City, N.Y.: Doubleday & Co., 1958, p. ix.

2. *Ibid.*, p. 7.

3. *Ibid.*, p. 107.

4. Joseph LaPalombara and Stephen Blank, *Multinational Corporations in Comparative Perspective*, New York: The Conference Board, 1977, p. x.

5. Raymond Vernon, *Storm Over the Multinationals*, Cambridge, Massachusetts: Harvard University Press, 1977.

6. For example, Richard J. Barnet and Ronald E. Muller, *Global Reach*, New York: Simon and Schuster, 1977.

7. *Ibid.*

8. Joani Nelson-Horchler, "U.S. Multinationals: Benefactors or Bandits," *Industry Week*, April 18, 1983.

9. John Diebold, "Multinational Corporations: Why Be Scared of Them?" *Foreign Policy*, Fall 1973, p. 79.

10. Obie G. Whichard, "U.S. Direct Investment Abroad in 1982," *Survey of Current Business*, Washington, D.C.: U.S. Department of Commerce, August 1983.

11. Edmund T. Pratt, "Foreign Direct Investment and U.S. Trade Policy." Paper presented to the National Foreign Trade Council, New York, October 23, 1979.

12. *Business Week*, "The Decline of U.S. Power," March 12, 1979.

13. Jean Jacques Servan-Schreiber, *The American Challenge*, New York: Atheneum House, 1968; Raymond Vernon, *Sovereignty At Bay*, New York: Basic Books, 1971.

14. Henry Brandon, *The Retreat of American Power*, New York: Doubleday, 1973.

15. Louis L. Snyder (ed.), *The Dynamics of Nationalism*, Princeton: D. Van Nostrand, 1964, p. 2.

16. John Fayerweather, *International Business Management*, New York: McGraw Hill, 1969.

17. Richard D. Robinson, *International Business Policy*, New York: Holt, Rinehart and Winston, 1964, p. 148.

18. Joseph LaPalombara and Stephen Blank, *Multinational Corporations and National Elites*, New York: The Conference Board, 1976.

19. Vernon, *op. cit.*, 1971.

20. LaPalombara and Blank, *op. cit.*, 1976 and 1977.

21. *Ibid.*, 1976, p. 3.

22. *Ibid.*, p. 8.

23. Daniel A. Lapres, "Principles of Compensation for Nationalised Property, *International and Comparative Law Quarterly*, 1977, p. 103.

24. See Paul B. Sigmund, *Multinationals In Latin America*, Madison, Wisconsin: The University of Wisconsin Press, 1980, Ch. 2; and Jessica Pernitz Einhorn, *Expropriation Politics*, Lexington, Massachusetts: Lexington Books, 1974.

25. *International Legal Materials*, Volume 9, 1975, p. 251.

26. Whiteman, *Digest of International Law*, Volume 8, 1967, p. 1020.

27. Theodore H. Moran, *Multinational Corporations and the Politics of Dependence*, Princeton, New Jersey: Princeton University Press, 1974.

28. Lawrence Rout, "Future Political Effect of Foreign-Debt Crisis Worry Some Observers," *The Wall Street Journal*, June 30, 1983.

29. *Ibid.*

30. As quoted in *ibid.*

31. Linda Sandler, "Is Discounting Sovereign Debt the Way Out," *Institutional Investor*, July 1983, p. 74.

32. *Euromoney*, "The IMF vs. The People," October 1983, p. 90.

33. Edward Boyer, "Why Lenders Should Still Be Scared," *Fortune*, December 12, 1983, p. 128.

34. *Ibid.*, p. 116.

35. LaPalombara and Blank, *op. cit.*, 1977, p. 3.

36. *Ibid.*, p. 31.

37. John M. Connor and Willard F. Mueller, *Market Power and Profitability of Multinational Corporations in Brazil and Mexico*. Report to the Subcommittee on Foreign Economic Policy, Committee on Foreign Relations, United States Senate, Washington, D.C.: USGPO, 1977, p. 5.

38. Robert E. Ebel, "Iran: A Post-Mortem for Industry," in Mark B. Winchester (ed.) *The International Essays for Business Decision-Making*, New York: AMACOM, 1979.

39. *The New York Times*, November 15, 1979.

40. As quoted in *Business Week*, December 17, 1979, p. 30.

41. See Joseph Jude Norton, "Extraterritorial Jurisdiction of U.S. Antitrust and Securities Laws," *International and Comparative Law Quarterly*, October 1979, p. 575; Terry E. Bathin, "A Congressional Response to the Problem of Questionable Payments Abroad: The Foreign Corrupt Practices Act of 1977," *Law and Policy in International Business*, 1978, p. 1253.

42. William L. Craig, "Application of the Trading With the Enemy Act to Foreign Corporations Owned by Americans: Reflections on Fruehauf v. Massardy," *Harvard Law Review*, January 1970, p. 579.

43. Louis T. Wells, "Social Cost/Benefit Analysis for MNCs," *Harvard Business Review*, March–April 1975.

44. Vernon, *op. cit.*, 1977.

45. Marilyn Much, "GM's Watchdog on Foreign Political Risk," *Industry Week*, March 31, 1980, p. 82.

46. Herbert E. Meyer, "Trudeau's War on U.S. Business," *Fortune*, April 6, 1981, p. 74.

47. *Business Week*, "Foreign Investment: The Post-Shah Surge in Political Risk Studies," December 1, 1980, p. 69.

48. Nils Howard, "Doing Business in Unstable Countries," *Dun's Review*, March 1980.

49. Carl A. Gerstacker, "Dow Chemical's Experience in Chile," in Jon P. Gunnemann (ed.), *The Nation-State and Transnational Corporations in Conflict With Special Reference to Latin America*, New York: Praeger, 1975, p. 14.

11

Anti-Americanism at the United Nations: Perception or Reality?

Edward Luck and Peter Fromuth

Anti-Americanism is to some degree an element in the political cultures of most of the 158 member states of the United Nations. Negative attitudes toward the United States are evident in some of the themes of the mass peace movement in Western Europe, are actively encouraged in Eastern Europe by government propaganda and official dogma, are in vogue in intellectual circles in much of the Third World, and are perhaps most virulent among disaffected groups in the United States itself. The world's most powerful nation, whose economic, military, and cultural reach touches every region, is bound to be the target of considerable criticism from many quarters. It is thus hardly surprising that hostility toward the United States, its values and its policies, is echoed from time to time in the halls of the United Nations.

This chapter will consider whether anti-American sentiments take on a special character in the U.N. system. It will examine the causes and consequences of this phenomenon and will suggest ways in which it could be dealt with more effectively by U.S. policymakers and diplomats. We believe, it is the first effort to address this problem and its implications in a systematic manner. But the analysis here is far from scientific. It is based on a review of recent voting records and speeches in the General Assembly, on numerous intensive interviews with diplomats from many parts of the world, including U.S. representatives and policymakers, and on a decade of experience observing the workings of the U.N. at close hand.

As a state of mind, anti-Americanism is difficult to define. Even its manifestations are difficult to identify and measure, particularly in the complex and often murky political culture of the United Nations. The United States will always be subject to criticism, whether it is deserved or not. The issue, however, is not only whether the charges are justified, but whether they are applied fairly in terms of the standards, practices, and charter principles of the organization. In other words, is the United States subject to a double standard at the U.N. relative to the treatment of other countries, whether friend or foe?

Some prominent Americans have clearly thought so. Two of the United States' most outspoken and articulate representatives at the United Nations, Daniel Patrick Moynihan and Jeane Kirkpatrick, have contended that the United States is isolated in the world body, that its basic values are under challenge there, and that the U.N. is an unfriendly, even dangerous, place in terms of forwarding U.S. objectives and protecting Western values.[1] This gloomy conclusion is certainly not shared by all U.S. policymakers; witness a statement endorsed by six former Secretaries of State, four former National Security Advisors, and seven former Permanent Representatives to the U.N. (including Senator Moynihan) that, "The United Nations provides this country with a forum for protecting and promoting our own interests as well as for seeking solutions to problems we share with other countries."[2] While there is a sense of uneasiness among U.S. diplomats that it has become increasingly difficult for the United States to gain a sympathetic ear in U.N. political forums,[3] interviews with non-American delegates reveal a striking difference in perceptions of the existence and extent of anti-American sentiment in the U.N.

To many seasoned observers, the very notion that anti-Americanism is a pervasive force in the activities of the organization seems patently absurd. The U.N., after all, is largely the product of U.S. ideals and aspirations in the post-war era. While the influx of scores of newly independent Third World countries has diluted U.S. dominance over U.N. political bodies, especially the General Assembly where the United States is frequently outvoted, it is generally believed that the United States continues to be the single most influential country in determining what can and cannot happen. U.S. influence is felt most keenly in the implementation by the Secretariat of resolutions from the political bodies, in matters before the Security Council, and in the specialized agencies. In short, the U.S. weight is felt whenever decisions are not made on the basis of the one-nation, one-vote principle. According to this viewpoint, anti-

Americanism is limited to remarks and maneuvers by a few extreme and highly partisan delegations. It has not, it is argued, become institutionalized in the fabric of the U.N. system itself.

There is substantial validity to this view; however, it would be a mistake to assume that because U.S. influence survives, the anti-American attitudes which do exist are unimportant. Such feelings can affect the climate at the U.N., especially the General Assembly, causing a lack of receptivity to U.S. initiatives. They can also affect the attitudes that ordinary Americans form not only toward the U.N. but toward international cooperation generally, conceivably making isolationist alternatives more appealing. Clearly, if high-level U.S. diplomats and policymakers perceive the U.N. to be a hostile environment—even if these perceptions exaggerate and distort reality—then the issue of anti-Americanism is already having a profound impact on U.S. attitudes toward and policies in the United Nations. Indeed, if Third World representatives respond to U.S. concerns on this subject by belittling them, then the result will be to exacerbate already strained relationships and to fuel a vicious cycle. U.S. diplomats, on the other hand, should be careful not to create a self-fulfilling prophecy by which they treat other delegations and the institution itself in such a way as to foster the very anti-American attitudes they seek to avoid.

To lessen tendencies toward these extremes, it is important to examine the roots of this issue in as straightforward and credible a manner as possible. This chapter will address these five basic questions:

1) Is anti-Americanism in the United Nations an isolated, sporadic phenomenon or institutionalized in some systematic way?
2) Does the United Nations tend to amplify, mirror, or moderate anti-American tendencies apparent in indivdual member states and in political groupings such as the Non-Aligned Movement (NAM)?
3) What are the chief causes of this problem and how might they be influenced by actions of the United States, other countries, or the U.N. itself?
4) Do these attitudes constitute a serious barrier to the achievement of U.S. goals in the U.N. system?
5) What are the implications for U.S. policy choices, and what U.S. strategies offer the greatest promise for the future based on this analysis?

The United States as Helpless Giant?

Much of the following discussion documents and analyzes situations in which the United States is on the defensive in the U.N. system. This is because our theme is anti-Americanism. It is not that we believe that taken as a whole these examples provide an accurate picture of the strength and stature of the United States in the United Nations. They do not. A genuine measurement of our power and influence in the world body necessarily involves an examination of such things as the number of U.S. nationals in high-level U.N. positions, the impact of U.S. views on U.N. and agency budget growth, the embodiment of U.S. values in U.N. charters and programs, and many more factors. None of these, however, can form more than a small part of this chapter. Yet it is these things, rather than the debates, or even the votes, of plenary bodies that determine the United Nations' essential character, and by all of these criteria U.S. influence is great.

AMERICA EMBATTLED?: U.N. VOTING

General Assembly votes are an often cited measure of U.S. isolation. Since 1981 the U.S. Mission and the State Department have kept a computerized record of all plenary votes cast in the General Assembly by every member state. While changes in methodology limit specific comparisons from one year to the next, the overall impression of a US minority position is clear. The following statistical examples typify the trend.[4]

1. From the 1981 General Assembly session through the 1983 session voting agreement between the U.S. and the U.N. majority has fallen from 30.6% in 1981 to 25.7% in 1982 to 25.5% in 1983.
2. During the same period voting agreement between the Soviet Union and the U.N. majority hovered between 70% and 80%.
3. Each year on a subset of 10 to 20 General Assembly votes considered to have special significance to Washington, the U.S. Mission mounted a lobbying campaign that was generally more vigorous than normal. Only in 1983, however, when the United States saw 4 of 10 votes go its way was voting agreement significantly better on this smaller vote sample.

As an index of the isolation of U.S. views in the U.N. the impression that these statistics give is generally correct. But like any quantitative measure it is important to separate what they do from what they do not tell us about anti-Americanism at the U.N.

First, voting differently from the United States does not signify opposition to the United States any more than voting the same way signifies support. In addition to national policy, countries cast U.N. votes for many different reasons. Contributing to the final numerical result is everything from bloc identification or group loyalty to a highly specific quid pro quo. Generally speaking, to regard a delegate's vote as an expression of his country's warmth or hostility to the United States is to see the U.N. through an ethnocentric lens. One might reasonably question, for example, whether the best index of friendship toward the United States is provided by Singapore's 25.6% agreement with our position in the U.N. or Costa Rica's 30.5% score.[5]

Second, voting disagreement with the United States does not signify support for the Soviet Union. The axis in the U.N. is from North to South not East to West. Very few U.N. votes regard East–West issues. When the ideological component is paramount in U.S. eyes it is rarely so in the perspective of the U.N. majority. Moreover, on many matters that unambiguously involve Soviet behavior—Afghanistan, Kampuchea, chemical weapons, the Korean airliner attack—U.S. interests have been upheld. In general, the reason that the Soviets are so often in the majority is that they use U.N. debates as a cost free way[6] of courting opinion in the Third World by paying lip-service to the southern side of North–South issues. Nothing more quickly reveals the folly of an East–West approach to U.N. vote counting than a comparison of some country percentages. In 1982 the Soviet Union joined the United States for 20.6% of General Assembly votes, a better score than almost half the countries of Africa. It was also more "sympathetic" than China and Kuwait and virtually the same as Jordan.[7]

Third, the voting totals compiled by the State Department and the Mission count only "yes" and "no" votes while disregarding abstentions. The premise is that the latter distort a member's support for U.S. policies since abstentions do not measure an act of will or commitment. There is, however, some difficulty with this approach. One of the purposes of U.N. voting analysis is to measure *disagreement* in addition to agreement between U.S. and U.N. majority positions. During the 1981, 1982 and 1983 General Assembly sessions, the United States abstained on approximately 25% of recorded votes.[8] Clearly, disregarding these votes magnifies the significance of the others.

Fourth, the U.S. approach to U.N. voting is not a constant. Although there are probably few cases in which a yes vote under one administration might be a no vote under another, different approaches to U.N. diplomacy can result in changes in a resolution's language sufficient to enable the United States either to abstain—or even to vote yes. Research conducted by *The Inter Dependent* newspaper[9] indicates that only since 1981, when U.S. "no" votes rose sharply as abstentions diminished dramatically, has the United States been on the losing side of most General Assembly recorded votes (yes votes, no votes, and abstentions).

Finally, votes in the General Assembly are only a partial and superficial measurement of attitudes and performance there. They do not reveal any of the other ways in which a country's behavior by behind the scenes efforts to minimize confrontation, to tone down offensive language in a resolution or to act as a braking force within a voting bloc may show sympathy toward the United States. The significance of these caveats is that attention to votes, as well as to the voting tallys, tends to overstate the degree of U.S. isolation at the U.N. On a cluster of key issues, however, the United States *is* isolated. For reasons having as much to do with the dynamic of U.N. voting blocs, and the political ethos of the organization as with the facts of the issue, South Africa, Israel and the North–South economic debate occupy much of the U.N. agenda. On these matters the United States is out of step with the U.N. majority.

SINGLING OUT THE UNITED STATES

Often cited as evidence of a special animus toward the United States is the tendency to single out the United States for criticism regarding practices in which many countries engage, and even occasionally for apparently fictitious offenses. U.N. treatment of the U.S. relationship with South Africa seems to fit this pattern. Last year, for example, the General Assembly passed a resolution castigating the United States for military and nuclear collaboration with South Africa.[10] There is no evidence that the United States has violated the South African arms embargo, a charge that U.S. delegates to the General Assembly vigorously deny. As to the matter of nuclear collaboration, U.S. companies, along with those from several other Western countries submitted bids for a technical services contract to beef up management capabilities in South Africa's Koeburg nuclear plant. A French company ultimately won the bid. Yet neither France nor any of the other home countries of the participating bidders was mentioned. In fact, France has long been the major supplier of nuclear materials and technology to South Africa even going as far as to sell that country its only nuclear reactor; yet, it has never been censured for doing so by any U.N. resolution.

Criticism of the United States is now part of the standard formulation of a condemnation of "foreign economic interests" which passes both the General Assembly and the Fourth Committee on a virtually annual basis. However, Great Britain is the largest investor in South Africa, and German investments are nearly as large as those of U.S. corporations. Both countries also trade heavily with South Africa. Moreover, IMF statistics show not only that South Africa trades with most countries in the world, but that in 1982, the most recent year for which numbers are available, its commerce with the rest of Africa exceeded $1 billion for the third consecutive year.[11] According to the South African Mission to the U.N., last year 49 African states—nearly every member of the OAU—participated in such trade.[12]

By raising these points we do not mean to imply that African objections to U.S. policies in South Africa and Namibia lack a rationale. On the contrary, the strategy of "constructive engagement" conflicts directly with approaches favored by Africans, and statements, such as President Reagan's in 1981 that South Africa is a "U.S. ally"[13] offend African sensibilities. These things, and the general conviction that U.S. power makes it more capable than any other country to pressure South Africa for change, have made U.S. policies in the region the object of considerable attention and frustration. Sometimes in the General Assembly these political frustrations are manifested in unfair treatment of unrelated matters.

Much of the criticism of the United States—fair or unfair—is the nearly inevitable result of its being on the "wrong side" of an issue important to a major U.N. voting bloc. This has obviously been true of the OAU regarding South Africa and Namibia, and the Islamic Conference regarding Israel and the Palestinians. More surprising and disturbing is the seeming gratuitousness with which some member countries, acting beyond the realm of any local interest join in attacks upon the United States. Occasionally this has produced some rather anomalous results, in which countries not involved in a problem or its solution are more confrontational than those which are. Such was the case with a 1982 resolution condemning the U.S. government for policies and actions giving support to apartheid.[14] Backed by only about half the membership of the OAU, the measure carried primarily on the strength of its support from Asian and Latin American countries.

DOUBLE STANDARDS

Another complaint U.S. critics raise about the U.N. is that many of its pronouncements regarding Soviet and U.S. actions seem to be guided by a double standard. Although the two situations are not equivalent, comparisons are often drawn between the treatment in the General Assembly of the Soviet occupation of Afghanistan and the U.S. invasion of Grenada. Although most members' positions are now well known, resolutions calling for withdrawal of foreign troops from Afghanistan are nonetheless thoroughly debated each year, before they are voted on. This was not the case with Grenada. When the General Assembly moved to consider a resolution deploring the U.S. action and calling for withdrawal of U.S. troops, it first passed a cloture motion preventing debate.[15] Second, the language on Afghanistan is considerably milder than that of the Grenada measure. Finally, a large number of states, several of whom maintain good relations with the United States, voted to condemn the United States on Grenada but abstained on Afghanistan.[16]

Elsewhere a double standard would also seem to underlie the selectivity of U.N. concern with certain problems or of its application of certain principles. For example, the U.N. Charter treats the process of self-determination, the act by which a people chooses its own form of government, as more important than the specific outcome—of which independence may be only one of several choices. The U.N. majority, however, rarely employs the principle of self-determination outside of the colonial context. It is not invoked, for example, over Libya's invasion of Chad. On the other hand, in the Committee of 24,[17] a subcommittee of the Fourth Committee, Puerto Rico continues to be treated as a colonial issue despite referenda in which the island's inhabitants overwhelmingly reject independence. Other examples of selectivity are the ways in which discussions of issues like refugees and human rights give more attention to problems and abuses in only a few states when the situation may be as bad or worse in many countries that are not mentioned.

THE UNITED STATES AND THE NEW NORMATIVE "ORDERS"

Finally, the United States, together with most of the industrial democracies, finds itself on the defensive with regard to the values and the claims asserted in various new "orders," such as the New International Economic Order (NIEO) and the New World Information and Communication Order (NWICO). Both of these reflect U.N. atmosphere, but there is a key distinction. The NIEO is an effort to use U.N. fora, UNCTAD for example, or the General Assembly itself, to press for changes which, however disagreeable to the United States, would have little direct effect on the strength of the United Nations or the principles for which it stands. The implications of the New World Information Order are more serious. In its concern to redress perceived imbalances in the flow of information it has provided a rationale for challenges to press freedom and other principles contained in the U.N. Charter. Fortunately, Third World support for the most interventionist aspects of the NWICO agenda seems to have crested.

ANTI-AMERICANISM?

While this foregoing summary suggests that the U.S. position at the United Nations is often an embattled one, there is little reason to believe that this is the result of anti-Americanism. To be anti-American in the strictest sense is to be predisposed to oppose the United States, its values, its policies and those things identified with them. Certainly there are members of the United Nations which do fit this mold, including the Eastern bloc, the handful of Soviet client states in the Third World, Iran and Libya. The fact is that most member states do not. Their official and unofficial bilateral relations with the United States generally reflect a balancing of specific pluses and minuses. The relationships are more determined by pragmatism than ideology. At the United Nations, these relationships change. But the reasons why they change have less to do with ideological or cultural antipathy than with the more abstract character of the United Nations agenda and the unique way in which certain voting groups participate in its decisions.

THE NONALIGNED MOVEMENT

Part of the explanation lies in the growth, over the last twenty years, of the Nonaligned Movement. Because of its numerical strength and the cohesion it maintains on certain key issues the NAM has had considerable success in ensuring that both its agenda and many of its positions become the agenda and resolutions adopted by the General Assembly.

Although the NAM has had a profound effect upon the U.N., and will therefore be examined at some length, its influence falls short of control and many of its more egregious declarations have been reversed by the larger body.

The initial objective of the Nonaligned Movement, which was first conceived during the Cold War atmosphere of the late 1950s, was to enable its members, most of which had only recently gained independence, to pursue a foreign policy independent of that followed by the two superpowers. In this way, nonalignment provided a ready vehicle for an assertion of sovereignty and nationhood by newly decolonized countries anxious to distance themselves from a colonial past. Consequently, most new nations were quick to apply for membership. It was perhaps inevitable then that as membership grew, from 25 members at Belgrade in 1961, to 101 last year in New Delhi, the common bonds of a postcolonial experience broadened and reshaped the meaning of nonalignment.

Over the last 23 years, the principle of foreign policy independence, though never disavowed, has grown less relevant to a NAM membership preoccupied with the problems of underdevelopment and anxious to use its numerical majority at the United Nations to elicit economic concessions from the industrialized West. During this period it was typical of NAM doctrine to explain the presence of economic underdevelopment by reference to the recent colonial past of many Third World countries. Today the number of colonies has dwindled to a handful. Yet anticolonialism, by growing increasingly abstract and expansive, remains a unifying theme. Now included under the anticolonial rubric are problems as diverse as North–South economic relations, Namibia, the Middle East, and even disarmament.

With the allegiance of 101 of the U.N.'s 158 members, and its frequent caucuses during General Assembly sessions, the nonaligned have achieved a very high degree of voting cohesion both in the General Assembly and in the Security Council. A recent study of the nonaligned and the United Nations, written by Richard L. Jackson, reports that on all 341 General Assembly votes in 1982 the nonaligned voted together 96.1 percent of the time. By contrast, for the 271 votes that year in which the United States was present and voting, agreement between the United States and NATO was 64 percent, ranging from a high of 80.1 percent coincidence with Great Britain to a low of 33.2 with Greece.[18]

Whereas in the General Assembly NAM coordination has resulted in nearly automatic voting majorities on core NAM issues, at the Security Council the permanent members' veto power prevents an equal degree of dominance. However, since a 9 vote majority is required for passage of Security Council resolutions, the presence of between 6 and 8 NAM members on the Council in any one year has given the nonaligned a nearly equal blocking power of its own. Furthermore, as NAM Council members have grown more assertive in recent years, forming a nonaligned subgroup in the process, they have also begun to exert an influence over the Council's agenda, the timing of its meetings, and the content of its resolutions.

With the growth in NAM numerical strength, activism and skill in Council procedures its members have also, on occasion, been able to underscore the isolation of a great power by forcing it to resort to a veto. The nonaligned are certainly not the first ones to appreciate that vetoes may be manipulated to score political points. Nor do they generally choose confrontation over compromise when a veto might be a foregone conclusion. Yet their numbers and cohesiveness make it far easier to stage confrontational Council proceedings when this is desired.

In the last decade no major power has been isolated more frequently—in either chamber—than the United States. Substantive disagreement between U.S. and NAM approaches to South Africa, the Middle East, North–South economic relations—issues generating the strongest feelings in important sections of the NAM—ensures conflict. Because the U.S. position on these issues usually reflects fundamental considerations of national policy to varying degrees underwritten by recurrent administrations, and because rightly or wrongly, the United States is seen as the key to progress in all three, until progress does occur, the United States will continue to incur some degree of hostility. Yet, while such opposition to the US may be unavoidable, its intensity varies in response to the internal dynamics of the NAM itself, to the way the US presents its position at the UN and elsewhere, and to minor shifts in US strategy.

The NAM Dynamic

The Power of the Chairman: To a limited extent the treatment of the United States in nonaligned summit and ministerial communiqués varies with the chairman, whose prerogatives include preparation of the first draft of summit communiqués. Although drafts are modified during plenary sessions in order to secure a consensus, skillful and aggressive use of the chair can ensure considerable influence over the final language. Thus, the stridency of NAM criticism of the United States was much greater in the communiqué of the Havana Summit of 1979 than it was in the declarations issuing from New Delhi in 1983. NAM communiqués often affect the tone of subsequent General Assembly sessions. Under Castro's chairmanship, however, this was generally not the case. Castro's effort, from 1979 to 1982, to lead the movement into the Soviet orbit caused widespread resentment among members. Although Third World moderates attempted to resist Cuban initiatives at NAM meetings it was at the United Nations where they were most successful. Emboldened by the greater degree of accountability at the General Assembly and by the presence of other moderate states the nonaligned delivered Cuba a series of defeats at the 1982 session.

Decision by Consensus: Ironically, a NAM characteristic that has tended more often to exacerbate than to moderate conflicts with the United States is its adoption of decisions by consensus rather than by vote. Since under consensus there are no records of countries' positions, a member may acquiesce in a policy declaration that it disapproves with the knowledge that it cannot be held accountable for it later. Further weakening accountability is the growing practice among moderate members of attaching reservations to nonaligned communiqués. Often phrased with deliberate vagueness, reservations enable members to disclaim responsibility for offensive sections rather than to oppose them in open debate.

Yet, why acquiesce at all? Since consensus maximizes the power of the dissenter, why don't NAM members unhappy with a resolution's treatment of the United States challenge it? Sometimes they do, but there are several disincentives. The membership of the nonaligned places a high value on unity, or at least the appearance of unity, since this maximizes its standing and power in multilateral fora. Second, as an Asian diplomat who is both friendly to the United States and a member of the NAM pointed out, it is far more difficult to stand against a consensus than to cast a no vote. Since the opponent of a consensus may thwart the will of the majority, the pressures against doing so can be very great. Third, taking a stand against the NAM is not cost free. Like most deliberative bodies its votes involve log-rolling. A member disapproving of anti-Western language on one item of a communiqué may not raise the matter lest it expose itself to attack on a subject of more immediate concern. A vigorous defense of the United States over treatment given to Puerto Rico, for example, might conflict with Pakistan's preoccupation with the Soviet presence in neighboring Afghanistan, with Morocco's need for support over the Western Sahara, with Singapore's campaign on Kampuchea.

The Power of Small Groups: Participation in controversial NAM debates thus tends to be limited to those countries with the most at stake politically or ideologically in the outcome. For the United States, this means that regional groups, and often within them, smaller groups of committed radical states, exert a determining influence on NAM positions regarding U.S. policy toward South Africa, U.S. bases in the Indian Ocean or at Guantanamo Bay, U.S. support for Israel, the status of Puerto Rico, and so on. Although in every major bloc within the NAM—the OAU, the Arab group, and the Latin American group— the radical states are a minority, lack of support for U.S. policy, for example on South Africa, may in itself be so widespread that few members within a group are likely to come to the United States' defense— especially at the risk of becoming targets themselves.

The NAM Agenda: Finally, NAM communiqués do not necessarily reflect matters that are most important to members; they reflect what they can agree on. Because NAM members have different and sometimes directly conflicting economic and political interests, institutional survival demands either a focus on a different and unifying set of problems or a reformulation of the same problems in a unifying way. In both categories, the United States often appears as a key antagonist. Thus, African sections of the text will take no position on the Libyan invasion of Chad, the conflict between Ethiopia and Somalia, or the war in the western Sahara and concentrate on South Africa and Namibia. Arab sections will ignore the Iran–Iraq conflict to dwell upon Israel. Economic sections will discuss high interest rates but omit references to oil cartels.

THE MODERATING INFLUENCE OF THE U.N.

All of these things—the consensual procedure, the dominance of regional groups, and the institutional focus on external problems—both weaken the group's cohesion and cause it to exaggerate the degree of Third World hostility toward the United States and the West. The U.N., however, has had some success in reducing these distortions. For one thing, the need to attract voting majorities forces more accommodation than is necessary under a vague NAM consensus. For many states that would have suppressed disapproval rather than thwart a consensus, voting is an easier way to register disagreement. Also, the very presence of spokesmen for the Western viewpoint creates both a more realistic atmosphere and offers the possibility of negotiation, compromise and a new set of trade-offs. The more extreme nonaligned consensus decisions reached at summit or ministerial meetings are often overturned or simply not raised at the U.N. because the same countries behave differently in the larger setting. Some notable reversals have occurred on challenges to Israel's U.N. credentials, on efforts to inscribe Puerto Rico on the U.N. agenda, on U.S. bases at Diego Garcia, and on Kampuchean representation.

ISSUES OR FUNDAMENTALS?

Our discussion thus far has focused on the way certain issues charge the atmosphere of U.S. relations with the U.N. majority. What would happen if in the near future there were substantial progress on the three most prominent areas of disagreement? For the sake of argument, assume that the Namibia ceasefire holds, and that the scheduled elections and constitution drafting result in a stable government acceptable to all parties. In the Middle East assume binding settlements to the questions of Palestinian autonomy and the occupied territories. On global negotiations imagine a softening of the U.S. position involving support perhaps for minor changes in the international trade and payments system. Do these and other isolated issues generate the primary obstacles to U.S. diplomacy at the U.N. or are they just lightning rods in a U.N. atmosphere that is incompatible with U.S. national interests in other ways?

We addressed this question to many of those interviewed for this chapter—to delegates from nonaligned countries and from allies, to members of the U.S. delegation, and to European and Third World officials of the U.N. Secretariat. Their comments and our own observations suggest that while disagreement on these matters is most conspicuous today, there are other important sources of tension.

Significant, though easily overlooked, is the influence of what one allied diplomat called "the eternal verity of small versus large." Because the United States is the "rich guy on the block," he said, its wealth and power always arouse a certain amount of jealously and resentment when these things are used primarily to benefit U.S. national interests. To some extent the same applies to the Soviet Union. However, the Soviets have been able to use the continued linkage between colonialism and underdevelopment both to encourage the anti-Western posture of many U.N. members and to minimize their own participation in development assistance. "The Soviet Union. . ." as a Russian author commented in 1976 "does not intend to bear responsibility for the plunder of the young states, committed by the colonialists and the present day neocolonialists."[19] Against such a rationale, the moral high ground of small against large would be futile if invoked with the Soviets. With the United States, a major source of multilateral assistance, it might be more persuasive. The pluralism of U.S. society and the presence of vocal U.S. constituencies for greater generosity toward the Third World reinforces the appeal of small versus large.

Second, as the chief factor in the world economy, the United States' support is crucial for the success of Third World efforts to restructure the international economic system. Nonaligned backing for both the strategy and the goals of the New International Economic Order has weakened considerably since 1974, the result of both a greater diversity of economic interest within the movement and the complete absence of meaningful dialogue with the developed countries on the rather one-sided terms contained in NIEO proposals. However, whether the call for a NIEO continues or is superseded for example by the emerging interest in a New International Conference on Money and Finance for Development, the Third World will continue to rally around calls for structural economic changes more favorable to developing countries. While OECD countries are virtually unanimous in their lack of enthusiasm for such changes, it is the U.S. leadership position that will probably receive the most attention and criticism.

It should also be borne in mind that Western-style democratic governments are a minority at the United Nations and an even smaller one among the nonaligned. Regardless of ideology, the governmental systems of most Third World countries are far more centralized than the United States. From market-based economic thinking, to press freedom, to human rights, democratic positions often require fuller explanations than do socialist ones.

Finally, though the nonaligned's "anticolonial" dogma is weakening and is increasingly challenged within the NAM itself, it continues to set the tone of the movement's many declarations and is often reflected in statements at the General Assembly. Rooted in theories such as *dependencia* which attribute internal economic conditions to external causes, "anticolonial" dogma has been reinforced by NAM institutional needs to focus on non–Third World sources for Third World problems. It has been further strengthened by the fact that most newly independent states are governed by small elite groups. For many of these the ability to explain the persistence of slow development and enormous poverty by external factors provides an important legitimizing function. Since U.S. and Western economic involvement is conspicuous in much of the Third World, it is a natural target for anticolonial attacks.

U.S. DIPLOMACY: STYLE AND SUBSTANCE

The current state of U.S. relations at the United Nations is a composite of four ingredients: the issues that dominate the agenda; the political ethos; the internal dynamics of the NAM; and the character of U.S. diplomacy. Oscar Wilde once remarked that "in all matters of importance it is style that counts." At the U.N., as a British diplomat recently said, it is the way you say something rather than what you say that so often is most important.

As membership in the United Nations has grown, so has the importance of the political skills of the U.S. representative. The United States is only one vote in 158 in the General Assembly and one in 15 plus its veto on the Security Council. Unlike the Soviet Union, which controls its own faction in the General Assembly as in the NAM, the United States has no pro-U.S. lobbies. Faced with this situation the success of U.S. initiatives or the defense of its interests depends upon old-fashioned politicking. The diplomatic community in New York, not unlike the U.S. Senate, forms an informal club, whose members are expected to treat each other with deference and respect even when they differ on key political issues. Moreover, there are times when the friendships and social ties formed between missions in the Delegates Lounge and in the many dinners, receptions and private gatherings that accompany a General Assembly session have more influence on voting outcomes than does the fairly predictable round of speeches filling floor debates. As an Asian diplomat noted, when a great power participates in the club it is an expression of esteem for the other members, a symbolic acceptance of their equality.

The degree to which U.S. representatives participate in this other U.N. varies significantly. Whereas Ambassador William W. Scranton treated such opportunities very seriously, developing many personal ties, Daniel Patrick Moynihan, his predecessor, participated much less. Like Scranton, Andrew Young also spent considerable effort cultivating the U.N.'s social periphery. In fact, a delegate who was present in New York during the Young period said that the ambassador's friendly and personable manner often became a factor when a nonaligned diplomat had to decide whether to support or abstain from a resolution critical of Washington. "You didn't want to embarrass Andy" he said. The same delegate and many others we spoke to labeled the U.S. approach under Ambassador Moynihan as bellicose and abrasive and contended that it cost votes on the Zionism equals racism resolution of 1975. Observers of U.S. diplomacy under Ambassador Jeane Kirkpatrick raise a similar point. Although more low-key than former Ambassador Moynihan, Mrs. Kirkpatrick's treatment of issues has been considered unnecessarily confrontational even by friendly delegates. "Diplomacy by assertion" was the phrase used by a high-ranking diplomat from one of the United States' closest allies. At the U.N. it is not enough, he said, simply to make declarative take-it-or-leave-it statements of a country's position and expect that their intrinsic merit will ensure support. What is most successful, he said, is a kind of reiterative "diplomacy by reasoning," setting out "rational explanations of where your national interests lie, explaining them a second time and then explaining them once more."

Another allied diplomat echoed the "diplomacy by assertion" theme. Representing a key NATO country he indicated that on some occasions the United States seemed to welcome, even to cultivate, the impression of isolation. He suggested, as others have, that the tactic caters to a domestic constituency already convinced that the United States and the Western democracies are a beseiged minority in the U.N. Whatever may be the reasons on the U.S. side, he said that the attitude which often came across to the allies, especially in 1981 and 1982, was that the United States as a superpower did not need to come to Europe to ask for support, but could "stand tall, and go it alone if necessary."

This kind of attitude inevitably affects the degree of U.S. coordination not just with allies, but with Third World states likely to be receptive to U.S. arguments on an issue. Our interviews suggest that to some extent this has been true both in the Security Council and in the General Assembly. One delegate complained that the United States' position on matters before the Council has often been unknown until the last minute and even then, prone to reversal. Another delegate recalled an occasion in the General Assembly in which efforts to pass a consensus resolution regarding peaceful uses of outer space, based on a U.S. draft, were actually stymied by U.S. opposition to its own draft. A point made by many observers is that the U.S. delegation, particularly the upper echelon, does not work the corridors often enough and certainly much less than its Soviet counterparts do. Furthermore, Third World delegates complain that when the United States does lobby it can be overbearing. "You have only one vote in 158," said an influential ambassador from a moderate African country, "You cannot get your way by threats." A high level African official with many years service in the U.N. Secretariat made the same point. Referring to the U.S. decision to link its foreign aid more closely to a country's voting behavior at the United Nations, he indicated the decision would backfire. "You'll insult their manhood," he said. The United States is not the only one to assert pressure, however, and there seems to be a consensus that both superpowers, in the words of one delegate, can practice a "fairly elephantine diplomacy."

A dominant theme in U.S. thinking about the United Nations, especially about the deliberations of the General Assembly, is that most issues revolve around matters of principle. Because the political apparatus of the U.N. is chiefly employed to make conceptual and normative statements, its many peacekeeping and functional activities aside, the United States has often tended to see the positions it takes as abstract statements, important more for their symbolism than their practical effect. As a delegate from Europe explained, in part because the Europeans have fewer world forums and in part because many of them have more at stake in their relations with the developing world, the European approach is more pragmatic. Hence on occasions in which the United States might tend to be peremptory and reject participation in something it considers fundamentally wrongheaded, a European strategy would be more subtly tactical. These European-American contrasts emerge in many subjects, such as the Third World call for global economic negotiations, the Indian Ocean Zone of Peace proposal, and the Committee for the Non-Use of Force in International Relations. As a general rule, then, the U.S. tendency to view its position in terms of principles rather than interests in a body in which the U.S. view is often a minority one has affected the impression of U.S. isolation.

Generalized comparisons between the approaches of different U.S. administrations to U.N. voting should be made with caution. Although there is considerable similarity in the subject matter of General Assembly and Security Council resolutions from one year to the next, the texts themselves are not a constant, nor of course are the external events that precipitate U.N. action. While the Reagan–Kirkpatrick strategy is more confrontational than the previous one, the language of resolutions on the Middle East, South Africa-Namibia, and disarmament has grown worse from the U.S. point of view. Thus it would be an oversimplification to attribute certain trends that may suggest increased isolation solely to changes in style and approach.

We have listed these caveats to discourage an automatic linkage between U.S. diplomacy and the fate of U.S. interests at the U.N. Yet it would be wrong to suppose that changes in indices like General Assembly or Security Council votes are unrelated to variations in the presentation of U.S. policy, and even, though to a much lesser extent, in the content.

In the Security Council for example it is difficult to attribute the high incidence of U.S. vetoes during the Kirkpatrick period entirely to outside factors. From 1945 to 1983, the United States has used its veto 38 times. Fifteen of these vetoes were during the last three years. This is more than in any other three-year period and more than triple the number under the last administration. For 12 of those 15, moreover, the United States was the only country to use its veto, suggesting an unusual degree of isolation. Undoubtedly external factors played a role, but so also did new U.S. policies on South Africa, on Central America, and on Israel in general and its settlement policy in particular.

Likewise, a satisfactory explanation of why the United States sided with the U.N. majority in the General Assembly three times more often in 1977 and 1978 than in 1981–83 is impossible without some examination of differences in U.S. diplomacy between the two periods.[20]

SPECIALIZED AGENCIES

This discussion has focused so far on the question of anti-Americanism as it is manifested at U.N. headquarters, but the U.N. is much more than the political bodies that meet in New York. More than 80 percent of the funding for the entire United Nations system supports a network of voluntary and specialized agencies largely independent of the parent organization. While NAM efforts to bring its agenda before the U.N. and to see its positions adopted there have explicitly included the specialized bodies, its success has varied greatly.

As a general rule, the more technical an agency's mission, the less inclined are its members to use it as a platform for political statements. Many of these organizations are providers of aid or technical assistance, chiefly to Third World countries, in such areas as health, agriculture, communications, and food. Most of the others are regulatory or quasiregulatory, like the International Civil Air Organization, the International Telecommunications Union and the Universal Postal Union. Thus, not surprisingly, the same less developed and least developed countries, which in more political surroundings provide the voting majorities for NAM demands, are generally less enthusiastic about such an approach when it could endanger the flow of aid-related contributions.

Yet many agencies with a relatively technical mandate have not been free of politicization. For example it is not uncommon for political issues to be cast in terms of an organization's special subject matter. Thus

Israel or South Africa might be injected in plenary session speeches by way of discussions of the effect of apartheid on health or labor in South Africa, or of Israeli settlement policy on agriculture, water, refugees, or medical services in the occupied territories. Occasionally such themes give way to action. In the early 1970s, for example, South Africa was expelled from most U.N. agencies. More recently Israel has been the nonaligned target. In 1982 alone, NAM activists sought expulsion of Israel from the World Health Organization, the International Telecommunications Union and the International Atomic Energy Agency. Although thwarted at WHO and the ITU by threatened U.S. withdrawals, the effort at the IAEA was briefly successful.

Much more prone to politicization are the agencies with a relatively abstract or open-ended mandate. The United Nations Conference on Trade and Development (UNCTAD) is political practically by definition. Established in 1964 to accelerate economic development by promoting international trade and regional trade harmonization, UNCTAD has become dominated by the Group of 77, the developing countries' economic caucus. Yet, given its mandate, and the influence of the G-77, UNCTAD doctrine and pronouncements on such things as commodity price stabilization, tariff preferences, debt reform and development finance naturally put forward a Third World view. Clearly this makes UNCTAD a political body, yet it is difficult to imagine how an international organization with universal membership explicitly concerned with the immediate economic interests of developing countries would not be political. It is also difficult to distinguish UNCTAD's "political" character from its original purpose.

The degree to which politicization can impede an agency's ability to perform its functions is a more relevant question if asked about UNESCO. The General Conferences of UNESCO over the last 10 years, with the notable exception of the 1983 gathering, have become the scene of pitched battles between delegates. The conflicts have been waged both over matters within UNESCO's sphere, such as press freedom, and subjects far beyond it, such as disarmament, human rights and the Middle East. The U.S. government, which has announced its intended withdrawal from UNESCO, charges that the politicization of the plenary meetings reappears in many of the agency's programs. The administration argues that these have been developed and administered by a staff sympathetic to the values of authoritarian governments in Eastern Europe and the Third World. It also asserts that UNESCO activities in the communications, social sciences and education areas often betray the principles of its charter.

We have not conducted an investigation of UNESCO comparable to the one recently completed by the State Department. However, we have had the benefit of wide-ranging interviews with Americans professionally involved in every area of UNESCO activities. The agency is certainly not problem free. In the communications area in particular it has been associated with some questionable activities. And there is clearly an anti-Western cast to the way a large number of its member governments view press freedom and press protection. While it is not yet evident to us that these problems have prevented UNESCO from conducting its essential functions it is clearly the most politicized of U.N. agencies.

Because of its status as a kind of flashpoint for the collision of radically differing views on press freedom, a subject fundamental to Western values, UNESCO deserves particular attention in a study of anti-American or anti-Western feeling at the U.N. Like the General Assembly itself, UNESCO is a key debating ground for much of the Third World. When themes recur in UNESCO speeches over time, they are a measure of the power and appeal that certain ideas have for many member states. The New International Information Order is this kind of theme. Its postulates, that Western wire services "monopolize" the flow of news, and provide a coverage and sense of the "newsworthy" twisted by a Western bias are very compelling in many Third World countries where U.S. newspapers need to place reporters. While developing countries have not lost interest in interventionist measures to redress "imbalance" in the international flow of information, recent emphasis has shifted more toward strengthening Third World news outlets.

The New International Information Order, like the New International Economic Order, has also exemplified a broader dissaffection in the developing world with the fundamental relationships between North and South and the perceived role of the U.N. and other institutions in preserving them. In a 1979 UNESCO conference the Prime Minister of Malaysia explained "It is because the exercise of the free press is loaded in favor of the developed countries that we have tried to fight for a new order." "All the principles of the U.N.," he continued, "were written by developed countries before the developing countries were admitted as members. Now...some of the loaded principles should be reviewed."[21]

Behind the Prime Minister's complaint is a tension surfacing in many areas of the U.N. system, between some of the Western values enshrined in founding charters, and an institutional need for U.N. bodies to respond to voting majorities that question some of those norms or their application. Although the United States is the most conspicuous embodiment of Western values, such criticisms are less anti-American than anti-

Western. How these pressures are resolved will influence the course and the survival of UNESCO and perhaps of the U.N. itself.

CONCLUSIONS

It is clear from the foregoing analysis that anti-Americanism does exist in the United Nations, as in the international system as a whole. At the same time, the evidence leads us to conclude that the phenomenon is much more apparent in the General Assembly and other general-membership political forums than in more purely functional bodies. There is little evidence of anti-American attitudes in the Secretariats of U.N. bodies, with the possible exception of UNESCO. On the whole, anti-American sentiments are expressed only sporadically, even in political forums, and do not appear to be a systematic characteristic by any means.

The United States tends to be on the losing side of most votes on controversial political issues, though a growing percentage of General Assembly resolutions (especially innocuous ones) are passed by consensus with tacit U.S. support. It would be wrong, however, to conclude that these voting patterns necessarily reflect anti-American sentiments, any more than a voting shift toward U.S. preferences on political issues would indicate pro-American attitudes. Countries cast General Assembly votes for a variety of reasons including national interests, group loyalties and norms, and simple horse-trading. They generally do not vote "for" and "against" the United States (or the Soviet Union). It would be extraordinarily ethnocentric, in fact, to think that international debates on global issues are decided primarily on the basis of which side of the issue the United States favors.

The polarization of East–West relations and the resulting competition for political support in U.N. political bodies certainly has led to increasing pressures from both sides on nonaligned countries to choose sides on highly charged issues, such as Grenada, Kampuchea, Afghanistan, Puerto Rico, and the downing of the Korean airliner in September 1983, which directly involve one of the superpowers or their immediate proxies. Most truly nonaligned countries have successfully managed to circumvent such pressures, which they greatly resent, and the recent record on these high-visibility East–West issues has hardly been anti-American, other than the double standard by which only the United States has been criticized by name (on rare occasions) in the General Assembly.

The high coincidence (about 80 percent) between Soviet and non-aligned voting patterns in the General Assembly reflects a concerted Soviet effort to court favor in the Third World through symbolic support for nonaligned positions.[22] The Soviets appear to vote with the nonaligned much more than the nonaligned follow the Soviet lead. As noted above, there are a handful of states professing nonalignment and active in the nonaligned leadership that act as proxies for the Soviet Union, but they are in a distinct minority in the movement and appear to have lost some ground in the past year or two. It was noteworthy, for example, that the Soviet Union (and the Ukraine) stood alone in opposing a recent Security Council resolution to expand the mandate of U.N. peacekeeping forces in Lebanon, which was supported by the Western powers and all eight nonaligned members of the Council, including Nicaragua. In effect, the Soviets, who have relatively little to offer or to give up in a reordering of North–South economic, social, and political relations, have been able to get a "free ride" in the North–South debate. Few experienced members of the U.N. community, whether from developed or developing countries, perceive the Soviet Union as the true champion of progressive change in the world. Instead, the Soviets are given credit for playing a cynical diplomatic game with considerable skill and dedication.

The United States is often on the losing side of votes in the General Assembly not because countries are anti-American, but because of its staunch support for Israel, its moderation on South African issues, and its generally status-quo approach to calls for a reordering of North–South relationships. The General Assembly and, to a lesser extent, the Security Council arguably are biased against Israel and South Africa, but this does not imply that they are anti-American. It is also not surprising that the United States and its OECD partners, as the major "have" nations, are usually outvoted in a forum heavily populated with "have not" countries on issues of economic development, redistribution of global resources, the utilization of the global environment, and the regulation of international commerce. On these questions, as well as on the growing batch of disarmament resolutions, the immediate national interests of the United States and developing countries diverge more often than they converge, regardless of how representatives of these countries view the United States.

These "objective" factors suggest that the United States will continue to find itself in the minority on a wide range of issues in the General Assembly until either 1) the United States radically alters its priorities and perceptions of its interests or 2) the developing countries substantially modify their tactics and objectives to a point where much greater accommodation and consensus are possible between North and South. Neither side appears prepared to beat such a hasty retreat in the foreseeable future. In all probability, the United States will continue to "lose" most votes in general U.N. forums for some years to come. Nevertheless, U.S. policymakers should rethink their priorities in order to sort out important principles from simple peevishness and to develop more positive initiatives. And there is great room for improvement in the style and competence of U.S. diplomacy in multilateral bodies. (Suggestions on both counts are outlined below.)

At the same time, the United States should be quick to exploit opportunities to strengthen its influence at the U.N. The most significant of these lies in the Nonaligned Movement itself. There are growing tensions in the NAM that create an opening for skillful U.S. diplomacy. After a decade of rhetoric about a New International Economic Order, about using oil and other commodities as "weapons" against the North, about an alliance between oil producers and least developed states, the near total failure of any of these campaigns to gain their objectives has challenged the strategy of confrontation that has dominated the NAM since its 1973 summit. India and many other moderates are demanding that the nonaligned find a more pragmatic vision. Clearly the United States would benefit from such a change and should be careful to avoid a confrontational diplomacy that would only serve to delay its coming.

But such a development will not, and should not be intended to, reverse the United States' minority status in one-country, one-vote forums. In general, it would be far more practical, and we think advisable, for the United States 1) to pay less attention to vote counting on essentially symbolic resolutions in the General Assembly, 2) to be more thick-skinned about criticisms aimed its way in the general debate and other rhetorical exercises, and 3) to get on with the tragically neglected work of building more reliable and viable multilateral machinery for undertaking peacemaking and peacekeeping efforts before local conflicts can take on global dimensions.

Ambassador Jeane Kirkpatrick is correct to take genuinely unfair treatment of the United States seriously and to reply forcefully, but there are signs that tit-for-tat and defensive tactics have begun to dominate the perspective of U.S. officials toward the larger strategic issues that shape the relationship between the global body and its most important member. An over-concentration on voting patterns can easily lead to a siege mentality in which the United States is seen as isolated in an essentially unfriendly and unsympathetic environment. Words like consensus, cooperation, and coalition-building begin to fade into the background as go-it-alone and damage limitation strategies come to the fore. If the United States is perceived to be in an adversarial position vis-à-vis the U.N. and much of its membership, it will be in a poor position to encourage the kinds of reforms it rightly believes are needed in the operations of the world organization.

These perspectives foster a style in and stance toward the U.N. which tend to perpetuate a series of negative and quite possibly self-fulfilling prophecies. The perception of anti-Americanism in the U.N. leads quite naturally to anti-U.N. sentiments and policies on the part of U.S. representatives and policymakers, leading to resentments on both sides. One representative of a moderate Third World country, denying the existence of widespread anti-American attitudes in the U.N. , noted, however, that many people in the U.N. community are beginning to ask "What has the United States done for the U.N. lately?" in response to U.S. complaints about bias in the U.N. system.

Style, moreover, is important in U.N. diplomacy. Representatives from smaller countries are particularly sensitive to being ignored or taken for granted by diplomats from the major powers. Small countries usually send their very best people to the General Assembly, because the U.N. plays a much more important role in achieving their national goals and in implementing their foreign policies than it does for the major powers. Many of these representatives use the U.N. as a forum for sharpening their diplomatic and rhetorical skills before moving on to higher positions in their governments. They place a high premium, therefore, on their participation in the speechmaking and vote-taking in the General Assembly both because of the symbolism of acting as equals to the great powers in a one-nation, one-vote forum and because they have higher expectations that their long-term national goals, and those of the developing world as a whole, will be served by Assembly declarations that often seem hollow to us.

It is true that small countries often lack the staff resources to permit a fully informed vote on highly technical issues, such as disarmament, and that voting with the nonaligned bloc is usually their safest and easiest choice. But paying attention to the interests, aspirations, and egos of Third World diplomats can make a major difference when the final votes are tallied. Prime examples of skillful and sensitive courting of Third World support by Western delegates would include the British on the Falklands issue, the French on the question of Lebanese peacekeeping forces, and the Americans on Puerto Rico.

By and large the U.S. Mission to the U.N. in recent years has been given poor marks by other representatives for its failure to develop close personal relationships with Third World delegates, for the tendency of Ambassador Kirkpatrick and her top aides to lecture other countries more than to listen to them, and for a general reluctance to "play the game" of multilateral diplomacy with any consistency.[23] These factors have evidently contributed to a decline in the percentage of times in which the United States has voted with the majority in General Assembly votes from 40.6 percent in 1977, when Andrew Young represented the United States, to 15.6 percent in 1983.[24]

Several representatives of Third World countries whom we interviewed did suggest that the U.S. Mission is beginning to pay somewhat more attention to them and to achieve better results in the Assembly. They complained bitterly, however, about the increasing linkage being imposed by the United States between bilateral aid levels and a recipient's voting pattern in the U.N. Some apparently felt that the "carrot" has been underemphasized in this "carrot and stick" approach. Others complained that aggressive voting records on North–South issues are a poor measure of how supportive or friendly a Third World nation is toward the United States. The United States is certainly justified in taking account of the attitudes and voting records of aid recipients in determining foreign assistance levels, but if this lever is to have the desired effect of promoting support for U.S. aims in the U.N., then the style and context within which this linkage is made must also be taken into account. In the long run, U.S. purposes in the U.N. will be better served by fostering an atmosphere of concerned participation rather than by intimidation. Soviet pressure tactics in the second year of the Afghanistan resolution, for example, failed badly for much the same reasons the U.S. campaign has made little headway.

Another frequent complaint about the conduct of U.S. diplomacy in the U.N. is that it is directed much more to domestic constituencies than to the other members of the organization. Every diplomat to some extent speaks to domestic audiences as much as to others in the General Assembly Hall and recognizes that his or her career depends more on reactions at home than on how well fellow diplomats respond. But for most of them, the criterion of success is how persuasive they are in rallying the support of other countries to their side of an issue. For U.S. diplomats, however, there is often more political capital to be gained at home by an eloquent expression of why the United States opposes the views of the majority than by seeking accommodation and consensus. The image of the lone U.S. spokesperson standing up for fundamental principles in the face of an unrelenting onslaught by a cynical alliance of socialists and Third World dictators has considerable appeal to a U.S. electorate already frustrated by the decline of U.S. influence in the post-Vietnam world.

The tendency to speak chiefly to home audiences, while perhaps most apparent in the U.S. representatives with a more confrontational style, may have deeper roots going beyond ideology or personalities. One Third World observer, for example, commented that Andrew Young, while sympathetic to and friendly with many nonaligned representatives, often seemed to be speaking to his domestic constituencies and to have his own agenda beyond the work of the U.N.

There are several possible explanations. The short tenure of most U.S. "Permanent Representatives" makes it less likely that they will join "The Club" and more likely that they will be interested in building a political base for the next step in their careers. Diplomats also have a natural desire to be shaping policy rather than just enunciating it, and the high visibility public forum of the General Assembly offers a tempting opportunity to influence policy by helping to shape public attitudes toward global issues and by acting as a prism through which Washington views the world. As a member of the President's Cabinet, and in Ambassador Kirkpatrick's case the National Security Council as well, the U.S. Permanent Representative is drawn into policy debates in Washington on a range of issues, which diverts time and attention from the U.N. Finally, the presence of the U.N. in New York may increase the tendency to play to domestic galleries, especially since the U.S. press corps so readily focuses on stories critical of the U.N.

There are thus many virtually cost-free things the United States could do to improve the style and effectiveness of its U.N. diplomacy and so counteract whatever anti-American tendencies exist in the organization. They entail a fuller and more outspoken commitment to the U.N. as an institution, a more attentive ear to the concerns of the Third World majority, more intimate and vigorous personal diplomacy, and a longer-term and more U.N.-oriented leadership at the U.S. Mission to the U.N. These steps would not guarantee that the United States could consistently attract the majority of members to its side, but they would create a more fertile and sympathetic environment for the airing of U.S. concerns.

The central issue facing the United States in the U.N. is not combating anti-Americanism, but deciding what it wants and what it really needs from the organization. What are our goals and what are our expectations? Where do our principles leave off and our interests begin? In other words, what is sacred and what is subject to negotiation? Some Americans have come to see important principles—worth fighting for and worth going-it-alone to defend—behind almost every political resolution in the General Assembly. They are idealistic both in their expectations of what the U.N. should and can be and in their faith in the universal attractiveness of traditional U.S. ideals and principles. They sometimes forget that our principles also serve our national interests and that, in a sharply divided and essentially pluralistic world, others will not necessarily rush to embrace our vision, however noble and just it appears to us.

From what we consider to be a pragmatic perspective, the key question is not whether U.S. principles are worth fighting for in multilateral forums—of course they are—but how this can be done effectively so that we further our objectives as well as satisfy our consciences. The U.N. is an imperfect instrument in an imperfect world, and we need to adjust our expectations and policies accordingly.

The U.N. cannot be a viable and effective institution without vigorous U.S. involvement. But this is a two-way street. When a radical minority endeavors to treat the United States unfairly and receives the acquiescence—even the support—of a General Assembly majority, as it did in cutting off debate about Grenada, it damages the credibility and reputation of the United Nations. Such actions are contrary to the principles of equity and consensus-building that are fundamental not only to the U.N. Charter, but also to the effectiveness of the work of the institution. When the rights of any member or minority group of countries at the U.N. are ignored or trampled—even if they are upheld most of the time—the values and even the viability of the whole organization suffer. Most member states apparently recognize the danger inherent in allowing a tyranny of the majority to dominate plenary bodies, especially since on many North–South issues the voting majority is a distinct minority in terms of financial contributions to the U.N. and of global economic and military power. Moderate nonaligned states need to be reminded of the need for continuous vigilance to prevent bloc politics from taking precedence over the fundamental principles of fair play which have largely determined where the U.N. has or has not been able to play an effective role—particularly in conflict resolution efforts—over the last 40 years. If the seeds of anti-Americanism (or anti-Westernism) are allowed to grow, then it will threaten the viability and utility of the whole organization and hence will harm the long-term interests of even the most radical nonaligned countries.

Gratuitous attacks on the United States and its values—while still relatively rare—can only alienate U.S. public and official opinion. In today's sensitive atmosphere such alienation can have serious consequences. It may well be, as we have argued here, that the U.N. and the bulk of its members are not anti-American. But in this case perceptions may be more important than reality. It is time for the U.N. membership to prove that it is not anti-American and for the United States to prove that it is not anti-U.N.

NOTES

1. This thesis has been expounded at length in A. Yeselson and A. Gaglione, *A Dangerous Place*, New York: Viking, 1974, and more recently in a series of contentious tracts by the Heritage Foundation's UN Assessment Project.

2. "The United Nations: A Statement of Support," sponsored by the United Nations Association of the USA, *The New York Times*, October 2, 1983.

3. See Richard Bernstein, "The UN versus the US," *The New York Times Magazine*, January 22, 1984.

4. *Report to Congress on Voting Practices in the United Nations*, February 24, 1984; Ambassador Jeane Kirkpatrick, press briefing, March 13, 1984; Kirkpatrick testimony, Foreign Operations Subcommittee: Senate Appropriations Committee, March 7, 1983 and March 2, 1984; State Dept. interviews, March 1984; State Dept. statistical record: "Country Agreement with US on 10 Key Votes in 1981"; also see Richard L. Jackson, *The Non-Aligned, the UN, and the Superpowers*, (New York: Praeger, 1983), pp. 144–45.

5. *Op. cit.*, *Report to Congress on Voting Practices in the United Nations*, February 24, 1984.

6. Soviet policy towards the Third World, as a western journal described it, amounts to "backing the poor on matters of high principle and the rich on matters of substance," "South Meets North," *The Economist*, December 2, 1978, p. 88.

7. *Op. cit.*, Kirkpatrick testimony, March 7, 1983.

8. Peter Fromuth, "UN Vote Watching," *The Inter Dependent*, March/April, 1984.

9. *Ibid.*, Study based on examination of United Nations official voting records contained the *Index to Proceedings of the General Assembly* for 1975–1982, and the preliminary compilation for 1983, *Resolutions and Decisions Adopted by the General Assembly During the First Part of its Thirty-Eighth Session*. The United Nations began to keep official end-of-session voting tallies in 1975.

10. A/38/L.26.

11. *Direction of Trade Statistics, 1983 Yearbook*, The International Monetary Fund, Washington, 1983.

12. Interviews with the South African Mission to the United Nations and the South African commercial consulate.

13. "Can we abandon a country that has stood beside us in every war we've ever fought, a country that strategically is essential to the free world? It has production of minerals we all must have and so forth... I just feel that, myself, that here if we're go-

ing to sit down at a table and negotiate with the Russians, surely we can keep the door open and continue to negotiate with a friendly nation like South Africa." President Reagan, in an interview with Walter Cronkite broadcast on March 3, 1981 and excerpted in *The New York Times*, March 15, 1981.

14. A/37/L.17, paragraph 21, December 9, 1982 (A/38/PV.103).

15. Procedural Motion, Rule 75, sponsored by Democratic Yemen (A/38/PV.43).

16. For textual and voting comparisons see resolutions 38/29 (Afghanistan), and 38/7 (Grenada).

17. The full title of the Committee of 24 (so named because it has 24 members), is "The Special Committee on the Situation with Regard to the Implementation of the Declaration on the Granting of Independence to Colonial Countries and Peoples." It is the principal U.N. body concerned with progress towards the self-determination and independence of peoples in dependent territories. Puerto Rico, however, acceded to commonwealth status in 1952 and by so doing placed itself beyond the legal mandate of the Committee of 24.

18. *Op. cit.*, R.L. Jackson.

19. Rais A. Tuzmukhamedov, *Soviet Union and Non-aligned Nations*, Bombay: Allied Publishers, 1976), p. xx quoted from R.L. Jackson, *op. cit.*, p. 204.

20. *Op. cit.*, *The Inter Dependent*.

21. Prime Minister Mahathir bin Mohamad, UNESCO Inter-Governmental Conference on Communication Policies in Asia and Oceania, Kuala Lumpur, Malaysia, Feb. 5-14, 1979; quote appears in "UNESCO: Getting Down to Cases," a paper delivered by Leonard Sussman, Executive Director of Freedom House, at an international conference of independent news media held in Talloires, France, Sept. 30, 1983, under the auspices of Tufts University and the World Press Freedom Committee.

22. It is interesting to note the degree to which China also had made a concerted effort to champion nonaligned causes at the U.N. In 1982, as noted above, China voted less often with the United States than did the Soviet Union in the General Assembly.

23. For a well-informed appraisal of the performance of the United States at the U.N. in recent years, see Seymour Maxwell Finger, "The Reagan–Kirkpatrick Policies and the United Nations," *Foreign Affairs*, Vol. 62, No. 2, (Winter 1983/84), pp. 436-57.

24. *Op. cit.*, *The Inter Dependent*. Ambassador Kirkpatrick cited just the opposite trend in her March 13, 1984 press conference, but the U.S. Mission subsequently released a correction after reviewing the figures.

12

Implications of Anti-Americanism for U.S. Foreign Policy

Richard E. Bissell

Anti-Americanism is generally perceived as a cultural or sociological phenomenon; at some point during its accumulation, its impact on the conduct of U.S. foreign policy has to be recognized. Before delving into the myriad implications, however, some bureaucratic truths about foreign policy and anti-Americanism require introduction. Hierarchical elements prevent our considering this issue with strictly academic analysis. Above all, the bureaucratic environment imposes certain limits to consider before allowing our imaginative implications to take control of the direction of this topic.

Those in the U.S. government who consider the issue of anti-Americanism to be a priority are not in major policymaking positions. Anti-Americanism is considered to be in the province of public opinion, whether mass opinion or elite opinion, and as such, is relegated to public affairs officers, both within the Department of State and even more, to the U.S. Information Agency, to deal with as a symptom, not as a matter of high policy.

Those in high policy positions do not pay attention to the emergence of anti-Americanism until it is brought to the doorstep of a U.S. ambassador or a foreign ministry. Thus, the U.S. government began to take a careful look at anti-Americanism in Iran *after* a student mob had occupied the U.S. embassy and taken the entire staff hostage. Anti-Americanism in Pakistan evoked a brief examination after the embassy was burned to the ground. But U.S. foreign policymakers did not dawdle long over this issue, encouraged by their counterparts in foreign ministries who pay much less attention to public opinion than does the State Department.

These bureaucratic considerations need to be considered not simply to make the discussion more difficult. They are essential for a full understanding of the contradiction at the root of this chapter, and indeed, to convey the terms of the challenge for U.S. policymakers wishing to do something about anti-Americanism: the gap between knowledge and capability for action that must be bridged when looking at implications. It may be that it can be done, and to be successful the strengths of existing perceptions and inclinations in Washington will have to be harnessed.

SOURCES OF ANTI-AMERICANISM

It can be more useful to deal with the "sources" of anti-Americanism than to attempt to provide a clearcut definition. There will inevitably be some disagreement over the grey areas to be included in anti-Americanism. But that should not deter the careful observer from attempting to stake out the main sources of the phenomenon. By way of general overview, however, I disagree with those who argue that anti-Americanism in the Third World is simply an elite phenomenon.[1] It is true that élites are generally those most aware of the outside world, and whose positions are most affected by the presence of the United States as a global force, and it may also be true that anti-Americanism among élites should concern us the most, given their role in determining attitudes in societies at large. More attention, though, should be paid to the fact that mass-based anti-Americanism does exist, and that it may need to concern us more in the future, by virtue of the very slim amount of knowledge generally at the root of such attitudes. The United States should worry greatly about the irrationality of the street mob, spurred on by a demagogic speech or by a foreign government trying to get a "message" across to the U.S. government, that proceeds to burn down the U.S. embassy. The expressions of anti-Americanism from the masses often occur less predictably, in a more violent form, and often untempered by the kind of love-hate relationship that characterizes élite attitudes toward foreign powers.

It may be useful to create an illustrative "laundry list" of recent symptoms of anti-Americanism. Such a list could not possibly be exhaustive, dealing as we are with the wide range of behavior that goes into attitudes; but some of the more obvious sources of anti-Americanism would need to include:

- an unpleasant contact with individual Americans abroad, such as a businessman or a tourist;
- a sense of being in competition economically with U.S. corporations;
- U.S. culture as a threat to cultural autonomy;
- a rejection of the materialistic manifestations of the U.S. life style;
- dislike for the style of U.S. public figures, such as President Reagan;
- resentment over feelings of economic or military dependence on the United States;
- frustration of Third World nationalists unable to achieve national autonomy;
- resentment of U.S. ideology as characterized by "capitalism" or "imperialism";
- a commitment to Third World ideologies (such as "neutralism" or "nonaligned movement"-ism);
- a loss of local elite influence by virtue of U.S. intrusions in cultural and economic affairs;
- the disparity between first world wealth and Third World poverty, possibly made evident by modern media;
- symptoms of U.S. vulnerability that make it an easy target;
- U.S. projections of their own low self-esteem or sense of guilt, sometimes called the "collapse of nerve";
- Soviet or West European attacks on the United States for cultural or ideological reasons;
- threatening perceptions to traditionalists of the United States as a modernizing, pro-technology force in the world;
- institutionalized anti-Americanism in forums such as the United Nations, where the attitude helps caucusing groups to maintain their coherence.

What needs to be emphasized in this extended list of possible sources of anti-Americanism is that they focus primarily on the environment of international relations, and not on the specific policies and measures taken by national governments in their pursuit of the national interest. It is common, for instance, for observers to confuse opposition to particular U.S. government policies with anti-Americanism. It is essential to keep them separate, and I hope that the list of sources conveys the extent to which there is a discernible phenomenon with plenty of substance, without also mixing in the question of antagonism towards U.S. foreign policy. It is especially important for policymakers attempting to sort out remedies for problems to relate specific tools to the issues.

It cannot be denied that U.S. foreign policy and the specific initiatives of a particular U.S. administration affect the projection of the United States into the international environment. The difference, however, should be maintained between opposition to short-term U.S. policies (or even perceived long-term U.S. strategies in the realm of high policy), and opposition to the United States as a diffuse cultural and ideological presence in the Third World. Each requires rather different policies on the part of the United States, and to confuse the two categories is to reduce our effectiveness in dealing with each. In this chapter, I shall not deal with opposition to U.S. foreign policy.

CAN ANTI-AMERICANISM BE QUANTIFIED?

How much anti-Americanism are we talking about, in this relatively diffuse area of cultural and ideological perceptions of the U.S.? We have much in the way of anecdotal evidence about its existence, both at the elite and mass levels. A widespread implication exists in the literature dealing with anti-Americanism that it has been increasing. As long as we deal with our own personal encounters with anti-Americanism or with newsworthy, violent symptoms of that attitude, we are unlikely to come to any conclusive answers. Quantitative efforts have been made over the years, however, to provide more careful measures of the extent of anti-U.S. attitudes overseas.

Among the many attitudinal survey questions used since the 1950s among better-educated, urban inhabitants of the Third World is the following: "How about the United States, do you have a very good, good, neither good nor bad, bad or very bad opinion of the U.S.?" A close variant of the question sometimes used is "Please use this card [with the same choices as above] to tell me your feelings about various countries. How about the U.S.?" With this type of question, survey researchers have been hard-pressed to find much anti-Americanism. Only on rare occasion has a majority of public opinion had a more negative than positive opinion of the United States. For example, in a series of five USIA worldwide surveys from 1963 through 1972 in at least 82 countries or major cities, in only one, Karachi, Pakistan in 1964, did the extent of general bad opinion of the United States exceed the extent of good opinion, and in only one, Dakar in 1965, were they approximately equal. Otherwise, majorities would be very strongly positive.[2] Even at the height of the Vietnam War, allegedly a watershed in anti-U.S. feelings around the world, such queries were obtaining very positive answers, and we can document the difference. Included in the same surveys in 1972 were questions about attitudes toward U.S. policies in Vietnam, which were coming up consistently and strongly negative while general attitudes remained strongly pro-U.S.[3]

Some may take issue with the notion of "general feelings" toward the United States; an alternative formulation also tried out was the issue of "respect" for the United States. In the same 1972 series of surveys, the margin of high respect over low respect for the United States was even greater than the measure of general feeling. And this was at a time of global opposition to U.S. policies in Vietnam! In Nairobi, for instance, high respect for the United States outweighed low respect by 84% to 15%. In Caracas, the proportions were 79% to 17%, and in Mexico City the positives outweighed negatives by 63% to 36%.[4]

The question of the direction of anti-Americanism is difficult to answer about the Third World countries. Surveys are not done consistently enough, and indeed, the demographics of many Third World countries are too unstable to conduct solid research. One important country frequently noted for its alleged anti-Americanism, however, is India, and recent surveys show that younger Indians in the early 1980s are more likely to have a favorable opinion of the United States than would their elders. In April 1982, for instance, more university graduates under the age of 36 (61%) expressed positive opinions of the United States than those between 36 and 50 (54%) and those over the age of 50 (50%).[5]

Quite clearly, the United States should not ignore that 36% in Mexico City or the 15% in Nairobi. But, in terms of the populations in Third World urban centers, there is a great difference between opposition to U.S. policies and being anti-American, and the latter group has historically been and remains a problem confined to a minority. Any policy responses to the problem should take that into account, ensuring that efforts to address the anti-American minorities do not jeopardize the reservoirs of goodwill already present in the general publics of the Third World.

IMPLICATIONS FOR POLICYMAKERS

Foreign affairs policymakers disagree about the meaning of this variegated pattern of anti-American sentiment for U.S. foreign policy. Honest analytical disagreements over its extent do exist, but an institutional problem comes into play: most policymakers prefer to deal with foreign ministries rather than with general populations, which are unpredictable and can generally "mess up" organized foreign policy. Such biases cause U.S. policymakers frequently to underestimate the potential damage to U.S. foreign policy.

In multilateral forums, for instance, we can say for certain that U.S. foreign policy is restricted by anti-American attitudes. It is evident at the United Nations that regional caucuses obtain their unity, to a considerable extent, by identifying an external foe (such as the United States) and ensuring that each General Assembly resolution, even if only remotely related to U.S. policies, includes an indictment of the United States. The United States is frequently associated, for instance, by the Africa bloc with resolutions on southern Africa, and by the Arab bloc on any resolutions including mention of Israel. Much of the residual unity of the Group of 77 (G-77) is based on the United States as a scapegoat for various local economic problems. The G-77, as well as the non-aligned (NAM) caucus at the UN can be steered to a striking extent by the current chair of those caucuses, given the ground rules of seeking consensus. Members of the U.S. delegation to the U.N., in fact, maintain that such a role for the United States—as a negative catalyst for caucus unity—has been fomented by particular radical states in each of the regional caucuses (e.g., the PLO in the Arab caucus, Cuba in the Latin American caucus), and that it has not been a spontaneous development at the U.N.

Policymakers also need to realize that anti-Americanism is a natural corollary to durable U.S. alliance relationships amid regional antagonisms. It is clear, for instance, that much of the anti-Americanism in India derives from the U.S. military support of Pakistan because the U.S.-Pakistani relationship has been sufficiently long-standing as to condition an entire generation of Indians to think of the U.S. and Pakistan in the same military camp. The United States has become a grey shadow behind the Pakistani threat, and as long as Pakistan remains a threat to India, and the United States retains its ties to Islamabad, the U.S. image will suffer. Anti-Americanism in that situation is hostage to the countries of South Asia settling their regional conflicts. Where regional conflicts are increasingly polarized, the United States is likely to suffer antagonism by involvement. In Africa, the extreme demands of the African states in the 1970s for complete diplomatic isolation of South Africa meant that U.S. maintenance of any ties with that country increased public African expressions of hostility toward the United States. Among the African press corps in particular, the hostility has become an anti-American reflex that might not even be reduced by settlement of issues between black and white Africa.

Policymakers should also not rush to judgment with a connection between specific U.S. policies and the emergence of anti-Americanism. Considerable resentment exists in the world—along with envy—for the standard of living and lifestyles of Americans. Such problems are fed by the widespread dissemination of U.S. television shows such as "Dallas" on a syndicated basis. The image of the United States as a crime-ridden society, emphasized so much on Radio Moscow, is reinforced by the syndication of "Hill Street Blues." The sources of anti-Americanism on a mass basis are more likely to be through such channels of popular culture than through events and policies primarily of interest to the elites, such as U.S. government foreign policy actions. The United States is not about to consider restricting the flow of U.S. popular culture abroad, but concern over the development of negative images of the United States abroad has to be placed in the context of the massive, nongovernmental flows overseas each year.

As a result, foreign policies should not be predicated upon converting latent anti-Americanism into pro-Americanism. Most of the sources of anti-Americanism in the Third World are not based upon antagonism toward specific policies. It is possible that perceptions of the pattern of U.S. foreign policies have contributed to anti-Americanism, but molding a specific foreign policy initiative to transform those attitudes will show little, if any, short-term payoff. Attitudes towards the United States generally are deep-rooted, as evidenced by persisting pro-American attitudes, and while it would be unwise to consistently create unpopular U.S. policies, there is good reason to think that undoing anti-Americanism will require actions at a level other than foreign policymaking.

Where anti-American attitudes have taken root, policymakers should consider taking a low-profile approach to implementation of foreign policy. Notable here is the reiterated theme in Latin America of the U.S. instinct for "interference" in hemispheric affairs. This form of anti-Americanism, developed over several hundred years and now part of almost all Latin American ideologies has to influence the visibility of the U.S. role in the region. The issue cuts both ways ideologically. Public opinion surveys have identified an equal sensitivity—or what others would call anti-Americanism—in Nicaragua and Guatemala to U.S. interventionism: in Nicaragua for U.S. support of the contras, and in Guatemala simultaneously for the U.S. holding human rights compliance over the heads of the government as a condition for obtaining military aid. That U.S. reputation for interference in Latin American affairs thus has to be taken into account in considering any specific foreign policy measure.

It is thus essential to include questions of foreign public opinion in the national security framework. This has been done in the Reagan administration more than in the past. The institutionalization of concern about foreign public opinion in the National Security Council has been accomplished, for the most part, and that suggests that anti-American attitudes are unlikely to be sloughed off ever again as a non-policy concern. This sensitivity is especially important in those countries or regions where public or elite anti-Americanism is large enough to threaten the ability of a foreign government to work with the United States in collaborative foreign policy ventures. In such instances, the United States simply could not use the phrase, "trust me," which is effective if based on a generalized pro-American attitude. The U.S. faces a distrustful environment in certain countries and regions, and policymakers increasingly have available to them the empirical research to warn them of such foreign pitfalls. The lessons of Teheran 1978 will long be burned in the minds of Washington policymakers, that inattention to public opinion can result in major losses for all sectors of the U.S. presence overseas.

WHAT IS TO BE DONE?

Discrete pockets of anti-Americanism do exist, and some sources of that phenomenon cannot be affected by virtue of the fact that the United States is simply a convenient scapegoat. Other major powers suffer the same fate by simply having a significant military or economic presence. At the same time, a range of possible actions should be considered to tackle the long-term aspects of anti-Americanism. The presence of that attitude cannot be answered with a "so what?" if the United States is to choose a course other than isolationism.

Actions need to be considered with care for several reasons. Generalizations across regions or even within regions are dangerous approaches to public policy, and dealing with the existence of anti-Americanism is not a matter for the U.S. government alone. Indeed, it is more likely that future levels of anti-Americanism will be determined primarily by the U.S. private sector. If one looks again at the list of the sources of such an attitude enumerated at the opening of this chapter, it is clear that private citizens, entities, and behavior generate much of the identifiable anti-Americanism. The importance of the private sector is at the root of the U.S. government's attempt to deal with foreign hostility; programs can be proposed by the government in Washington, but they are nearly always carried out in the private sector and abroad only with the active support and concurrence of experts who know attitudinal conditions among the specific foreign audiences. Nevertheless, let me propose a range of responses that should be considered for possible development in the United States and possible dissemination to foreign audiences:

- Expand the channels for foreign elites to get their "messages" to the United States in order to balance the avalanche of "messages" emanating from the United States to overseas audiences. Here I include as "messages" cultural forms, television and print output, and policy-relevant views on issues of general international concern. Unless Americans show that they can listen as well as project, foreign elites will opt out of the international dialogue. Concrete measures here would include expansion of foreign language studies in the United States as well as training of more area experts who spend considerable time in foreign countries.
- Reexamine recent trends in the flow of international student and faculty exchanges, with a goal of establishing a balance in that flow. It is my impression, backed up with limited statistics, that the period since the 1960s has been marked by a major tilt in that balance toward a far greater number of foreign students being in the United States than vice versa. We all know the commercial reasons for that occurring; sensible notions about cultural balance would argue for a more generous distribution of the U.S. academic presence overseas.
- The U.S. business community and the private sector generally need greater attention, in the sense of bringing them into the process of combating anti-Americanism. As mentioned above, the foreign behavior of U.S. multinationals is one source of anti-Americanism, and surely it is in their interest to pay greater attention to the problem, if they do not want to face an implacably hostile environment. Some argue that they have made progress, but much more can be done.
- Focus increasingly in foreign information programs on "expectations."

It is often said that anti-Soviet attitudes are rare owing to low expectations of Soviet behavior in the first place, which creates a double standard penalizing the United States. It is for the United States and its allies with an interest in sustaining international values to press harder for the establishment of common expectations. Certain Third World countries will object, of course, believing that they cannot meet commonly accepted political and economic standards. But with some sensitivity, the process of dialogue on such issues may bring into play more realistic expectations of the United States, the Soviet Union, and the countries in the Third World, all of whom suffer by inappropriate expectations.

These suggestions are made without any expectation of "solving anti-Americanism." But is is necessary to avoid any tendency toward the polarized and unnecessary choice between designing policies to minimize anti-Americanism and unilateralist pursuit of policies that would erode the long-term reservoir of foreign goodwill toward the United States. Recommendations from the first perspective eventually become a U.S. mirror of foreign anti-Americanism, and the latter perspective eventually results in isolationism. Neither approach results in a peaceful world or a healthy foreign policy. Instead, a constructive approach would result in an increased U.S. awareness of foreign public attitudes—especially where anti-Americanism has emerged—that would temper the pattern of policies pursued by the United States through a process of dialogue. The United States may not have major problems now, but it is far less painful to avoid their emergence than to find remedies once the United States has been stigmatized by unpopularity.

NOTES

1. One could argue that U.S. intellectuals are particularly susceptible to the perception of foreign elite anti-Americanism, since their most common contacts with foreign publics are with foreign intellectuals, generally among the most outspoken elites in any foreign society.

2. USIA Report R-27-72, "U.S. Standing in Foreign Public Opinion Following the President's Visit to China," 1972; and USIA Report R-176-65, "U.S. Standing in Worldwide Public Opinion—1965."

3. USIA Report R-39-72, September 1, 1972.

4. Ibid.

5. USICA Research Memorandum, "Twelve Year Trend: Elite Indian Opinion of the U.S. and USSR," July 26, 1982.

Index

A

Africa, 91, 94, 100, 105, 171–
190; historical involvement
with the United States, 173–
175; perception of the U.S.
role, 100, 106–107, 109–110,
173–180

Ajami, Fouad, 102, 114

al-Afghani, Jamal al-Din, 71, 75

Allende, Salvadore, 13, 16, 26,
55, 196, 205

Amin, Samir, 99

Angola, 106–107, 212

Anti-Americanism, and the
Arab world (historical roots),
67–84; 110–120; and the
Palestinians, 73, 77–78, 103,
112, 159, 232; in Mexico, 32,
44–46

Arbenz, Jacobo, 13, 15

B

Baykurt, Fakir, 121, 124, 125

Betancourt, Romulo, 61

Burns, Arthur F., 50

C

Cabral, Amilcar, 88

Cárdenas, Lázaro, 40

Camp David, 80, 104

Cantú, Gaston Garcia, 32

Castro, Fidel, 21, 23, 25, 32, 56,
86, 230

Chace, James, 57

Cuba, 21, 33, 40, 42, 45, 56,
182, 213

Cultural dimensions, 2–7

Cyprus, 129

About the Editors

and Contributors

About the Editors and Contributors

RICHARD E. BISSELL is Executive Editor of *The Washington Quarterly*, and formerly Director of Research at the United States Information Agency. Among his published works are *South Africa and the United States*, and *Apartheid and International Organizations*.

ADEED DAWISHA is Deputy Director of Studies at the Royal Institute of International Affairs, London. In 1983–84, he was Visiting Professor in the School of International Studies, Johns Hopkins University. In addition to numerous articles, he is the author of *Egypt in the Arab World: The Elements of Foreign Policy*, and *Syria and the Lebanese Crisis*.

AINSLIE T. EMBREE is Chairman of the Department of History, Columbia University, and past president of the Association for Asian Studies. He was Counselor for Cultural Affairs at the American Embassy in New Delhi, 1978–80. His books include *Charles Grant and British Rule in India*, *India's Search for National Identity*, and *Pakistan's Western Borderlands*. He is past president of the American Institute of Indian Studies and of the Association of Asian Studies.

AHMET EVIN is Director of the Middle East Center at the University of Pennsylvania. His most recent book is *The Origins and Development of the Turkish Novel* (1984). In addition, he is Editor of *Modern Turkish Architecture* (1983) and *Modern Turkey: Continuity and Change* (1984).

PETER J. FROMUTH is Editorial Director of the Multilateral Project of the United Nations Association of the USA and Associate Editor of *The Inter Dependent* newspaper published by UNA–USA. He has served on the legislative staff of the Alaska State Legislature (1976–78) and of U.S. Senator Ted Stevens (1981–82), and as an international economist with the U.S. Commerce Dept. (1983). He holds a B.A. from Georgetown University, an M.A. from Oxford University, and an M.A. from the Johns Hopkins School of Advanced International Studies.

HARVEY GLICKMAN is Professor of Political Science at Haverford College. He is the author of a number of articles, reviews and parts of books on political change in Africa, including the analytical chapter on "Political Science" in *The African World, Handbook of the African Studies*

Association. He has served as consultant to the African Section, Bureau of Intelligence and Research, U.S. Department of State, and to the Social Sciences Division of the RAND Corporation.

GEORGE W. GRAYSON is John Marshall Professor of Government and Citizenship at the College of William and Mary, where he has taught since 1969. He has served in the Virginia State Legislature since 1974. His published works include *The United States and Mexico: Patterns of Influence,* and *The Politics of Mexican Oil.*

DAN HAENDEL is an attorney with the U.S. Department of the Treasury where he specializes in international financial law. He previously served with the Department of State, Department of the Army, and Citibank. He has taught at the University of Pennsylvania, Georgetown University, and the American University. He received his Ph.D., J.D., M.B.A., and B.A. from the University of Pennsylvania and his M.L.T. from Georgetown University.

MOHAMMAD BESHIR HAMID is Professor of Political Science at the University of Khartoum (Sudan). In 1983–84, he was Visiting Fellow, Center of International Studies and Program in Near Eastern Studies, Princeton University, and Visiting Scholar, Center for Contemporary Arab Studies, Georgetown University. His published works include chapters on the Sudan for the annual volume of *Africa Contemporary Record* since 1977; *The Politics of National Reconciliation in the Sudan,* CCAS Reports, Georgetown University; and articles in journals such as *Third World Quarterly* and *Journal of Arab Studies.*

ROBERT C. HORN is Professor of Political Science at California State University, Northridge. Dr. Horn has published numerous articles, chapters, and reviews on Soviet foreign policy in Asia and on the policies of major powers in Southeast Asia. His study of *Soviet-Indian Relations: Issues and Influence* was published in 1982. He spent 1983–84 on a Fulbright–Hays Visiting Lecturer Award in Malaysia, conducting research and teaching at the University of Malaya in Kuala Lumpur and the National University of Malaysia in Bangi.

IRVING LOUIS HOROWITZ is Hannah Arendt Distinguished Professor of Sociology and Political Science at Rutgers University and Editor-in-Chief of Transaction/SOCIETY. He has held major visiting professorships at Stanford, Wisconsin, California, Princeton University's Woodrow Wilson School of Public and International Affairs, and Washington University. Among his extensive writings on problems of Latin American development and the Third World are: *Three Worlds of Development: The Theory and Practice of Stratification*; and a sequel, *Beyond Empire and Revolution: Militarization and Consolidation in the Third World*.

EDWARD C. LUCK is President of the United Nations Association of the USA. In his former capacity as Vice-President for Research and Policy Studies, he oversaw research programs on Soviet-American relations, arms control and national security problems, and U.N. affairs. He has been a consultant to the Social Science Research Department of the Rand Corporation and he has published and testified widely in the fields of arms control, national security policy, Soviet foreign policy, and multilateral diplomacy.

ALVIN Z. RUBINSTEIN is Professor of Political Science at the University of Pennsylvania and Senior Fellow of the Foreign Policy Research Institute. He has published extensively on the Soviet Union and the Third World. His books include: *Soviet Foreign Policy Since World War II: Imperial and Global*; *Red Star on the Nile: The Soviet-Egyptian Influence Relationship Since the June War*; and *Yugoslavia and the Nonaligned World*.

DONALD E. SMITH is Professor of Political Science at the University of Pennsylvania. He is author of *India As a Secular State*, and *Religion and Political Development*. He is Editor of *Religion, Politics, and Social Change in the Third World*.